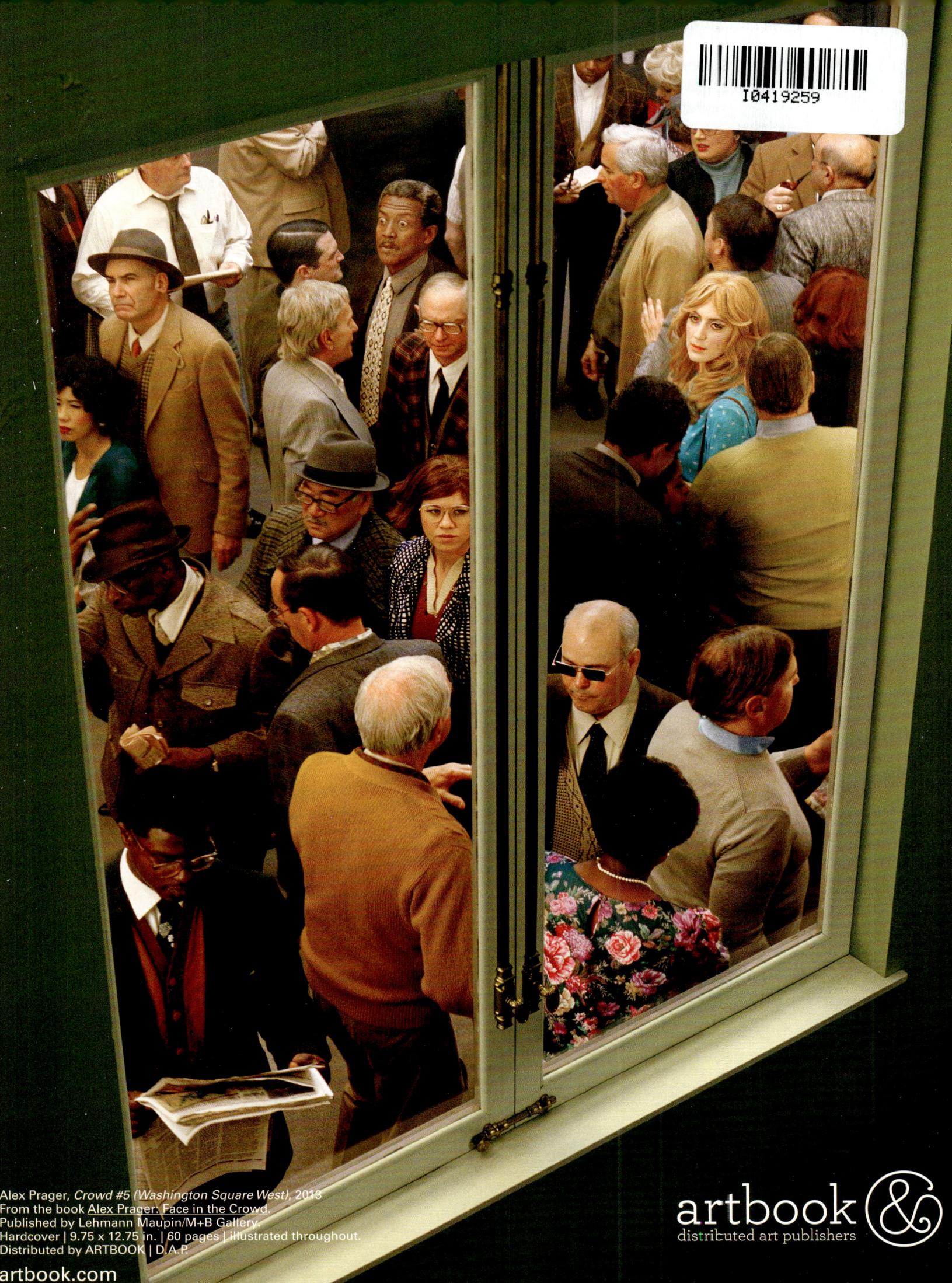

Alex Prager, *Crowd #5 (Washington Square West)*, 2013
From the book Alex Prager: Face in the Crowd.
Published by Lehmann Maupin/M+B Gallery.
Hardcover | 9.75 x 12.75 in. | 60 pages | illustrated throughout.
Distributed by ARTBOOK | D.A.P.

artbook.com

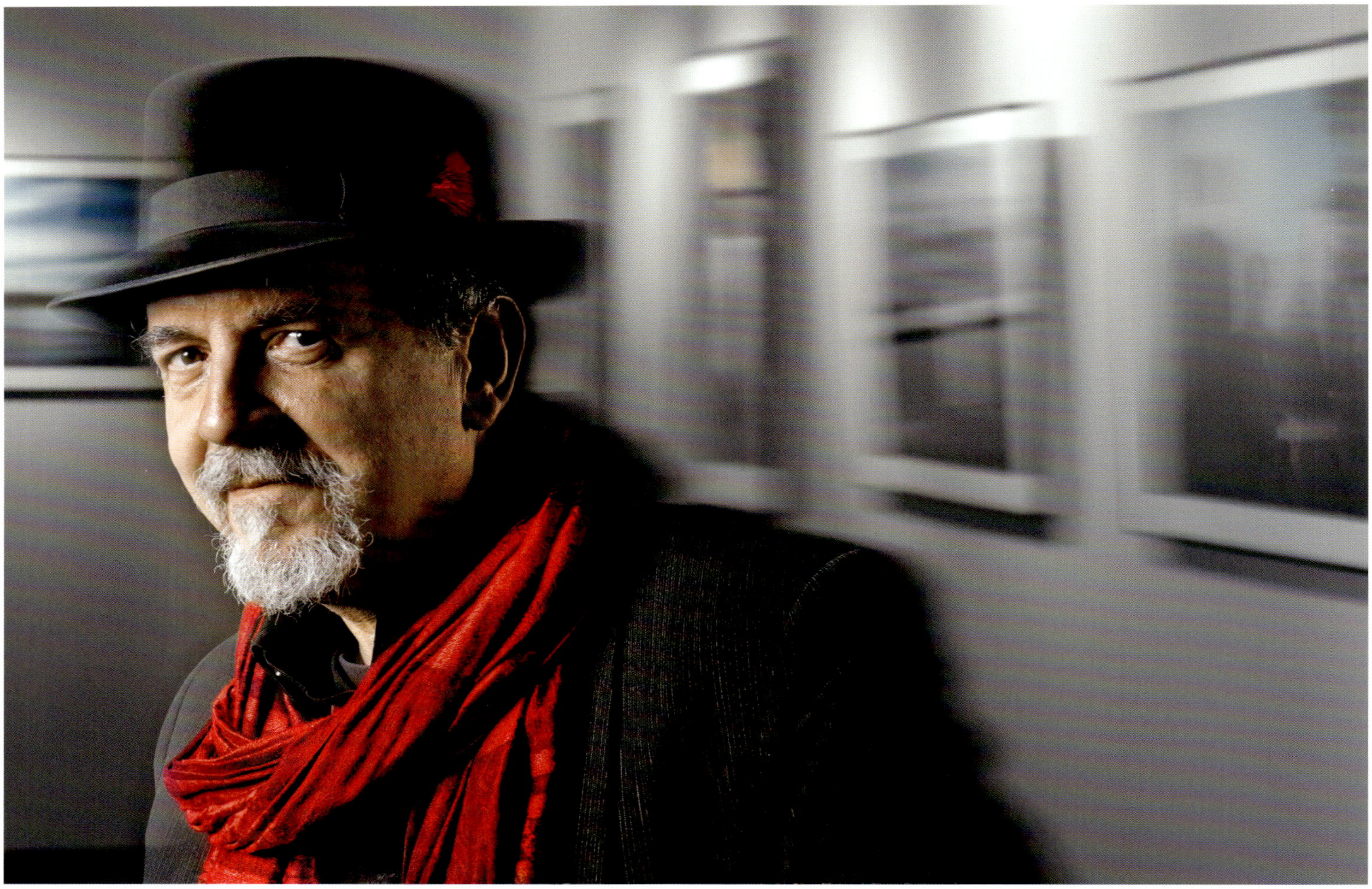

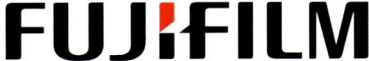
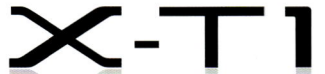
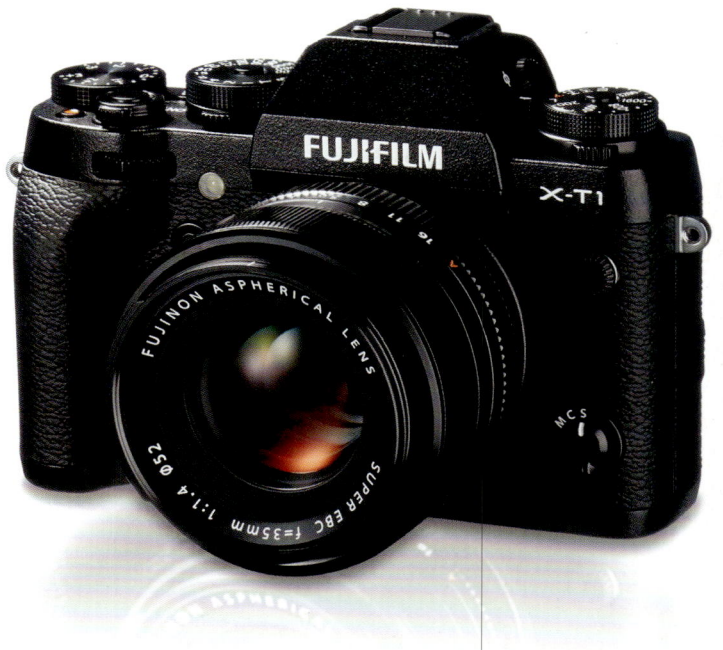
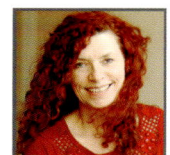
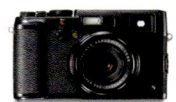 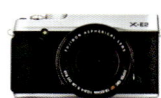 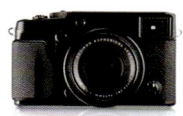
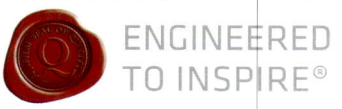

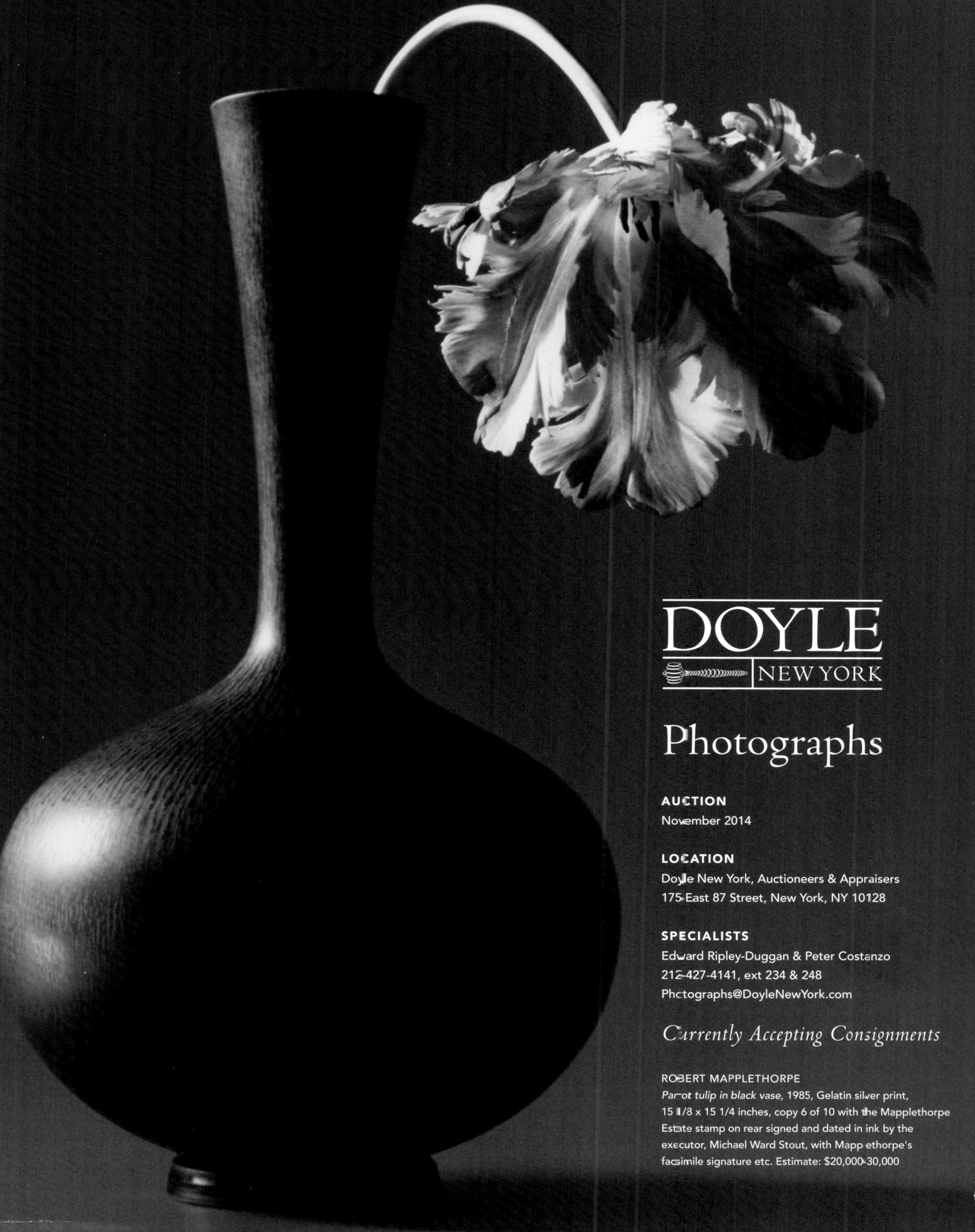

DOYLE
NEW YORK

Photographs

AUCTION
November 2014

LOCATION
Doyle New York, Auctioneers & Appraisers
175 East 87 Street, New York, NY 10128

SPECIALISTS
Edward Ripley-Duggan & Peter Costanzo
212-427-4141, ext 234 & 248
Photographs@DoyleNewYork.com

Currently Accepting Consignments

ROBERT MAPPLETHORPE
Parrot tulip in black vase, 1985, Gelatin silver print,
15 1/8 x 15 1/4 inches, copy 6 of 10 with the Mapplethorpe
Estate stamp on rear signed and dated in ink by the
executor, Michael Ward Stout, with Mapplethorpe's
facsimile signature etc. Estimate: $20,000-30,000

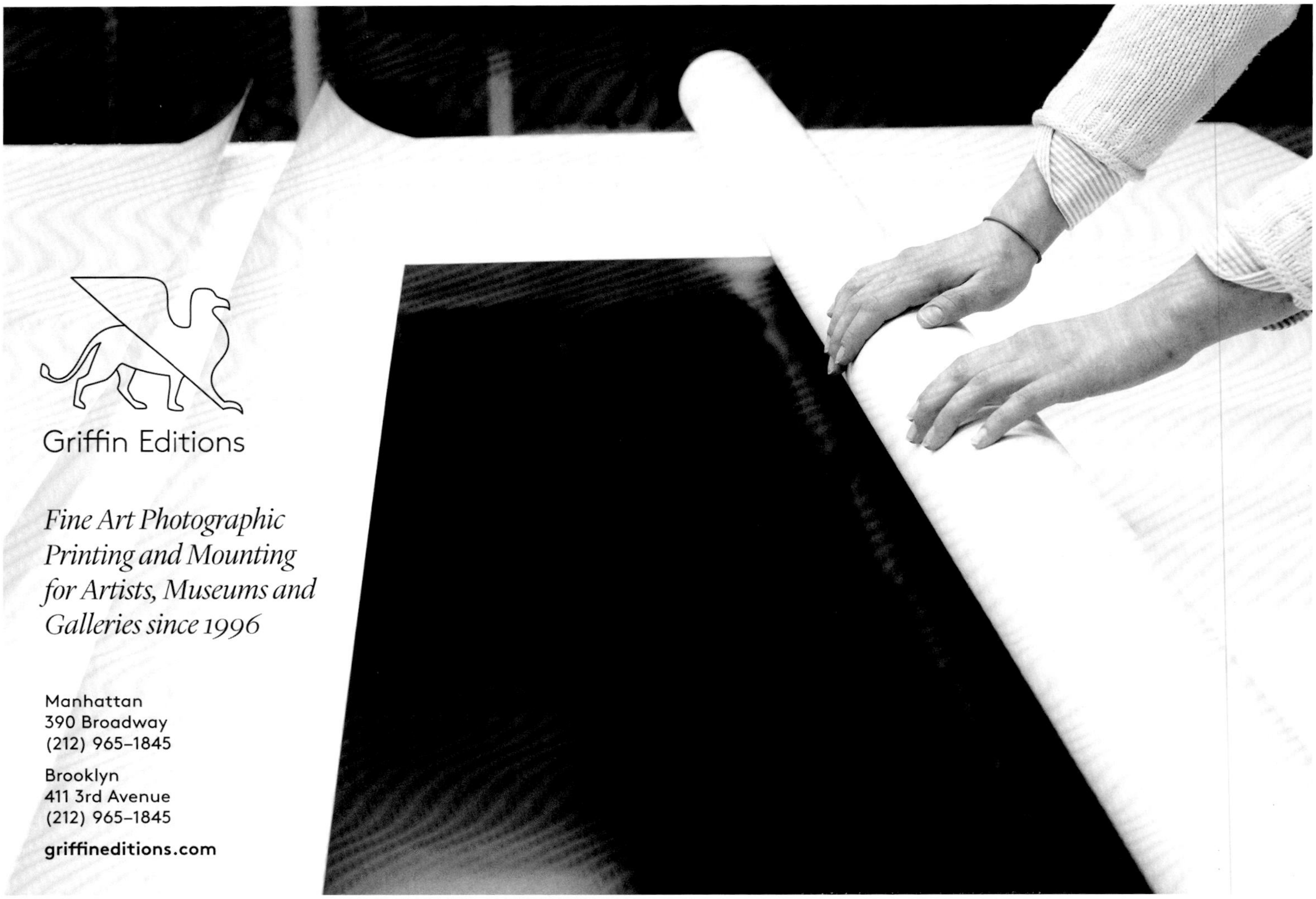

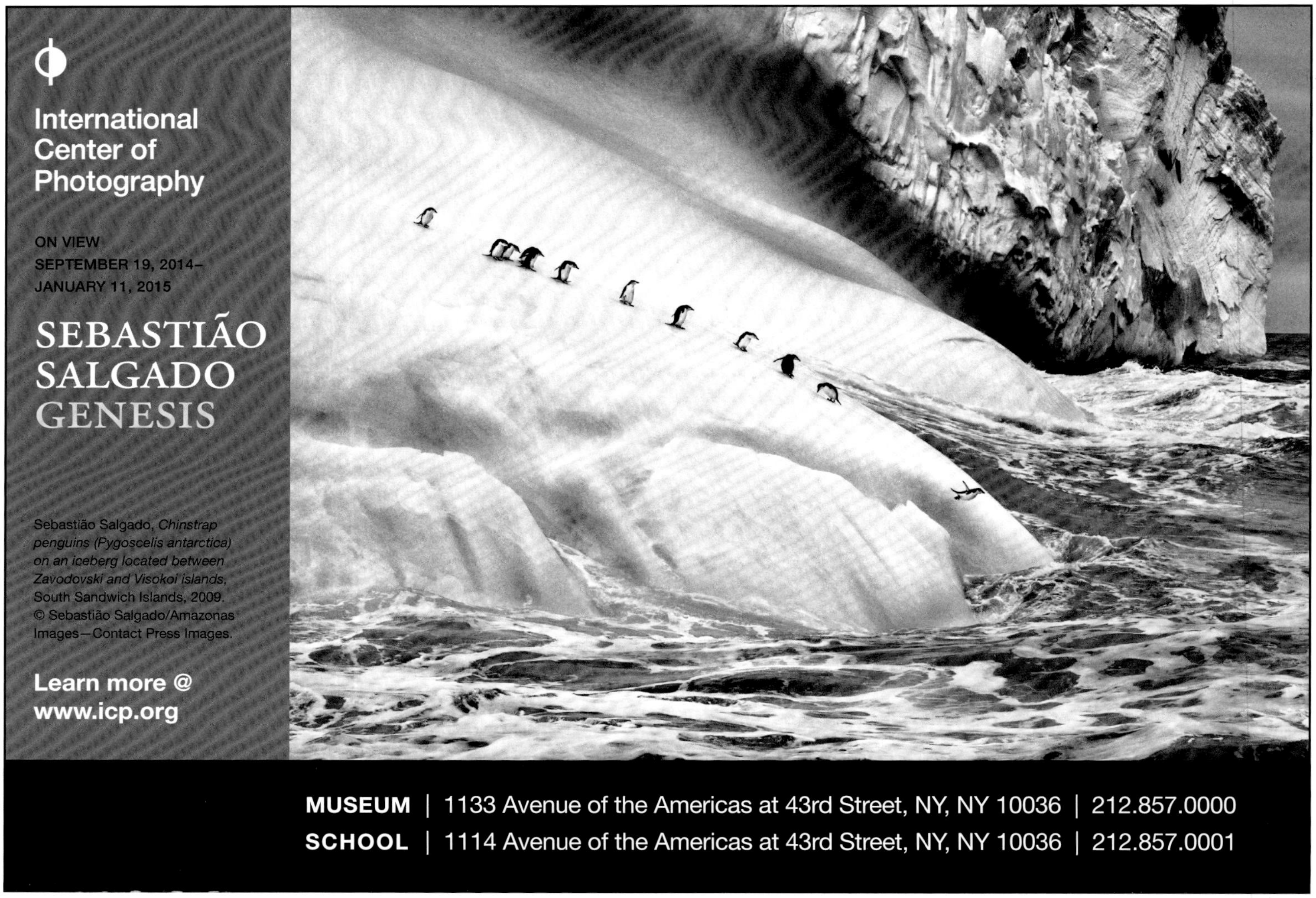

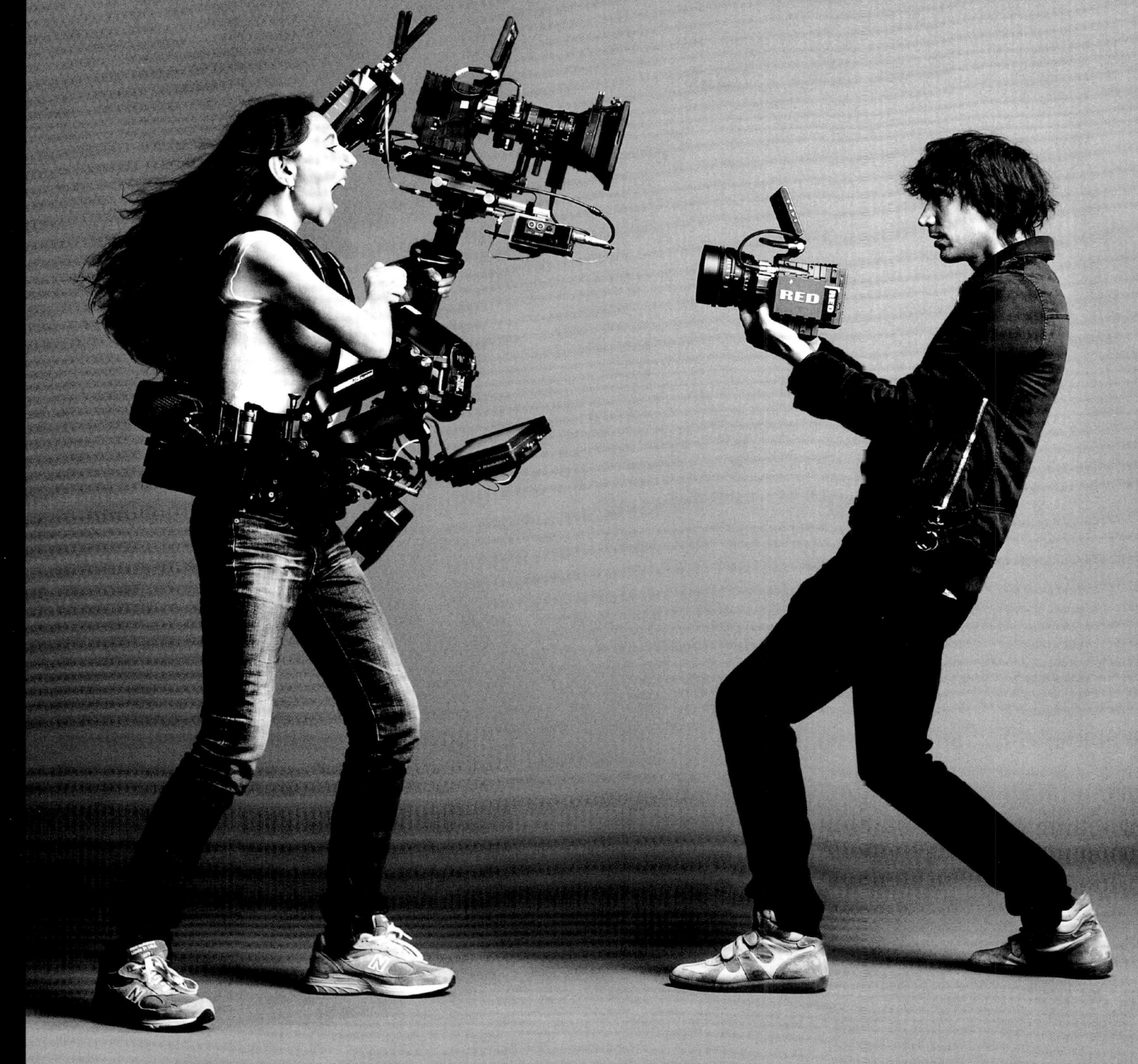

Minor White
Manifestations of the Spirit

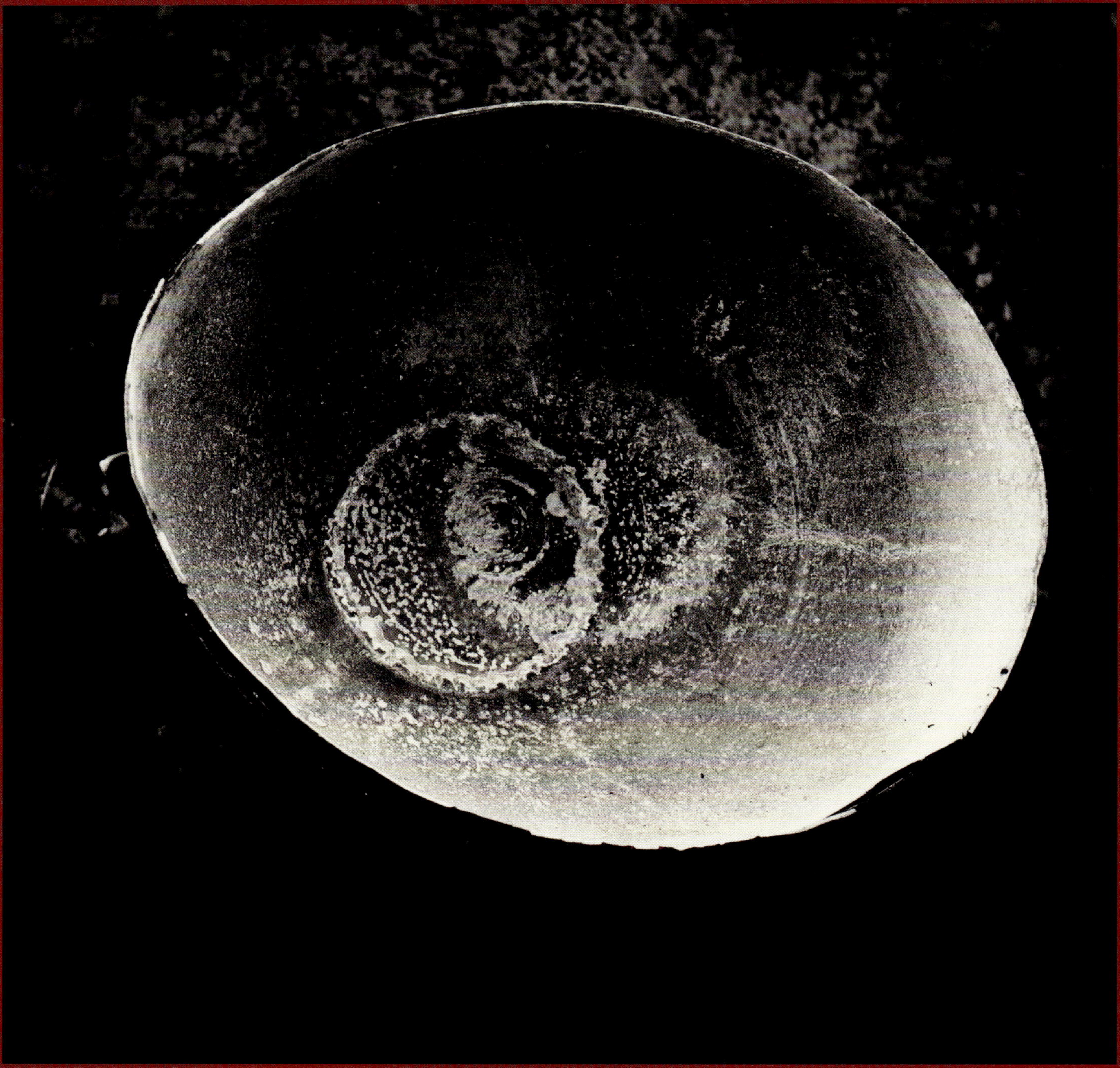

July 8–October 19, 2014
At the Getty Center

www.getty.edu

The J. Paul Getty Museum

At MICA's BFA in Photography, accomplished visiting artists and curators are working alongside our students to shape the future of the medium.

PAST ARTISTS AND CURATORS INCLUDE

Abelardo Morell	Richard Renaldi
Elinor Carucci	Hank Willis Thomas
Debra Klomp Ching	Liz Wells
Jen Davis	Mary Coble
Brian Paul Clamp	Gabriela Bulisova
Mark Alice Durant	Ernesto Bazan
Emmet Gowin	Paul Emmanuel
Justine Cooper	Sant Khalsa
Andy Grundberg	Robert and Shana
Larissa Leclair	ParkeHarrison

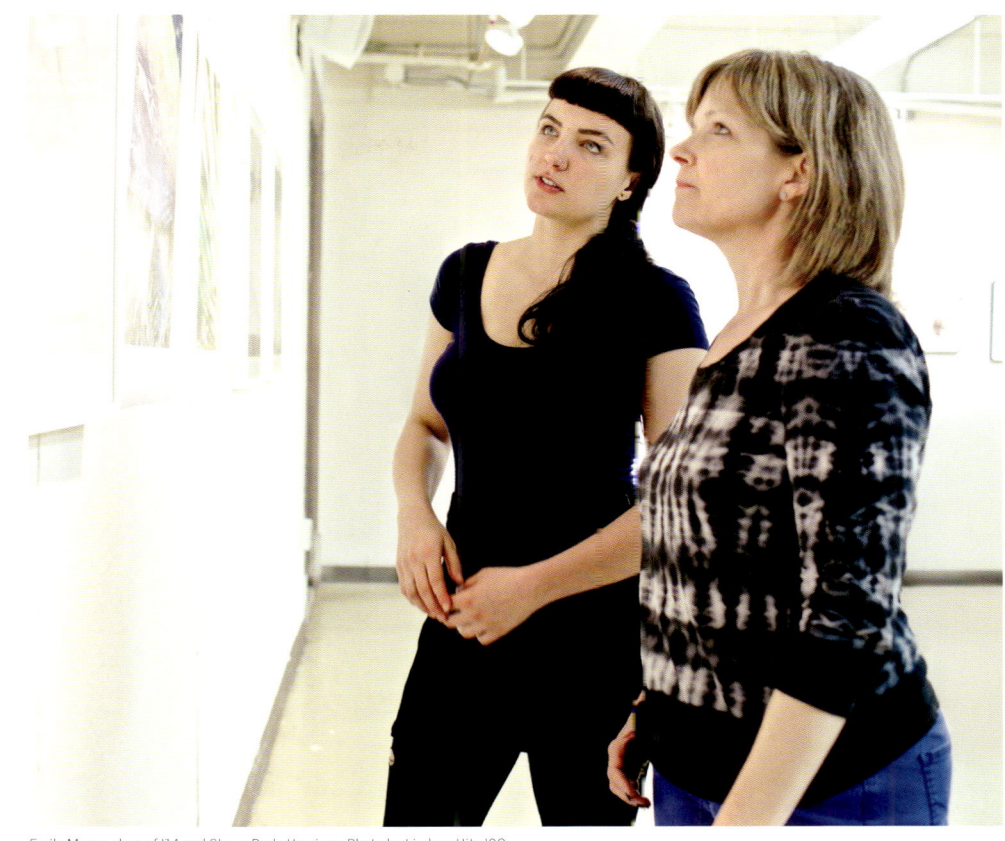

Emily Mason class of '14 and Shana ParkeHarrison. Photo by Lindsay Hite '08

M|I|C|A MARYLAND INSTITUTE COLLEGE OF ART   MICA.edu/bfaphoto

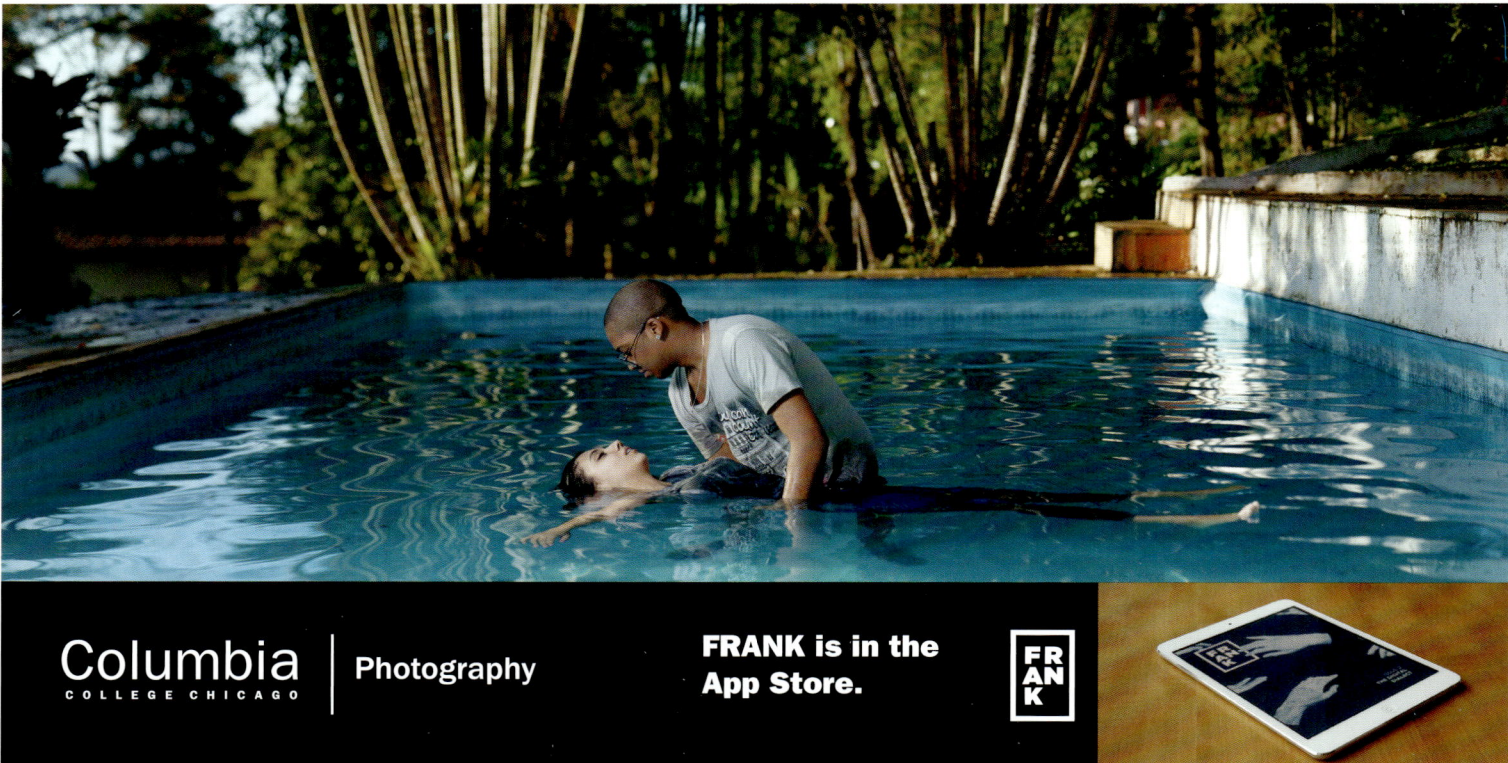
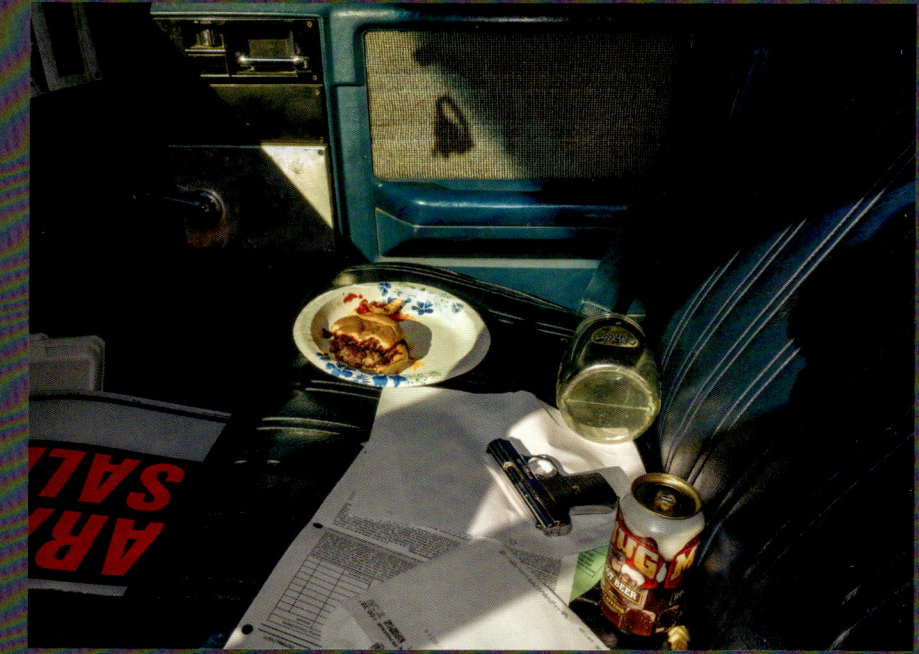

THE PARIS PHOTO — *aperture foundation* PHOTOBOOK AWARDS 2014

WINNERS TO BE ANNOUNCED AT PARIS PHOTO, NOVEMBER 13–16, 2014, AND IN *THE PHOTOBOOK REVIEW*, ISSUE 007

An exhibition of all thirty-five short-listed books will be exhibited during Paris Photo and will launch simultaneously at Aperture Gallery, New York, and at IMA Concept Store and Gallery, Tokyo, in December 2014.

**CALL FOR ENTRIES:
MAY 5–SEPTEMBER 12, 2014**
aperture.org/photobookawards

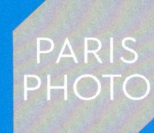 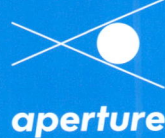

Aperture Foundation
547 West 27th Street, 4th Floor, New York, N.Y. 10001
212.505.5555 aperture.org

FIRST PHOTOBOOK PRIZE

PHOTOBOOK OF THE YEAR PRIZE

PHOTOGRAPHY CATALOGUE OF THE YEAR

NEW CATEGORY AND PRIZE!

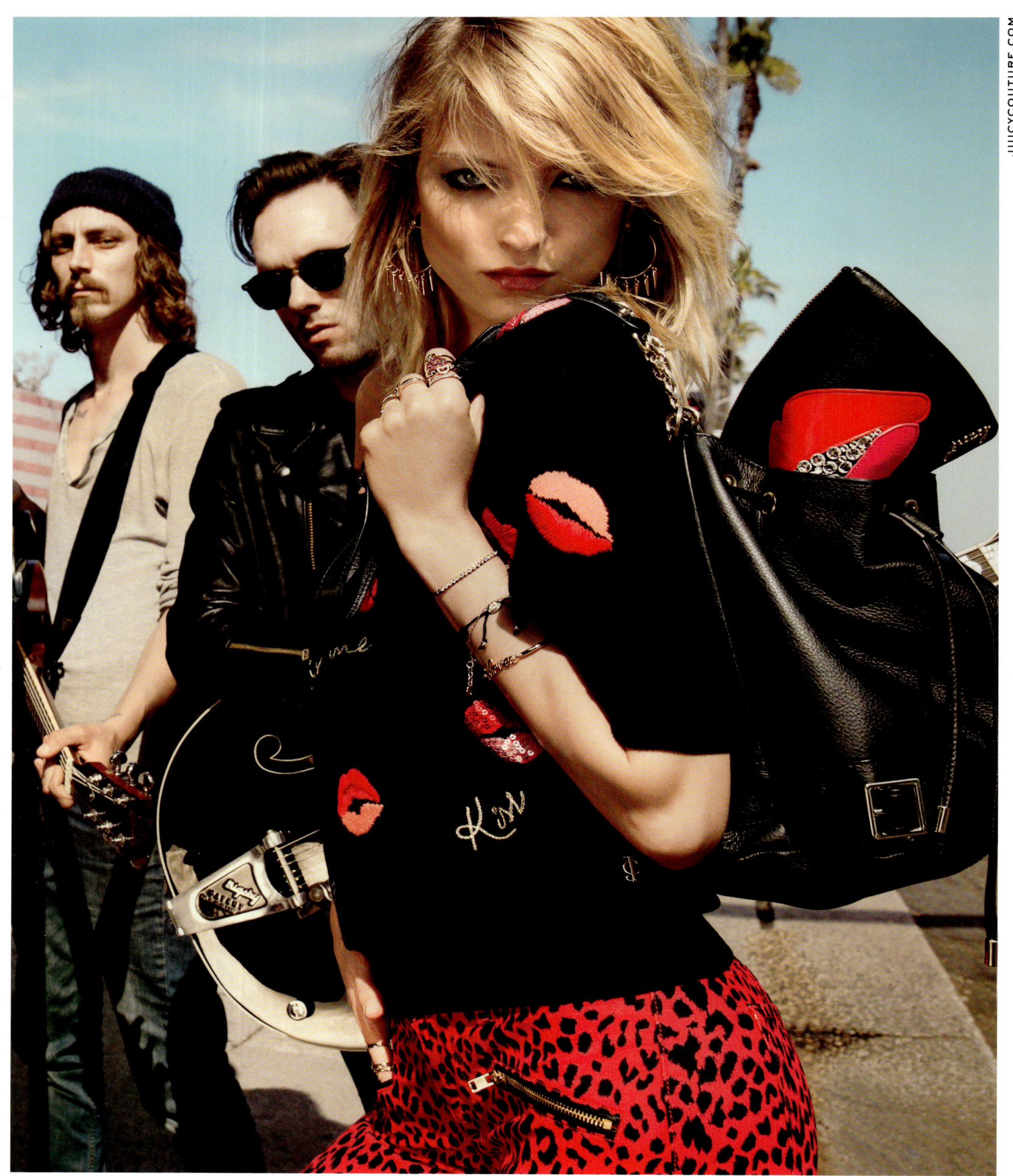

Juicy Couture
los angeles, california

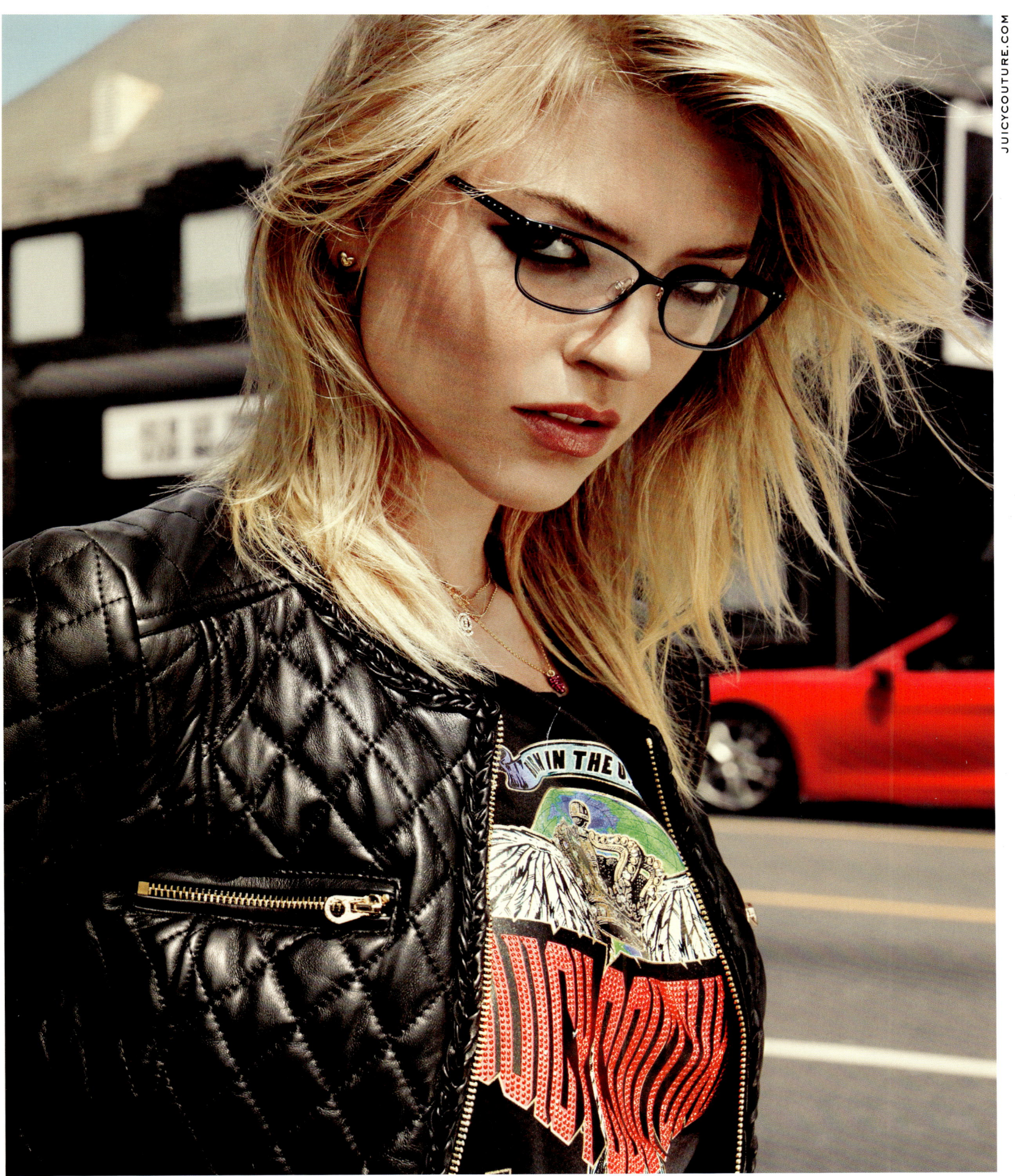

Juicy Couture

los angeles, california

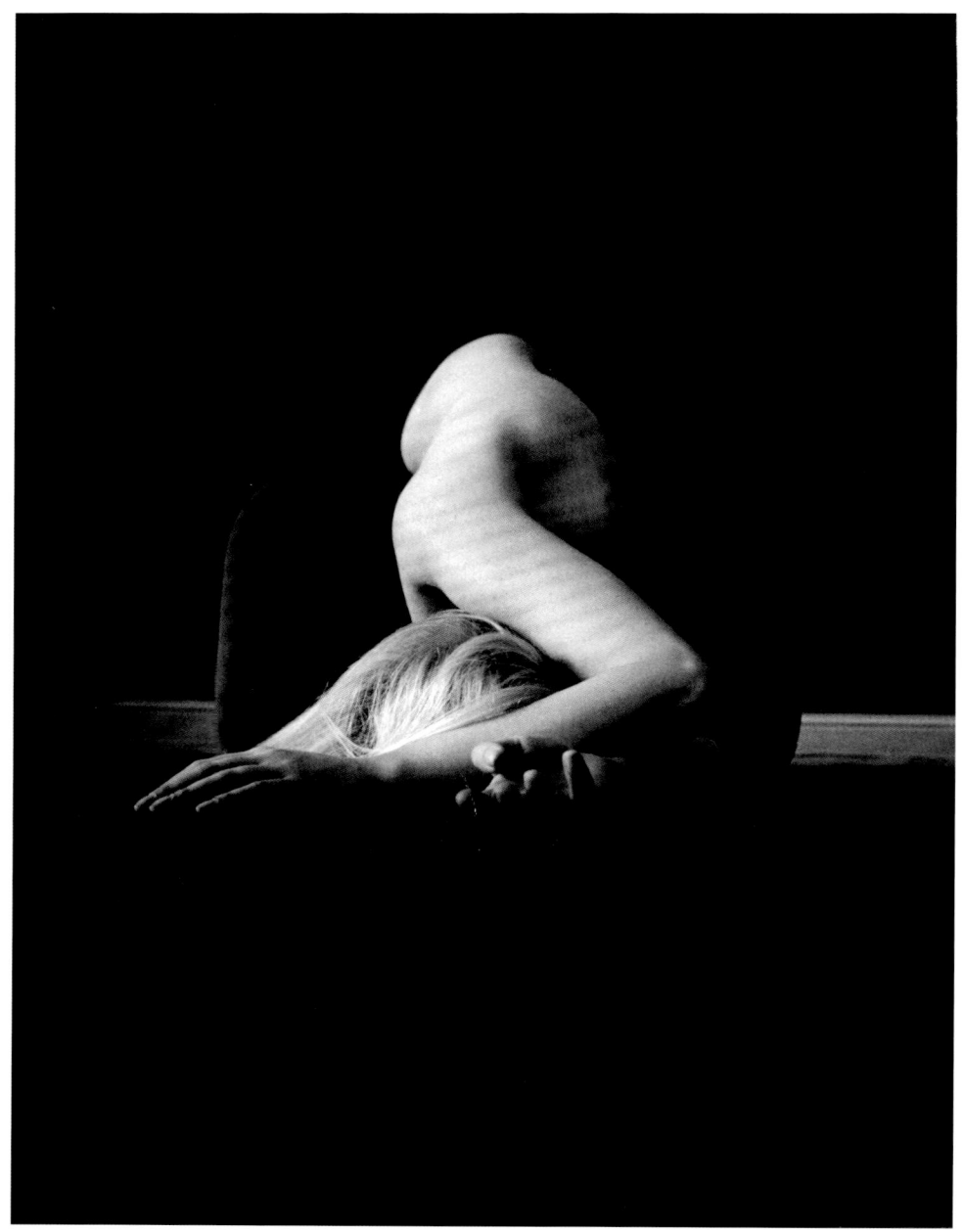

Fall 2014

Opposite:
Karin Székessy,
Nude on red chair, 1969
© Karin Székessy
(See page 82)

Front cover:
Richard Hamilton,
Fashion-plate, 1969–70
(offset lithograph, collage,
silkscreen, pochoir,
and cosmetics on paper)
© R. Hamilton,
and Tate, London;
all rights reserved ARS,
New York/DACS, London
(See page 82)

Editor
Michael Famighetti

Managing Editor
Paula Kupfer

Copy Editor
Claire Barliant

Production Manager
Matthew Harvey

Production Assistant
Luke Chase

Work Scholars
Jessica Lancaster, Hannah Max, Emily Myerscough

Art Direction, Design & Typefaces
A2/SW/HK, London

Editor-at-Large
Melissa Harris

Publisher
Dana Triwush
magazine@aperture.org

Manager, Special Projects
Andrea Hill
ahill@aperture.org

Advertising
Bill Besch
631-665-0467
bbesch1@verizon.net

Cultureshock Media
Sarah Haviland
+44 (0) 20 7735 9263
ads@cultureshockmedia.co.uk

Switzerland and Liechtenstein:
Affinity-PrimeMEDIA Ltd.
Eva Favre
+41 (0) 21 781 08 50
e.favre@affinity-primemedia.ch

Executive Director,
Aperture Foundation
Chris Boot

Minor White, Editor (1952–1974)

Michael E. Hoffman, Publisher and Executive Director
(1964–2001)

Aperture, a not-for-profit foundation, connects the photo community and its audiences with the most inspiring work, the sharpest ideas, and with each other— in print, in person, and online.

Aperture (ISSN 0003-6420) is published quarterly, in spring summer, fall, and winter, at 547 West 27th Street, 4th Floor, New York, N.Y. 10001. In the United States, a one-year subscription (four issues) is $75; a two-year subscription (eight issues) is $124. In Canada, a one-year subscription is $95. All other international subscriptions are $105 per year. Visit aperture.org to subscribe. Single copies may be purchased at $24.95 for most issues. Periodicals postage paid at New York and additional offices. Postmaster: Send address changes to *Aperture*, P.O. Box 3000, Denville, N.J. 07834. Address queries regarding subscriptions, renewals, or gifts to: *Aperture* Subscription Service, 866-457-4603 (U.S. and Canada), or email custsvc_aperture@fulcoinc.com.

Newsstand distribution in the U.S. is handled by Curtis Circulation Company, 201-634-7400. For international distribution, contact Central Books, centralbooks.com.

Help maintain Aperture's publishing, education, and community activities by joining our new general member program. Membership starts at $75 annually and includes invitations to special events, exclusive discounts on Aperture publications, and opportunities to meet artists and engage with leaders in the photo community. Aperture Foundation welcomes support at all levels of giving, and all gifts are tax-deductible to the fullest extent of the law. For more information about supporting Aperture, please visit aperture.org/join or contact the Development Department at membership@aperture.org.

Library of Congress Catalog Card No: 58-30845.

ISBN 978-1-59711-282-6

Printed in Turkey by Ofset Yapimevi

Aperture magazine is supported in part by an award from the National Endowment for the Arts and with public funds from the New York City Department of Cultural Affairs in partnership with the City Council.

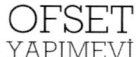
OFSET
YAPİMEVİ

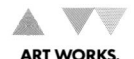
ART WORKS.

National
Endowment
for the Arts
arts.gov

aperture.org

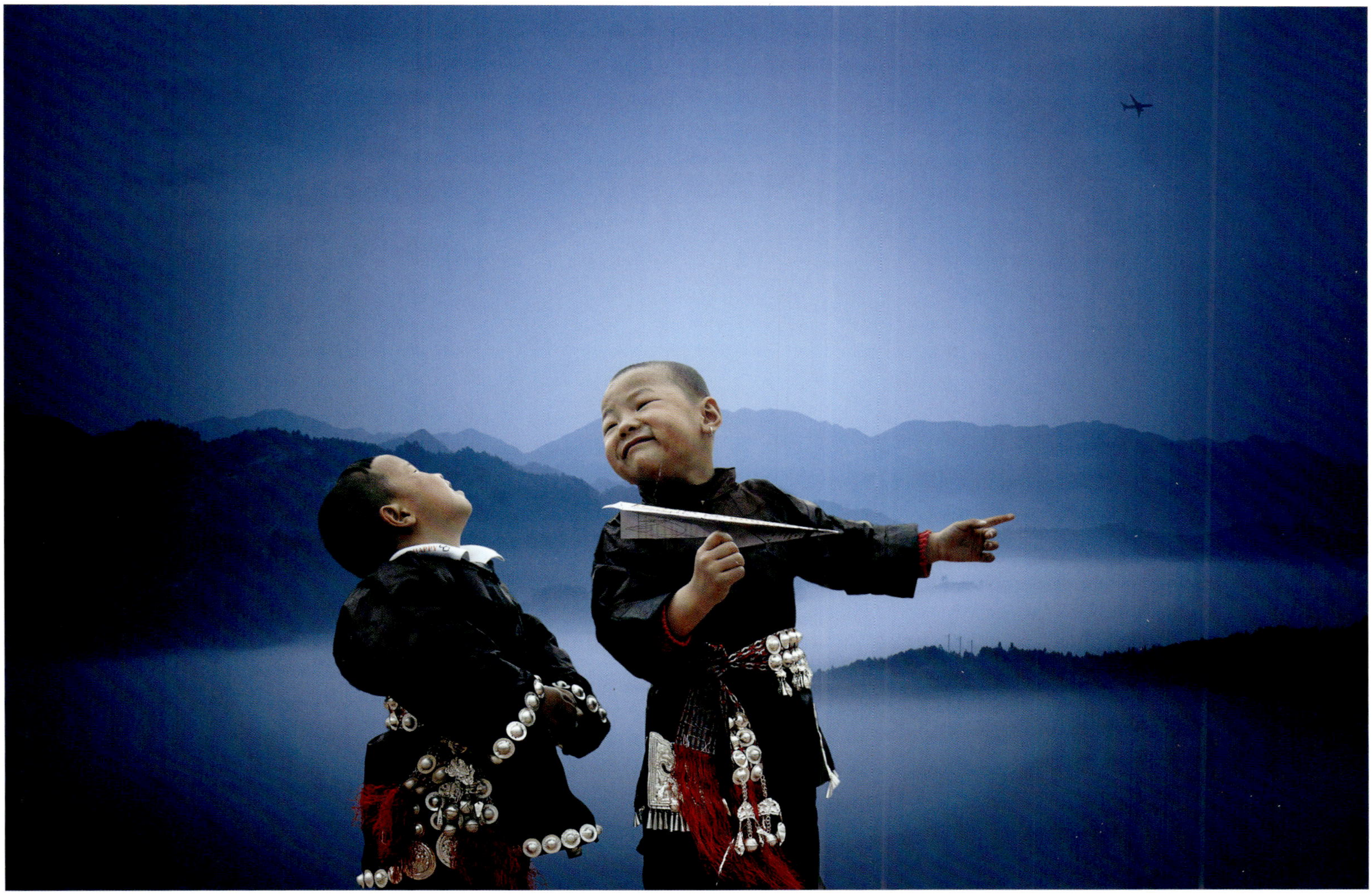

LIFE IN COLOUR

جائزة حمدان بن محمد بن راشد آل مكتوم الدولية للتصوير الضّوئي
HAMDAN BIN MOHAMMED BIN RASHID AL MAKTOUM INTERNATIONAL PHOTOGRAPHY AWARD

www.hipa.ae

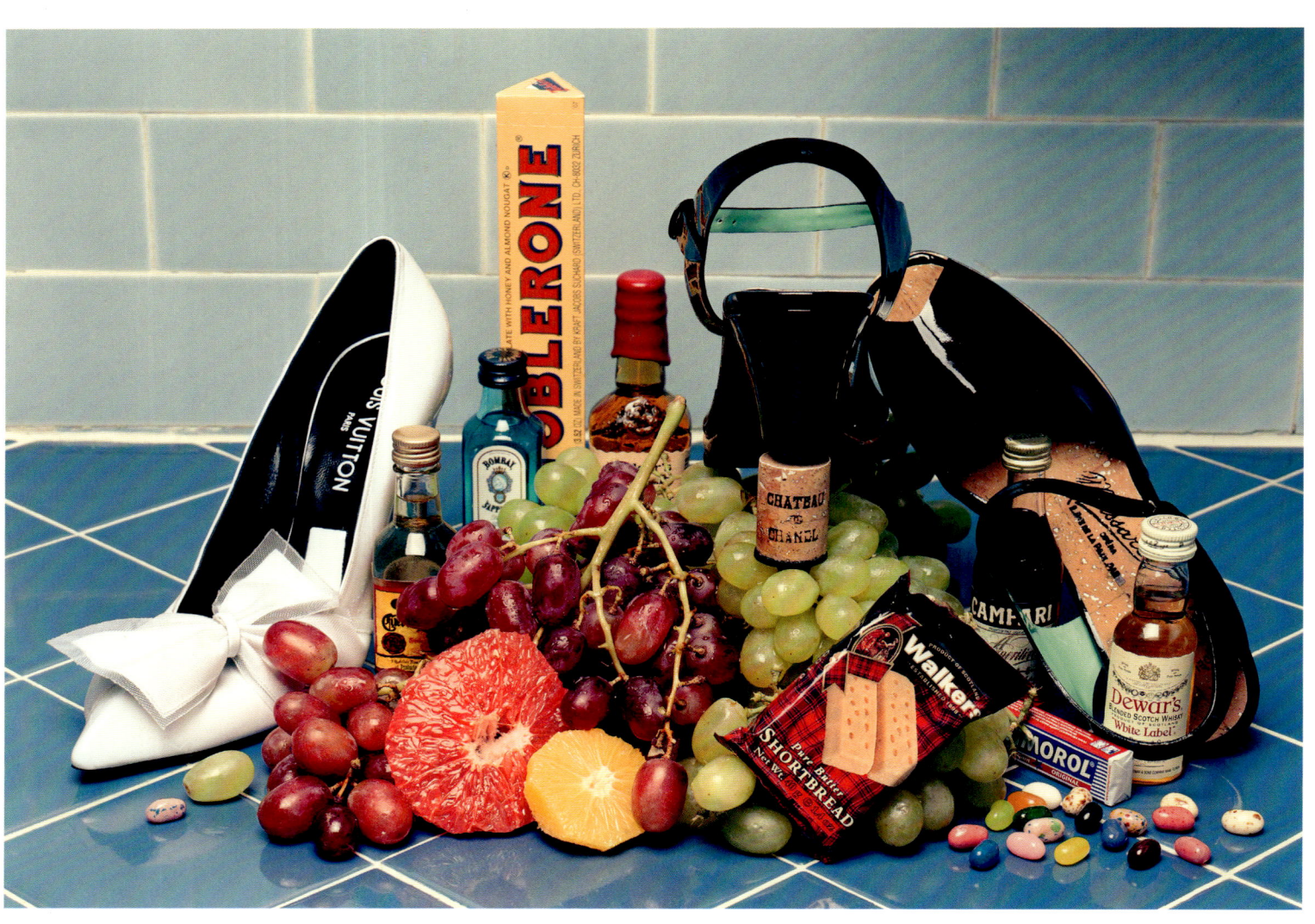

"Fashion"

With guest editors Inez & Vinoodh

Though this issue's title appears in quotation marks, the intention is not to be ironic, or to suggest skepticism. Rather, the quotes allude to image quotation and reference, which are part and parcel of any creative act but are essential to the world of fashion. "In today's professional climate… you're only as good as your references," guest editors Inez & Vinoodh note in their introduction to a portfolio of images by fashion's most iconic and imitated photographers. Referencing is delicate, requiring thoughtful handling to avoid crossing the line into copying. Curator Charlotte Cotton remarks in her contribution that fashion photography's often transparent use of references may be one reason why the genre is criticized from other corners. But in the end what matters is how a reference is used: when adequately transformed, you may sense a quotation but won't recognize its source.

Transformation, in a broader sense, is a hallmark of Inez & Vinoodh's work. The husband-and-wife team has collaborated for more than twenty-five years, breaking ground in the 1990s with their early digital interventions into fashion photography. Their work is marked by restlessness and curiosity about photography, a tension between illusion and reality, the beautiful and the grotesque, and a desire to explore the medium's generous flexibility. The protean nature of their output has earned them both commercial success and art-world kudos. In these pages, writer Donatien Grau describes their agnostic practice as a "collaboration embedded within collaborations," noting their frequent partnerships with artists, graphic designers, even pop stars.

The "Pictures" section comprises key influences and references for Inez & Vinoodh. Some choices may be surprising, as not all emerge from the field of fashion but instead reference styles from various periods, as in the work, spanning the 1950s through the 1980s, of Ed van der Elsken, the influential Dutch documentary photographer. A selection of the wonderfully beguiling ads produced in decades past for the Shiseido cosmetics company are a reminder that commercial art often warrants serious consideration. A collage from Pop artist Richard Hamilton's *Fashion-plate* series appears on our cover, an image that playfully underscores the artifice, construction, and illusion that is fashion image making. This 1969 collage is part of a portfolio that considers photographs that have served as references for painting. Hamilton sourced his material from fashion magazines, the medium through which the story of fashion photography is often told. A new generation of photographers has gleaned much by flipping through back issues of the pioneering magazines *i-D*, *The Face*, and *Jill*, all of which fostered the careers of many major photographers and stylists. (The dog-eared and even cut-up copies of these publications in the Fashion Institute of Technology's library attest to their consistent use as reference material.) Closing the "Pictures" section are two emerging photographers who reference photography's recent past: the street tradition for Daniel Arnold and a casual diaristic touch in the work of Margaret Durow.

In "Words" we consider the growing area of fashion film, the complex relationship between documentary photography and fashion, and a conversation between two of fashion's most influential magazine editors, Penny Martin of *The Gentlewoman* and Emmanuelle Alt of *Vogue Paris*, details the production of fashion photography and the sensitivities of using archival references when working with photographers. Alt notes that "your first music and visual influences stay with you forever…. You live with what was around when you first became curious." Indeed, much of what forms this issue is culled from what was around when Inez & Vinoodh first became curious, as they note, echoing Alt's observation, that fashion is nostalgic and based on a "string of memories." — The Editors

Collectors
The Painters
On Recent Acquisitions

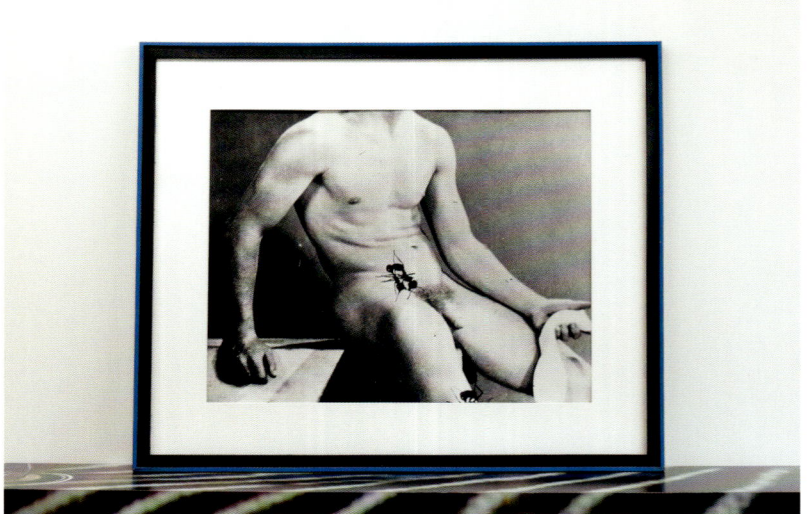

David Wojnarowicz, *Untitled (nude and ants)*, 1988–89 Courtesy P.P.O.W., New York

Wade Guyton

Untitled (nude and ants) (1988) is the first thing one sees upon walking into my studio. It's sitting on a table sculpture I made with Kelley Walker. David Wojnarowicz was an early influence for me. Growing up in Tennessee before the Internet, discovering art, music, and writing was a slow process.

I found his incredible book *Tongues of Flame* in a used bookstore in 1992. My generation followed his, which suffered first from the AIDS epidemic, and their tragedy became our heritage. I hadn't yet seen contemporary art in museums so it was through Wojnarowicz that I first understood art as it was interlaced with politics. An image could be a protest against mass media, power, and ambivalence. And the act of making images could be about fighting for one's life, as well as (fighting) for what the images of one's life could be.

Photographer Peter Hujar, his close friend, died the year before Wojnarowicz made this image, which was four years before his own premature death. I read it as layered with their friendship and experience. Wojnarowicz placed the plastic ants across this picture from Hujar's collection and took the photograph. He designed the black wood frame with a blue face. The blue could have many symbolic meanings, or it could just be a fanciful flourish. But I'm reminded that the best art, whatever its form—even in the midst of intense urgency and anger—always pays attention to its framing.

Wade Guyton lives and works in New York. His work was the subject of an exhibition at the Whitney Museum of American Art, New York, October 2012–January 2013.

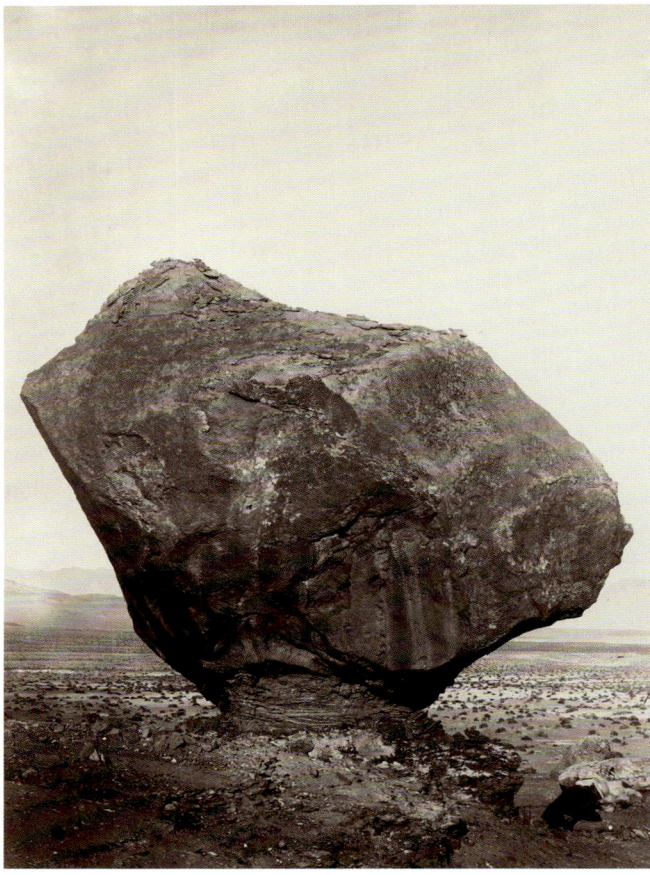

William Bell, *Perched Rock, Rocker Creek, Arizona*, 1872 Courtesy Library of Congress Prints and Photographs Division, Washington, D.C./Collection of Ellsworth Kelly

Ellsworth Kelly

In 1990 I was invited by the Museum of Modern Art to select works from the museum's collection for a series called "Artist's Choice." My presentation was titled *Fragmentation and the Single Form*. I included two photographs, Edward Weston's *Mexico D.F. (Anita)* (1925) and William Bell's *Perched Rock, Rocker Creek, Arizona* (1872). Photography isolates the world via an aperture and gives the photographer the means to see differently, to achieve a spontaneous vision that is direct and uncompromising. William Bell photographed *Perched Rock* during a geological survey in Arizona. Presented by Bell as an image of a single form in space, the natural icon stands like a piece of sculpture, anticipating abstract painting in its formal concerns.

Ellsworth Kelly is regarded as one of the most important abstract painters, sculptors, and printmakers working today. In 2012, Kelly was presented the National Medal of Arts by President Barack Obama. He lives and works in Spencertown, New York.

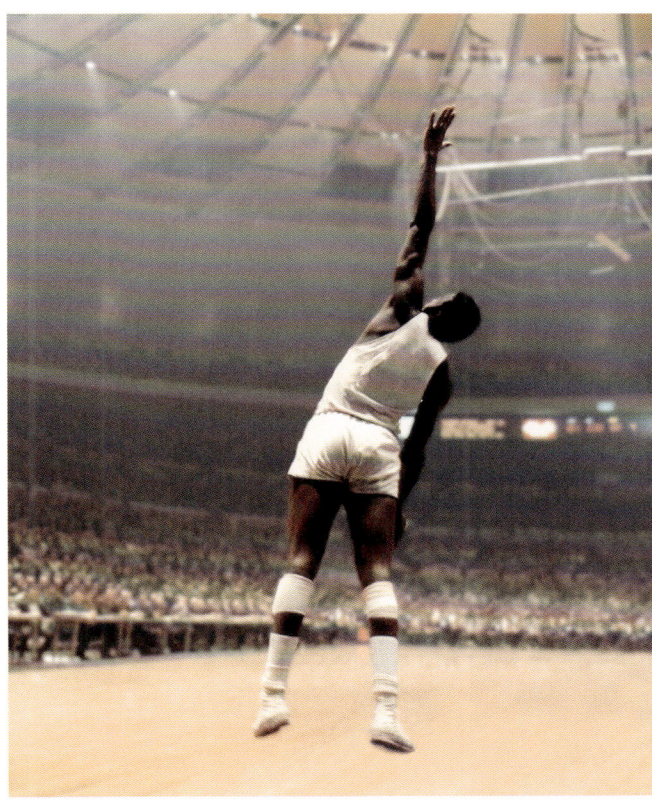

Paul Pfeiffer, *Four Horsemen of the Apocalypse (6)*, 2001 © Paul Pfeiffer and courtesy Paula Cooper Gallery, New York

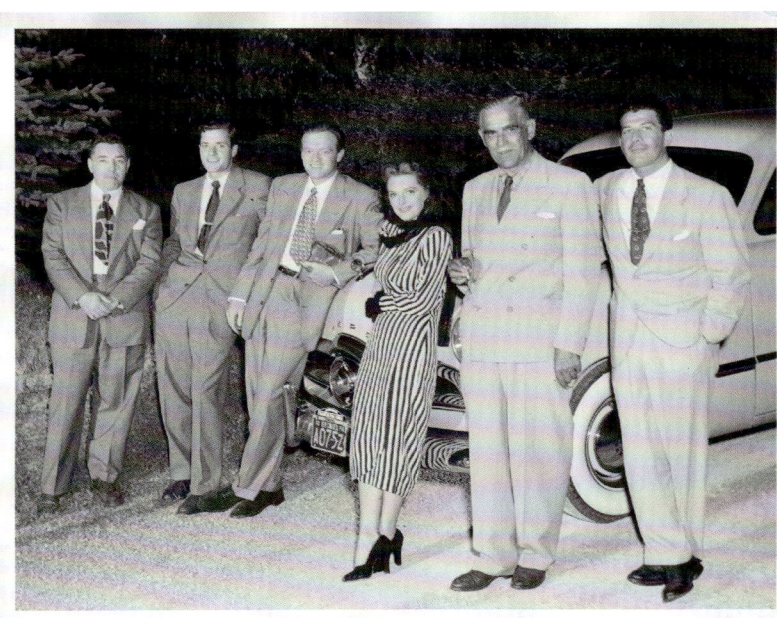

Vintage found photograph (Uncle Jack, far right) Courtesy Amy Sillman

Amy Sillman

When my great-uncle Jack died, I volunteered to snoop around in his Harrisburg, Pennsylvania, apartment before the cleaning woman arrived. I discovered a disorganized treasure trove of interesting narcissism. Jack, a confirmed bachelor and Air Force officer, was a Rock Hudson look-alike who owned a Ford dealership and a racetrack in Cuba. In family albums he just looks like the eldest in a set of Jewish sons, barely cracking a smile, but the unofficial photos disclose his mirth and vanity, plus his homoerotic interests. He hung with various swells, beauty queens, and arm candy, including a former Miss Pennsylvania named Jackie, but the bulk of his photos are of his buddies, their names neatly inscribed in pencil on the back, gaily drooped over one another on barstools and boats, in convertibles, and on the backs of camels. I threw a handful in a box. I should have saved them all.

Amy Sillman is a painter living and working in Brooklyn. Her first survey show was recently on view at the Hessel Museum of Art at Bard College.

Julie Mehretu

A man in flight hovers between ascension and the wooden floor of the basketball court, suspended in a moment of total silence. A space of complete spectacle, the stadium disappears; the entire crowd becomes invisible, faces and bodies blurred; all the noise, markers, flags, numbers, other players, erased.

An African man in flight, touching the sky, palming the light; what can that be? Incredible. We walk by this photograph every day; our boys love the jumping man, his reach, his feet humming as they keep him hovering. "Good morning, jumping man," they say. But I have caught glimpses of them watching him, lost in the moment/ momentum of his flight.

This photograph by Paul Pfeiffer evokes in feel and emotion the greatness of a Renaissance painting. Think of Titian's *Martyrdom of St. Lawrence* or Veronese's *The Ascension of Christ*. There are few works of art in our home that I look to for inspiration, that I keep close, so that I can make something in the studio that day that moves and affects me as much as *Four Horsemen of the Apocalypse*. Paul's piece, so dear to our whole family, is one of those rare ones. We feel fortunate and grateful to witness it daily, to move past it, to feel that reach, to remember what that can mean, what can be held there.

Julie Mehretu is an artist based in New York. Her work will be on view this fall at carlier/gebauer, Berlin, and White Cube, São Paulo.

HILLMAN**PHOTOGRAPHY**INITIATIVE
CARNEGIE MUSEUM OF **ART** PITTSBURGH

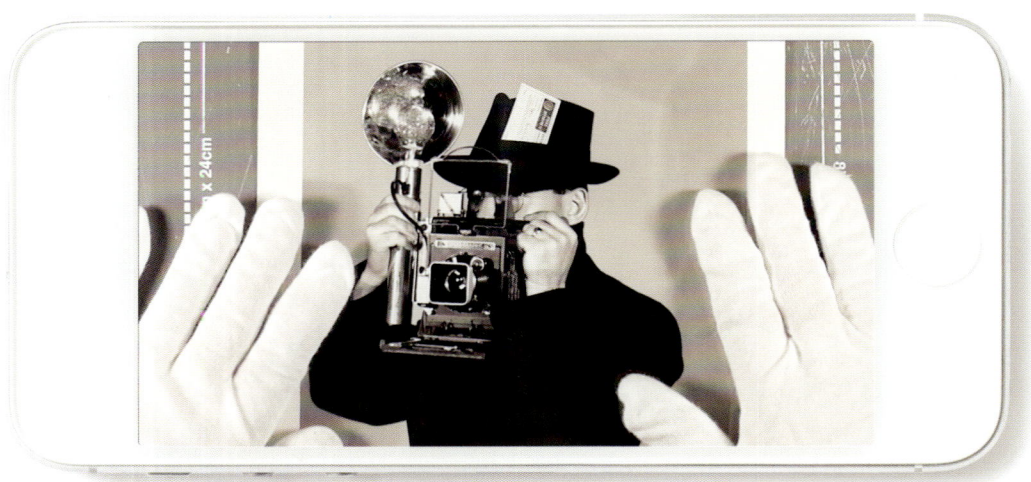

© Bettmann/CORBIS

Let's talk about photography.

It pervades our world.
Every day, millions of images are created,
appropriated, and erased from existence.
Join the conversation today.

nowseethis.org

What Matters Now?
Photography, Technology, and the World

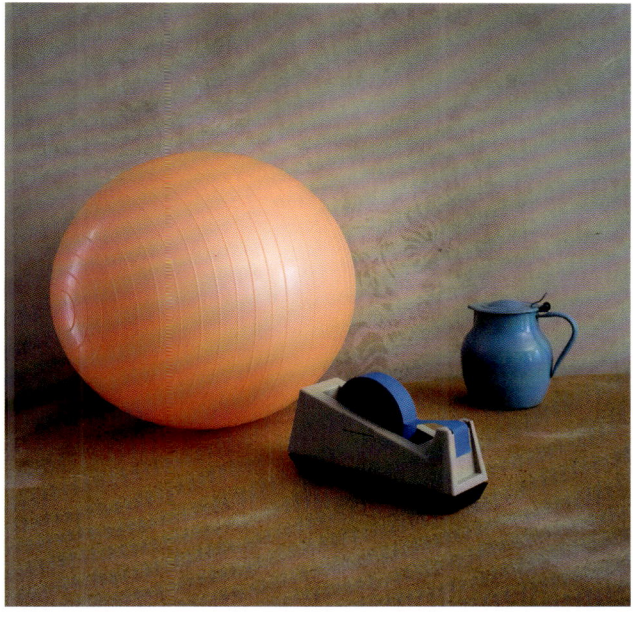

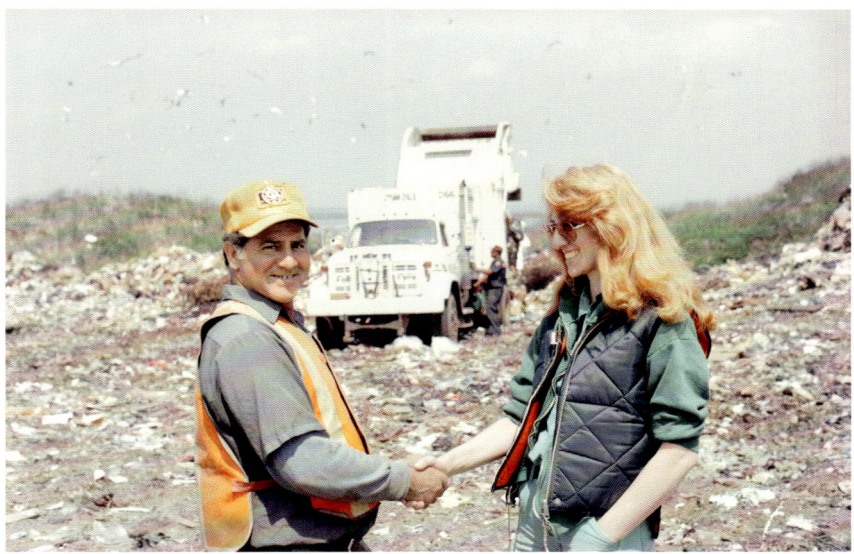

Handshake Ritual

This is the image I share with students when I discuss the work of Mierle Laderman Ukeles—a defining artist in the history of performance, feminism, and socially engaged art who has been the official artist in residence with New York City's Department of Sanitation for more than three decades. Photography plays a major role in her work—a record of repetition, a relic of the everyday, a monument to labor, and the embodiment of relationships. This picture of "Handshake Ritual" is evidence of the eight thousand five hundred sanitation workers she touched while saying, "Thank you for keeping New York City alive." It is more than proof; it is the catalyst for the story. It embodies the sincerity of her gesture. Socially engaged art is mediated by images, and photography can either be an ally or condemn one's work to looking like ambiguous social interactions. This image continues to be a benchmark for me of what documentation can achieve for socially engaged art.

—**Jen Delos Reyes, founder and director of Open Engagement, a conference on socially engaged art**

Mierle Laderman Ukeles, *Touch Sanitation* ("Handshake Ritual"), 1977–80
Courtesy Ronald Feldman Fine Arts, New York

Too Much Information

For decades, the photography lover cherished looking at an 8-by-10-inch contact print. Rich with information, the contact print was the be-all and end-all. However, in the final years of the twentieth century, the possibility of grand scale and moving things around in a picture digitally became real options. Photography and what photography could be changed.

Harry Callahan, when presented with a digital enlargement from one of his 4-by-5-inch Kodachromes, said, "It's too sharp." Harry simply did not like seeing more information than he was used to seeing in his analog prints.

Though the digital revolution has been afoot for decades, things today are different because, among other reasons, millions of people are equipped with sophisticated cameras in their pockets.

Digital innovations have marched forward, and the resulting photographs created with large sensors and prints made on pedestrian printers with pedestrian ink look very different; to me, they look more like the world we live in. The color is richer and more dense, and the rendering of space seems to be more closely aligned with reality. One can only imagine Vermeer scratching his head.

—**Peter MacGill, president of Pace/MacGill Gallery, New York**

Susan Paulsen, *Katonah*, 2014, an example of a hyper-real still life
© and courtesy the artist

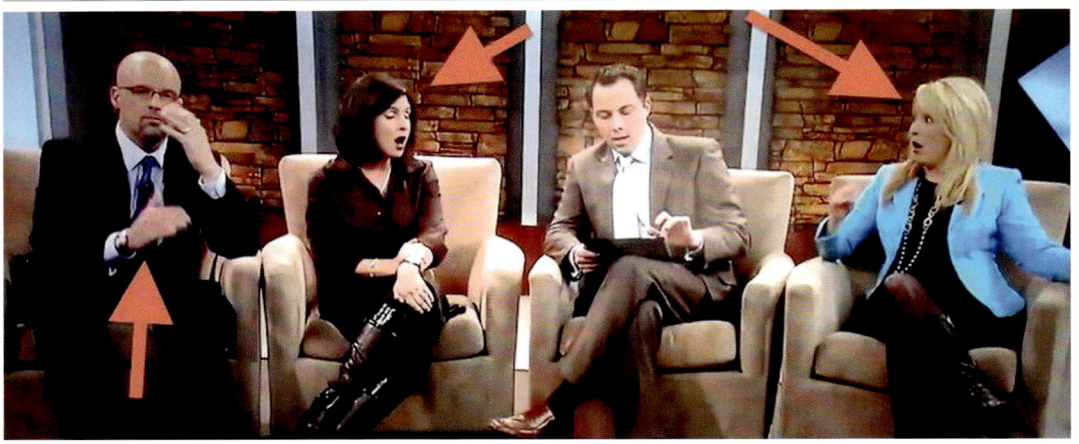

Above:
Fox News–affiliate
news hosts in
shock following
the accidental
broadcast of
a Twitter photo of
an exposed penis,
March 18, 2014.
This image with
arrows quickly
went viral.

NSFW

"Oops," in analog days, was a word seldom uttered during the distribution of photographic images. Today, it only takes one errant tap of a touch screen for an image intended for a single pair of eyes to go wildly astray or viral, with no turning back. Pictures whose flight paths spin out of control are routinely making and breaking reputations and turning into public-relations fiascos. This past March, a Fox News–affiliate station, covering a helicopter crash, scrolled right past an accident-scene photo on a newsroom team member's Twitter feed only to land on and broadcast, live, a shot of an erection. US Airways, in response to a passenger's tweet complaining about service last April, replied, "We welcome feedback, Elle" but illustrated that, somehow, with a NSFW image of a toy plane being inserted into a lower-body orifice. The moral: look twice and count to three before you link, flip, or leap.

—**Marvin Heiferman, curator and writer, most recently, of** *Photography Changes Everything* **(Aperture, 2012)**

Nir Evron,
Endurance, 2014 (still)
Courtesy the artist

Time, Space, and 16mm

In the coming months, families will start moving into the first houses in the new Palestinian city Rawabi, north of Ramallah, which is planned to be the home of forty thousand people. *Endurance*, my new 16mm film, is based on the measurement of space in one of Rawabi's model apartments, and was made without using a camera. It shows grayscale rectangles depicting doors, windows, and furniture abstracted from the architectural plan. Every shot represents the length of one wall, using the formula 1 meter=5.4 seconds, when shooting 16mm film at 24fps. In that sense, the duration of the film equals the total length of the apartment and can potentially surround the whole living space.

As technology advances, I feel it is urgent to counter it with the use of 16mm film. This feeling does not stem from nostalgic sentiment or fascination with the unique descriptive qualities of celluloid but rather from the belief that only the cinematic apparatus can embody such an interesting relation of space and time. *Endurance* is a severe consideration of the space of filming and the duration of viewing.

—**Nir Evron, artist and filmmaker based in Tel Aviv. Evron's work was included most recently in the 19th Biennale of Sydney (2014).** *Endurance* **premiered last summer at LA→←ART in Los Angeles.**

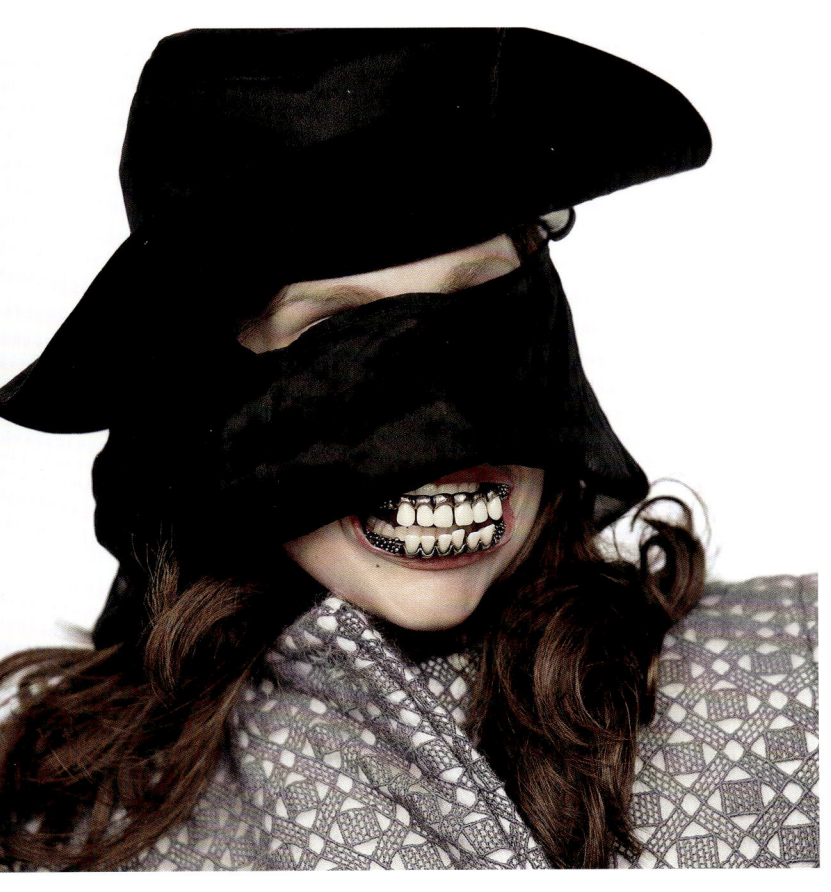

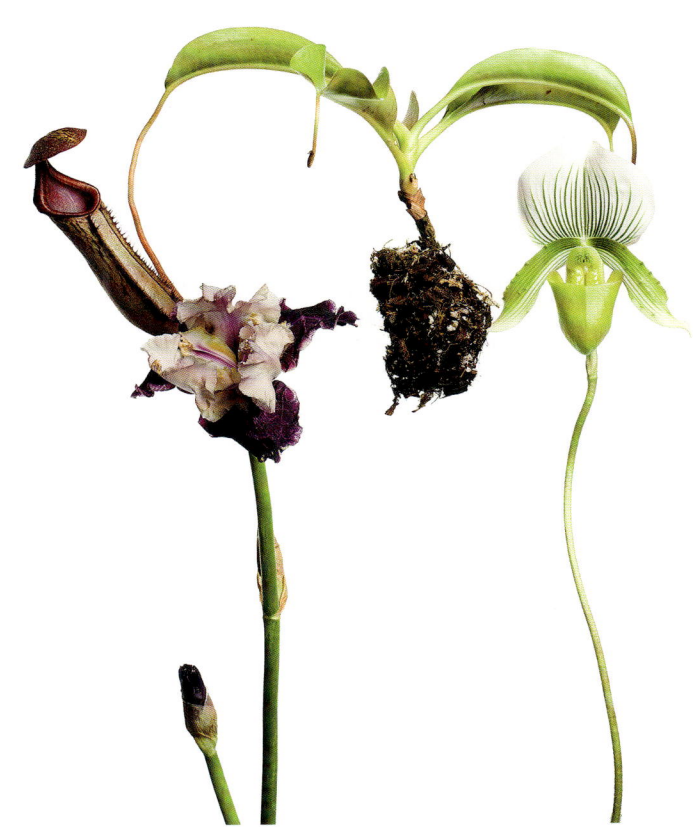

Lady Gaga / Dope - Artpop 2013

1 Pitcher Plant, 1 Purple Iris, 1 Lady Slipper Orchid 2013

INEZ &
VINOODH

Curriculum
A List of Favorite Anythings
by Alec Soth

Frank O'Hara

Whenever I'm asked to make a list, I have the desire to formulate some sort of manifesto. I like rules and guidelines, as in Lars von Trier's filmmaking movement "Dogme 95" (the film must be in color, the shooting must be done on location, and so on). But then I reread Frank O'Hara's "Personism: A Manifesto" and remember that his whimsical, rule-free manifesto is probably the most I'd ever be able to adhere to. "Personism has nothing to do with philosophy, it's all art," writes O'Hara. "But to give you a vague idea, one of its minimal aspects is to address itself to one person (other than the poet himself), thus evoking overtones of love without destroying love's life-giving vulgarity...."

The Family Photo Album

Picasso famously said that it took him four years to paint like Raphael but a lifetime to paint like a child. In a similar way, the struggle of many professional photographers is to make images that have the same purity of heart as the family snapshot. As someone whose primary ambition is to make photobooks, I've found the ultimate guide in the vernacular album. After years of collecting these albums, it was great to see this art form acknowledged in the recent Aperture book *Photographic Memory: The Album in the Age of Photography* (2011).

Masahisa Fukase's *The Solitude of Ravens* (1991)

When asked to name my favorite photography book, I always answer *The Solitude of Ravens* by Masahisa Fukase. Made after his divorce, it describes the feeling of a broken heart as lyrically as a Roy Orbison song.

Chantal Akerman's *News From Home* (1977)

In an era when just about every still photographer is experimenting with video on their DSLR, it is eye-opening to revisit Chantal Akerman's 1977 film of barely moving images. Every frame is perfect. But it is the voice-over of Akerman in New York reading letters from her mother, who is back home in Belgium, that gives this film its haunting beauty.

Robert Frank's *Pangnirtung* (2011)

Though I've never met Robert Frank, I feel like I've been having an ongoing conversation with him for the past twenty years. In many of our conversations, I question his later work. But with his modest 2011 book about a five-day visit to a remote Inuit village, I ceased to question and now simply enjoy being in the company of a master.

Pedro Meyer's *I Photograph to Remember* (1991)

I own an original CD-ROM of Pedro Meyer's multimedia piece *I Photograph to Remember*, but it no longer opens on my computer. Fortunately, Meyer eventually put the essay online, though that presentation feels dated too. What doesn't feel dated is Meyer's heartfelt tribute to his parents. The love, humor, and vulnerability of Meyer's intimate family slide show stands the test of time.

Leonard Cohen's *Ten New Songs* (2001)

A number of years ago in a frigidly contemporary German hotel room I discovered Cohen's CD in a drawer. As always with Cohen, the lyrics are the biggest draw. Nobody is able to describe the full spectrum of yearning—from physical to spiritual—the way Cohen does. But what I love most about this album is that Cohen isn't singing alone. In almost every song the vocalist Sharon Robinson accompanies him. Since that first night in Germany, the blend of their voices has served as a tonic to my loneliness in a hundred hotel rooms.

What Was True: The Photographs and Notebooks of William Gedney (2000)

There is so much meat on the bones of this book about the underappreciated photographer William Gedney. There are Gedney's wonderful photographs, of course. But these fragmentary glimpses of grace are made all the more meaningful by reading about Gedney's process in transcriptions from his notebooks and in two illuminating essays by Geoff Dyer and Maria Friedlander. Every (as-yet) unsung photographer grappling with the medium would do well to own this book.

Wim Wenders's *Im Lauf der Zeit* (*Kings of the Road*, 1976)

Since I first rented the double-cassette VHS as a teenager, Wenders's depiction of two lonely men on the road together has felt like some sort of prophecy. So when I started traveling extensively with the writer Brad Zellar a couple of years ago, you wouldn't believe my shock when he told me that *Kings of the Road* was one of his favorite movies.

Larry Sultan's *Pictures From Home* (1992)

One of the hardest things to do with photographs is accompany them meaningfully with words—particularly those written by the photographer. *Pictures From Home* achieves this goal better than any other book I've seen. But I only allow myself to read the book every few years because (1) it is so heartbreaking and (2) it is so good that it makes all of my work seem trivial.

Alec Soth is a photographer born and based in Minnesota. He is the author of more than a dozen publications including *Sleeping by the Mississippi* (Steidl, 2004), *NIAGARA* (Steidl, 2006), and *Broken Manual* (Steidl, 2010).

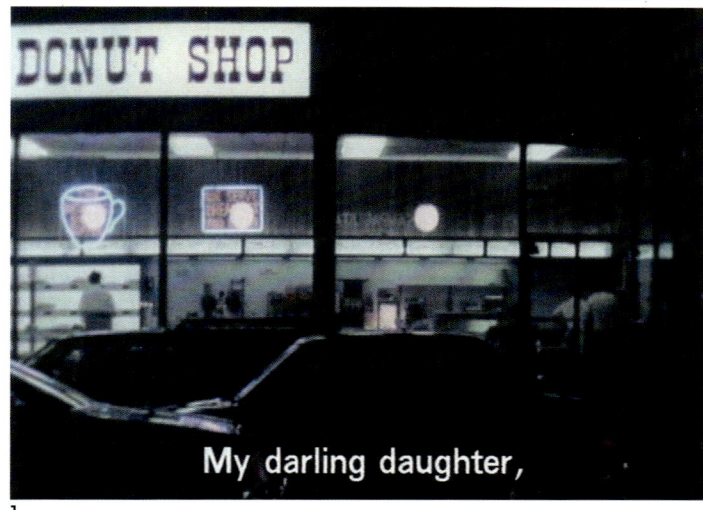

1

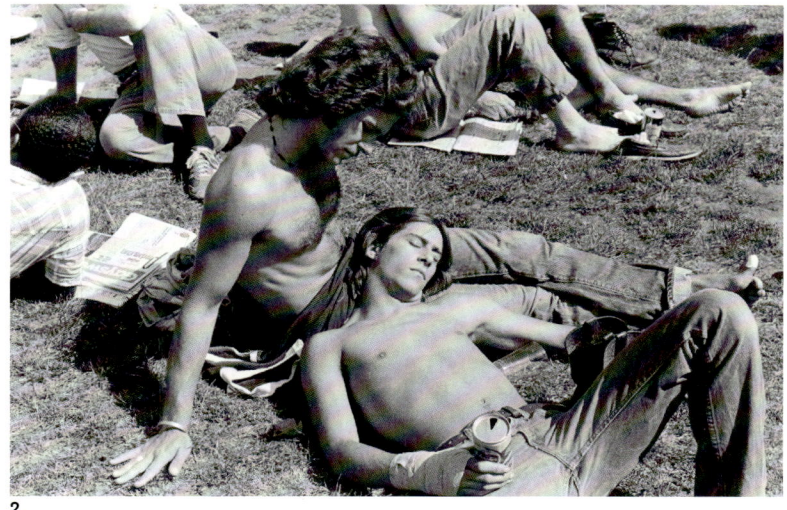

2

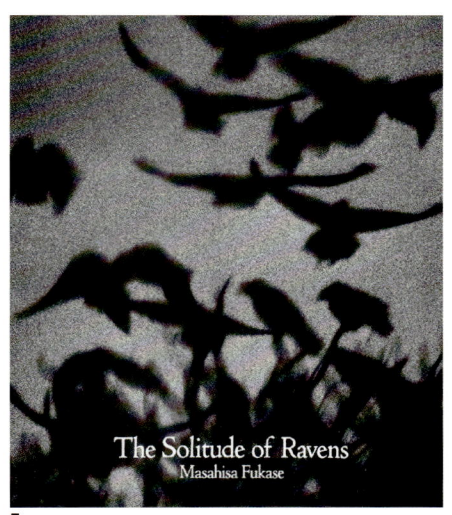

3

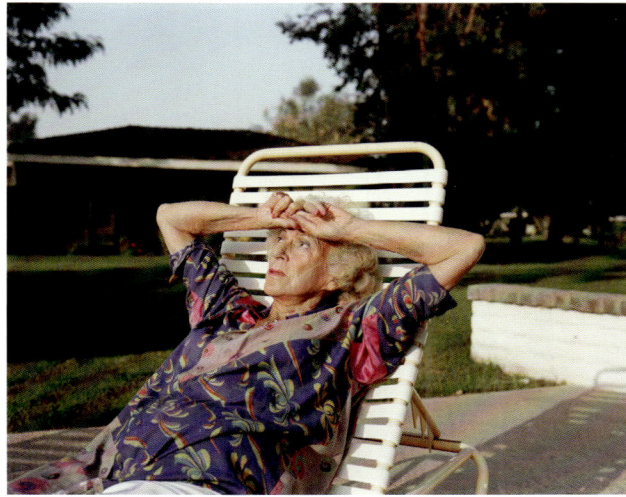

4

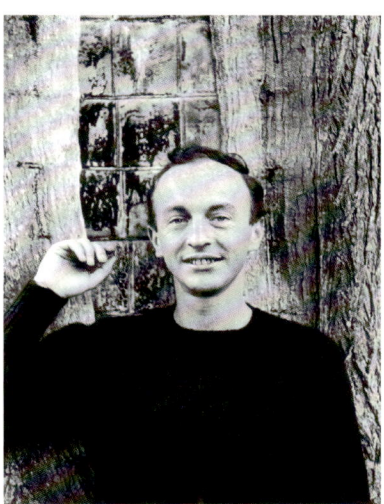

5

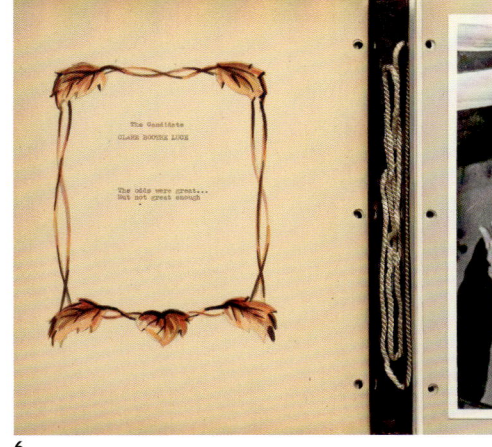

6

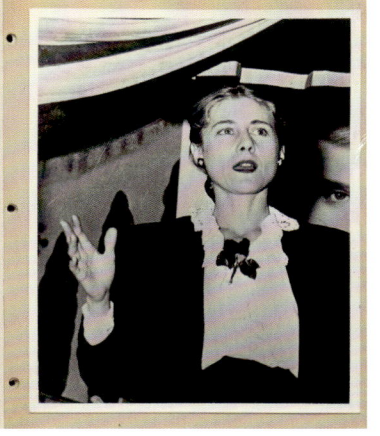

7

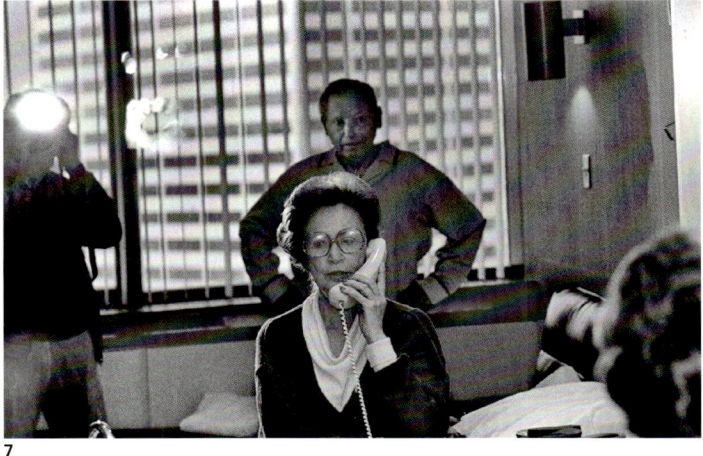

8

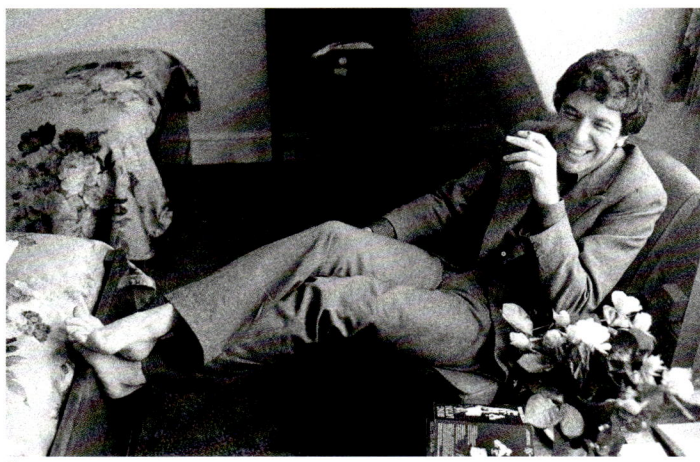

9

Art | Basel
Miami Beach | Dec | 4–7 | 2014

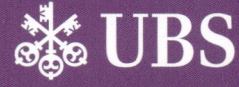

Redux
Rediscovered Books and Writings

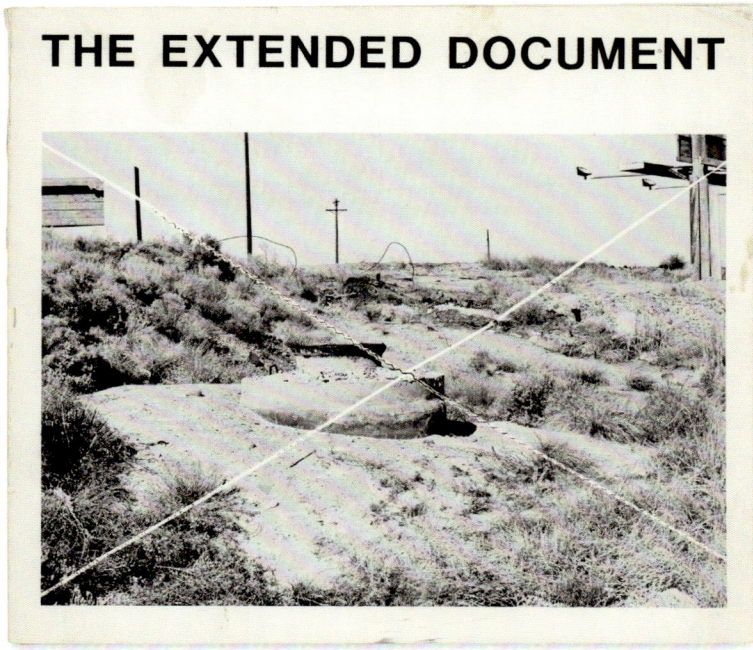

THE EXTENDED DOCUMENT

The Extended Document
Mary Statzer

In 1975, George Eastman House curator William Jenkins stood in the back room at New York's Sonnabend Gallery with Ealan Wingate, then director of the gallery, and video artist and photographer William Wegman, who was accompanied by his dog named Man Ray. Jenkins was making selections of Wegman's work for the upcoming exhibition, *The Extended Document* (February 1–April 30, 1975). Performance artist Vito Acconci walked in and called from across the room, "Hey, Man Ray, how ya doin'?" The dog didn't move. Acconci got on his hands and knees and cajoled, "Hey! Man Ray! Come here! Come see Vito!" Man Ray got up and began walking over to him until Wegman calmly said, "Don't do it." As soon as the dog heard Wegman's command, he flattened himself to the floor and refused to budge.

Jenkins shared this anecdote about witnessing an impromptu piece of performance art during a recent conversation with me. I found it both funny and significant as it places Jenkins, a museum curator little known outside of photography circles, in a powerful contemporary art gallery and working with cutting-edge artists, suggesting that these worlds were not as distinct or rigidly defined as previously thought.

The exhibition catalog for *The Extended Document* was typical of those produced at the time—a small, slim, soft-bound book containing a short essay, the checklist, brief biographies, and several serviceable black-and-white reproductions that represented a fraction of the works on view. Designed in-house, with a print run of approximately two thousand five hundred, it sold for three dollars and remains the most complete record of the exhibition. Underwhelming in its physical presence, this catalog and others like it belie the importance of the ideas contained therein and the groundbreaking territory of the exhibition.

The Extended Document was a significant gesture made from within an established institution of photography that not only attempted to close the gap between photographers and artists but also critiqued photography's documentary function, then considered a fundamental aspect of the medium. The impetus for the show was Jenkins's belief that photographic truth was suspect. He sought out works that expanded on that thesis by photographers Thomas Barrow, Michael Bishop, Marcia Resnick, and Richard Schaeffer as well as non-photographers John Baldessari and William Wegman.

Jenkins knew Barrow's, Bishop's, and Schaeffer's work well, as all three had ties to the photography community in Rochester, New York. Resnick's series *See*, in which a surrogate viewer placed in the landscape performs the act of seeing for the camera, was discovered during a routine portfolio review. Jenkins contacted Baldessari at Resnick's suggestion—she had been a graduate student at CalArts—and explained the premise of the show, which he enthusiastically embraced. His *Seeing Is Believing*, created especially for *The Extended Document*, is composed of three panels in which a lit cigar appears to be frozen in a chunk of ice with smoke curling illogically above it. In reality, Baldessari had photographed a cigar lying in a cast glass ashtray, made prints of the photograph, and airbrushed loops of "smoke" that spelled out the phrase "Seeing is believing." Jenkins could not have asked for a pithier summary of his exhibition's premise.

The Extended Document took aim at the spectrum of examples that traded on the notion of photographic truth. Jenkins's catalog essay "The Extended Document: An Investigation of Information and Evidence in Photographs" outlined dramatic shifts in documentary photography during the previous century. Photographs made by Lewis Wickes Hine or Timothy H. O'Sullivan were considered evidence because of the presumed "indisputable accuracy of the lens" to record what was before it. Jenkins noted, however, that photographic truth was a matter of faith and that Robert Frank's *The Americans*

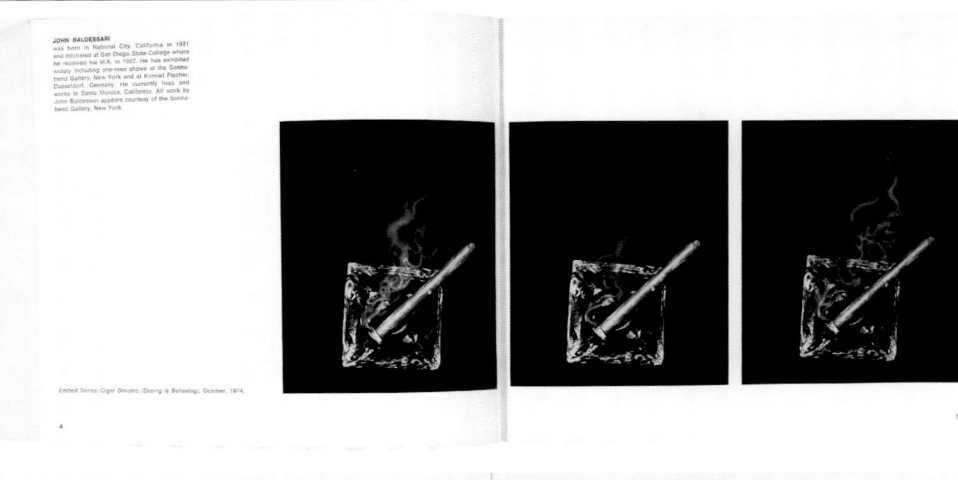

Embed Series/Cigar Dreams (Seeing Is Believing), October, 1974.

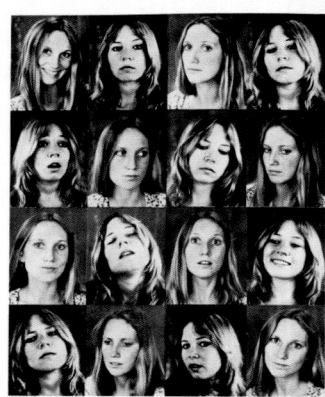

Blondes-Brunettes, 1974.

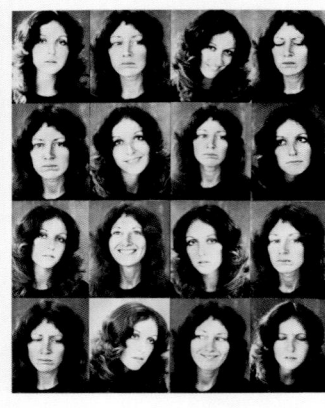

Previous page:
Exhibition catalog for
The Extended Document
(International Museum
of Photography, George
Eastman House, Rochester,
1975)

This page: Pages from
the exhibition catalog
showing John Baldessari,
*Embed Series/Cigar
Dreams* (*Seeing Is Believing*),
October, 1974 (top) and
William Wegman, *Blondes-
Brunettes*, 1974 (bottom)

(1959) had struck a fatal blow to the belief in the "camera as an impartial witness." Photographs by Garry Winogrand and Lee Friedlander, introduced in the 1967 MoMA exhibition *New Documents*, were equally subjective. And yet Frank sought to show something about American life in the 1950s, as did Friedlander and Winogrand in the 1960s and '70s, and thus the meaning and impact of their photographs was "still totally dependent on the implied relationship between the photograph and the photographed."

Jenkins also posited that photographs "can and often do contain meanings quite apart from their visual subject matter." Baldessari's *Seeing Is Believing* is not really about cigars, ashtrays, or smoke; rather it questions how truth in photographs is generated. Most photographers resisted picturing humorous subjects or trivial actions, but Conceptual artists who employed photography used these strategies to signal the viewer to look beyond literal subject matter for underlying meanings. In Wegman's case, it helps to see several photographs of Man Ray to understand that Wegman is a jokester and his well-trained Weimaraner his accomplice. Jenkins had no idea whether his audience, accustomed as they were to serious photography, would get the joke.

Jenkins conceived *The Extended Document* and his follow-up exhibition, *New Topographics: Photographs of a Man-Altered Landscape* (October 14, 1975–February 2, 1976), as two parts of a single argument, yet the latter is much better known and venerated. Perhaps it is because *New Topographics* was the straight man, as it were: the meanings of the pictures were contained in the photographs. These photographs were about what they "said" they were about—environmental issues, stark changes to the landscape, and the built environment. Even though *New Topographics* reflected important shifts in what it meant to make a landscape photograph, Jenkins considers *The Extended Document* a more crucial and far-reaching proposition because it confronted, in his words, "photographic veracity and untangling how photographs come to mean."

Few people paid attention to *The Extended Document*, but Charles Desmarais, who wrote a mixed review of it in the March 1975 issue of *Afterimage*, nevertheless implored photographers to learn from art-world uses of photography. In selecting artists who used photography in their work as well as self-identified photographers who arrived at the same conclusion, that photographs can lie, Jenkins successfully blurred the distinction between fine art and photography and laid claim to a critique of the medium made from both sides of the divide. Jenkins's efforts now seem prescient, anticipating photography's eventual absorption and integration into the art world.

Mary Statzer is a PhD
candidate in the history
and theory of art at the
University of Arizona.
She is editor of the book
*The Photographic Object
1970*, to be published by
the University of California
Press next year.

Words

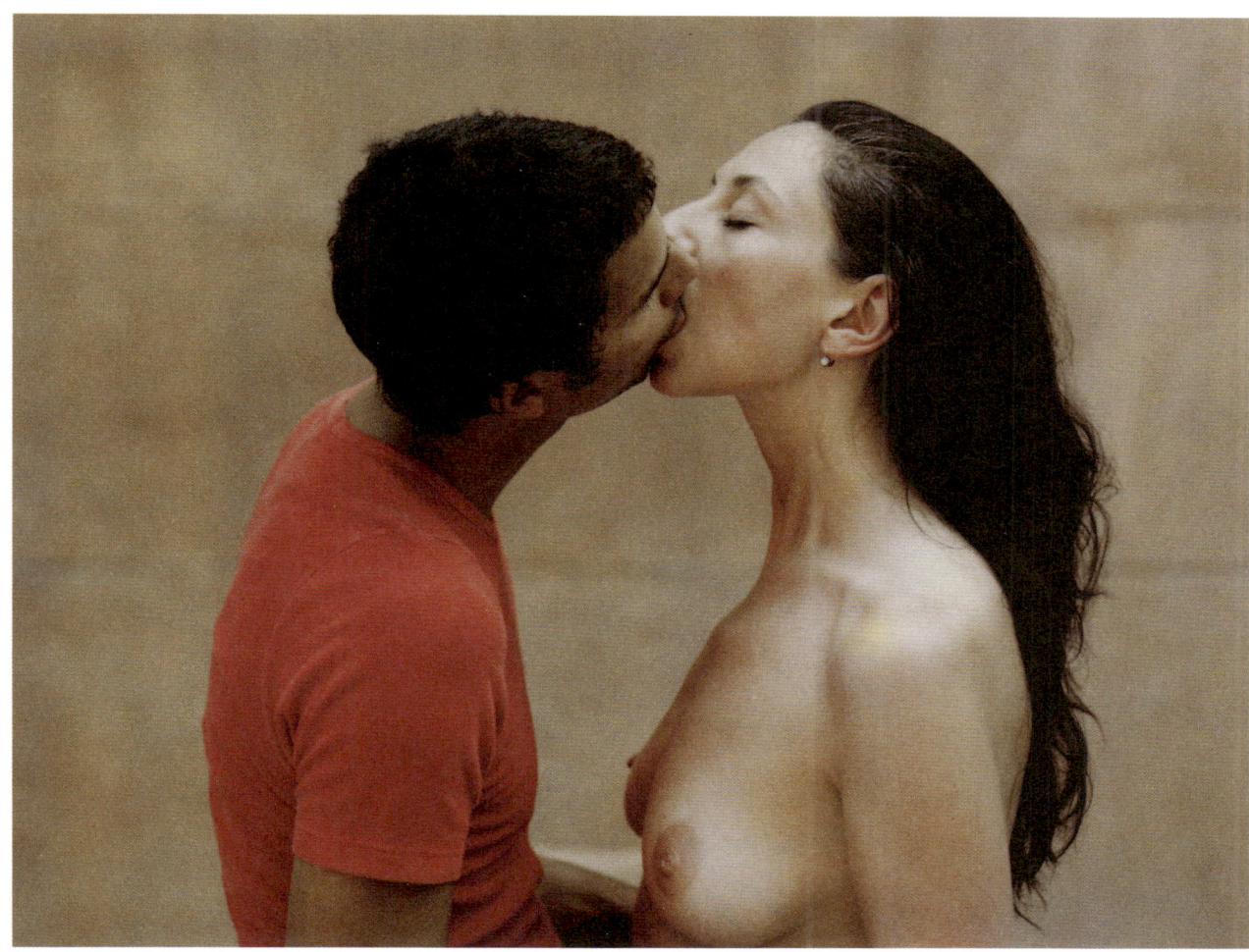

Inez & Vinoodh: The Art of Transformation

Donatien Grau

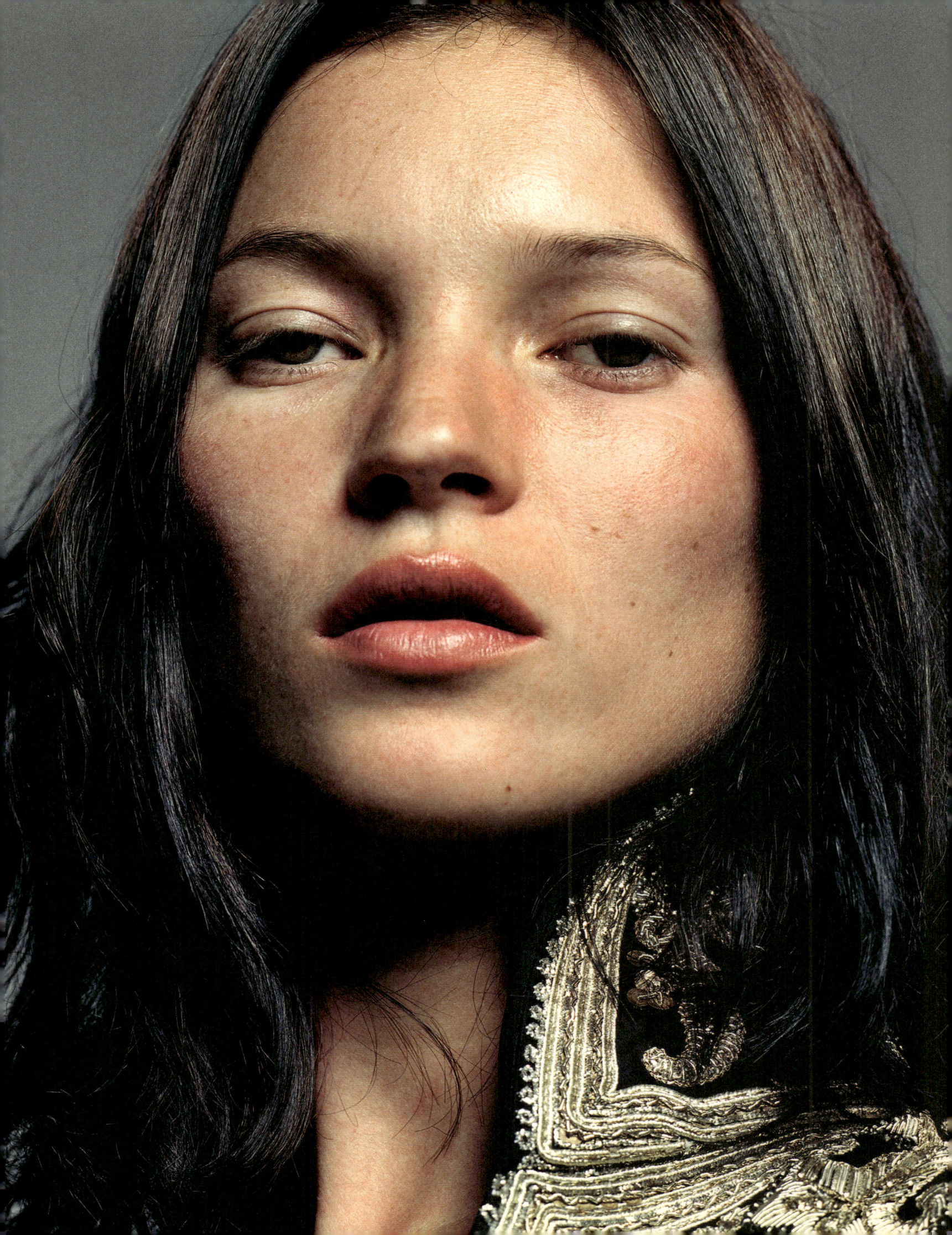

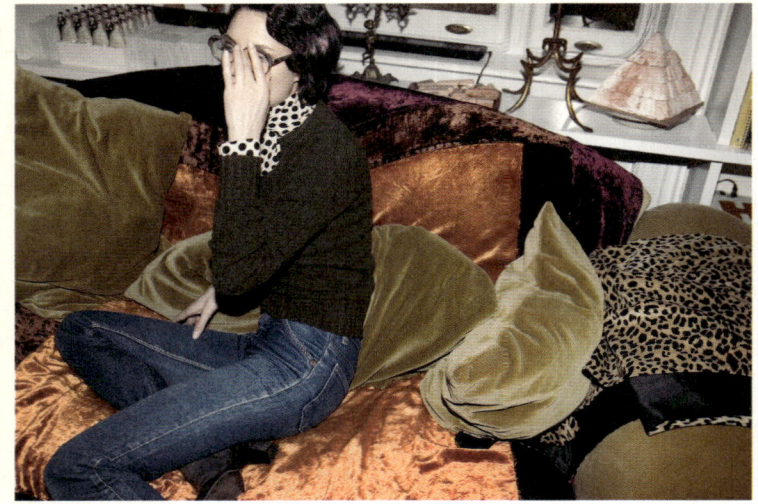
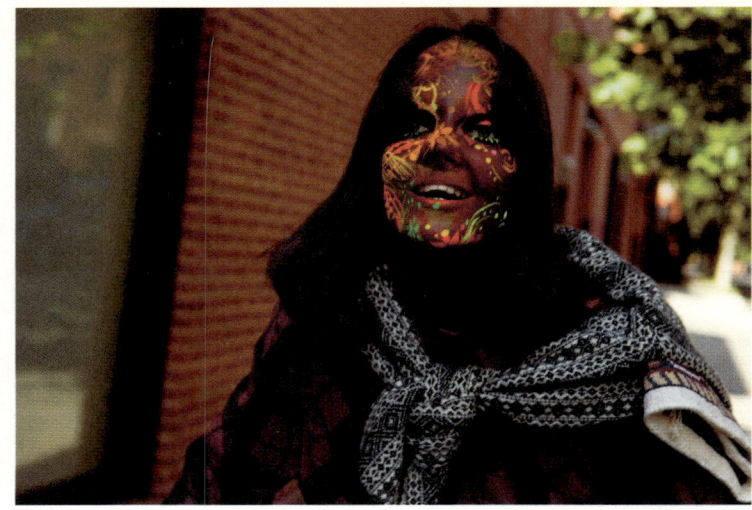
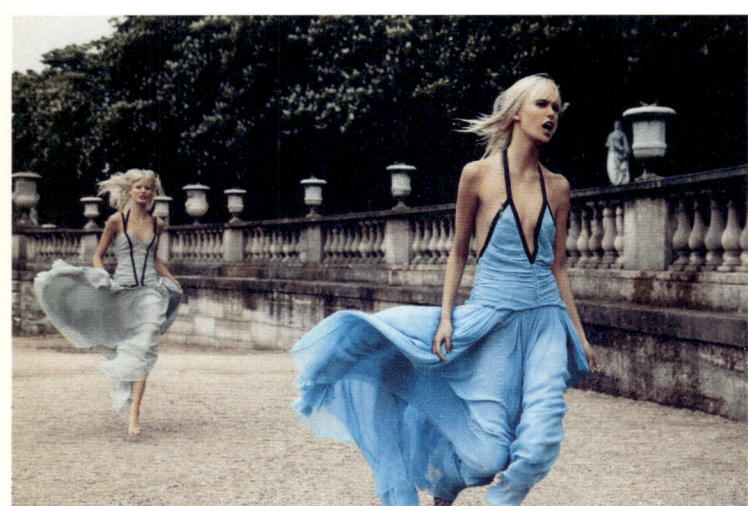
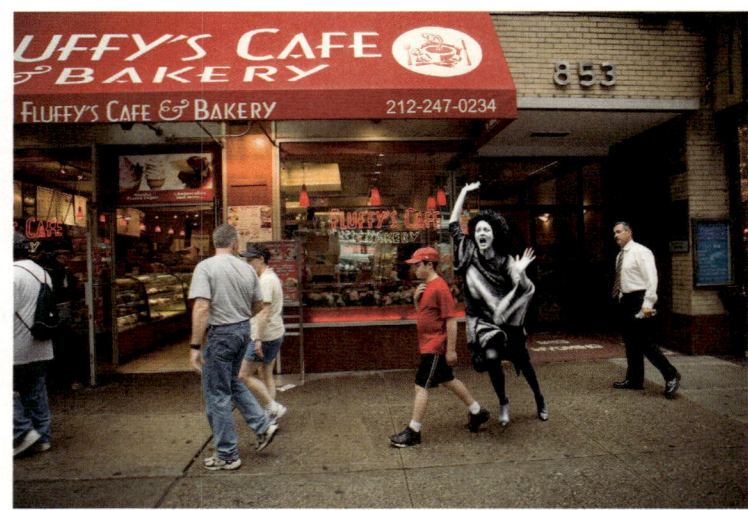
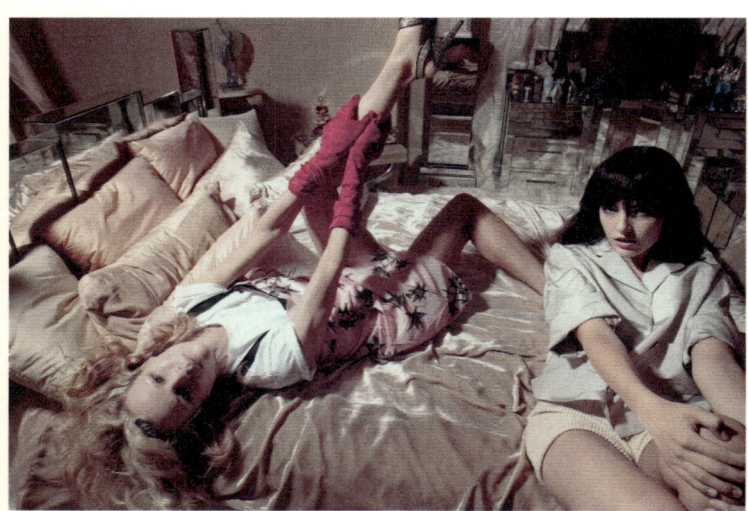
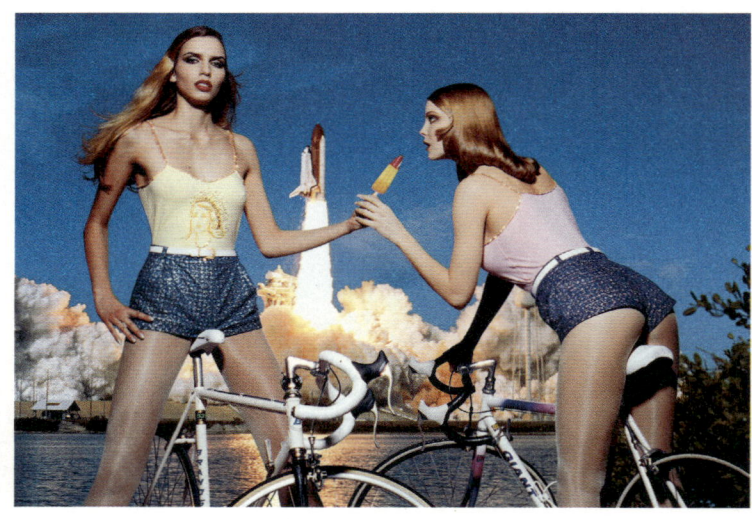
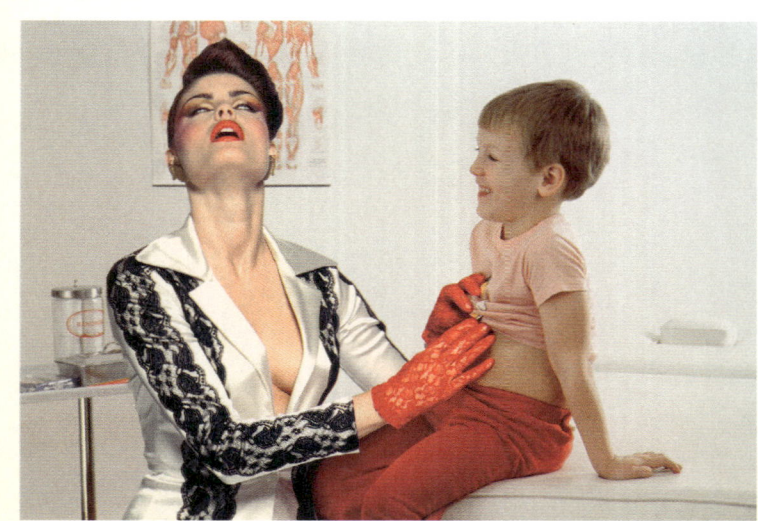
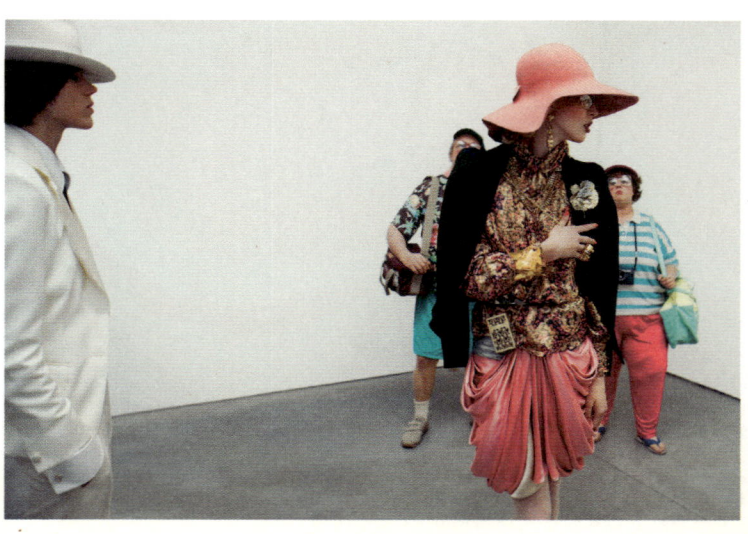

Guest editors Inez & Vinoodh have collaborated for more than twenty-five years, creating an uncommon range of distinctive fashion imagery, fueled by a curiosity about the flexibility and possibilities of photography. Here, writer Donatien Grau reflects on how their powerful creative union underscores their restless output.

Shalom in NY, 2006

Dewi Driegen and Carolyn Weinberg, Chloé Campaign, 2004

Kim Basinger and Camilla Belle, Miu Miu Campaign, 2006

A Two-Tone Stretch Satin and Lace Pantsuit by Bertrand Marechal, The Face, 1994

Eniko Mihalik in Isabel Marant, Self Service, 2008

Shalom Harlow at 853 7th Avenue, Self Service, 2006

Well Basically Basuco Is Coke Mixed With Kerosene..., The Face, 1994

Freja and Raquel With Tourists by Duane Hanson, W, 2009

Inez & Vinoodh: two people, one name; a couple, in life and for art. Such a creative situation is rare in the field of photography. In many ways, photography is the art of the individual. If we take for granted, as Robert Doisneau once described it, that photography's original goal is to "capture what is ephemeral," then, we need only one perspective, not two, to capture it. The gesture of capturing a timely moment provides a person with the opportunity to explore his or her own intimacy, dreams, and fantasy, in the process of selecting, stealing, and appropriating from reality. The situation with Inez & Vinoodh is different. Over the twenty-five-plus years that Vinoodh Matadin has been collaborating with fellow Dutch artist Inez van Lamsweerde, their work has changed art and fashion photography, first altering the way art photography was perceived by bringing harmony and elegance into it in the late 1990s, at a time when reality was the rage; then bringing strangeness into fashion imagery; and eventually, today, creating their synthetic world that is displayed in a range of contexts: from magazines to fashion exhibitions as well as on the walls of some of the world's most prominent contemporary art galleries. This kind of crossover and experimentation is exceptional both in contemporary photography and fashion.

An early photograph from 1999, *Me Kissing Vinoodh (Lovingly)*, might well be the visual emblem of their union. It brings together the different components involved in the making of their works: the presence of art, the symbols and ethics of love. This picture can be paralleled with Gustav Klimt's 1907–08 painting *The Kiss*, the composition of which is echoed in Inez & Vinoodh's photograph: a man on the left kissing a woman on the right. Vinoodh's black hair is strikingly reminiscent of Klimt's male model. But the dynamics are different: in Klimt's painting, the kiss itself is a rather small, albeit central, part of the image; in Inez & Vinoodh's, the kiss is located in the same area of the image but is far more conspicuous. In 1907, the man is in a dominating position, taller and leaning over the girl, whose eyes are closed, as are Inez's. In *Me Kissing Vinoodh*, Vinoodh is leaning his head too, but he reaches out to Inez, and doesn't affect a posture of protection. Another key difference: in 1999, the picture is

They want to make people look beautiful—though not in a classical, ordinary way but often in a rather uncanny fashion. Their style is restless and all-encompassing, as is their subject matter.

taken by a woman, Inez—hence the title. She is the one engaging Vinoodh, the one "kissing" him, and not, like the passive woman in Klimt's painting, the one being kissed. Femininity is activated symbolically by Inez's situation in the picture, through the appearance of her bare breast. It is a picture about Inez van Lamsweerde, and yet it signals the importance of the couple, both creatively and personally—they are both represented and they co-author the photograph.

This notion of shared exchange is one of the best lessons Inez & Vinoodh's work provides. Their generation of artists and creatives, which blossomed in the 1990s, valued collaboration and conversation. Inez & Vinoodh collaborate not only with each other, but also with other artists, critics, editors, and designers—producing a twofold displacement of the authorial figure, a collaboration embedded in collaborations. It is difficult to think of any other photographers who would be as much at ease with the video and installation artist Philippe Parreno, a prominent figure of relational aesthetics, as with Lady Gaga or Kate Moss. An immediate parallel from their generation is M/M (Paris)'s Mathias Augustyniak and Michael Amzalag, the collaborative duo that hybridized graphic design and other practices, notably engaging in an ongoing artistic dialogue with Inez & Vinoodh. Bringing together the initials of their first name, M/M (Paris) decided to coin a new name for a new way to collaborate with other creatives, ranging from design and art direction to filmmaking and art.

One of the reasons why *Me Kissing Vinoodh (Lovingly)* is such an important picture has to do with the fact that it signals that very tension. It is the sign of a movement toward a new unity beyond individuals: a couple, a synthesis. The adverb set between parentheses—"lovingly"—carries much weight: it signifies the feelings of two human beings toward each other, but it also conveys a more universal meaning. All of Inez & Vinoodh's pictures might be viewed as acts of love: they are words in a global declaration of love to the world in which they live. Collaborating, conversing: these are gestures of interest in others. It could be argued that their passion for portraiture somehow emanates from their love, which is at the same time very specific, open, and generous: they portray very different kinds of people, models as well as actors as well as singers as well as their friends. They want to make people look beautiful—though not in a classical, ordinary way but often in a rather uncanny fashion. Their style is restless and all-encompassing, as is their subject matter: they make photographs of flowers, turn mass-market products into contemporary still life, portray people in black-and-white or in vivid color, zoom in on a face or situate a portrait in a complex environment. They never gave up on the notion of beauty, an idea that was not popular among their generation of photographers. They want to see the beauty in people and allow other people to seize the objects of their love.

This ever-expanding embrace explains their interest in the language of fashion photography as well as their collaboration with the pop star Lady Gaga: fashion is designed, among other things, to make people feel good about themselves, to give them a sense of belonging; Lady Gaga's message is based on the idea of welcoming people who seldom feel as though they belong anywhere. Inez & Vinoodh, by taking the language of fashion and making it their own, by challenging and twisting it, help us understand that those who feel different from the rules of common existence have a place to stay, a place of fantasy.

Therein comes a crucial notion: transformation. Inez & Vinoodh's pictures are not mere depictions of reality. They intervene heavily in the making of them: they very obviously

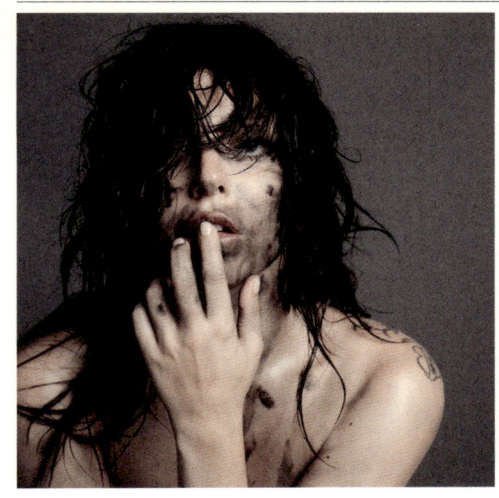
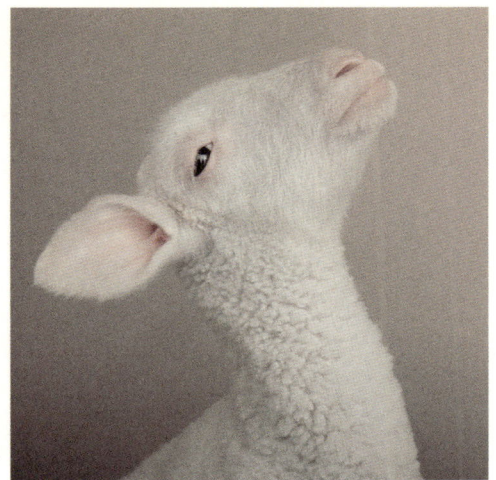
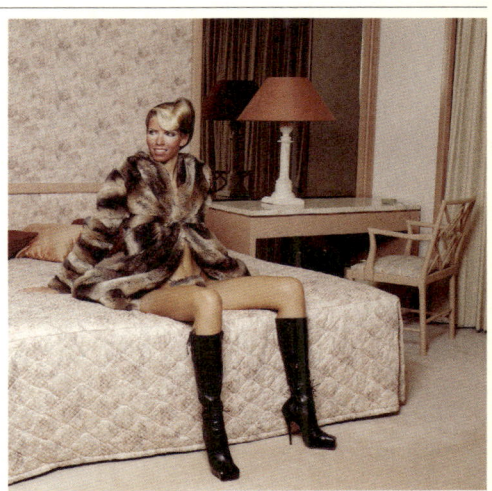
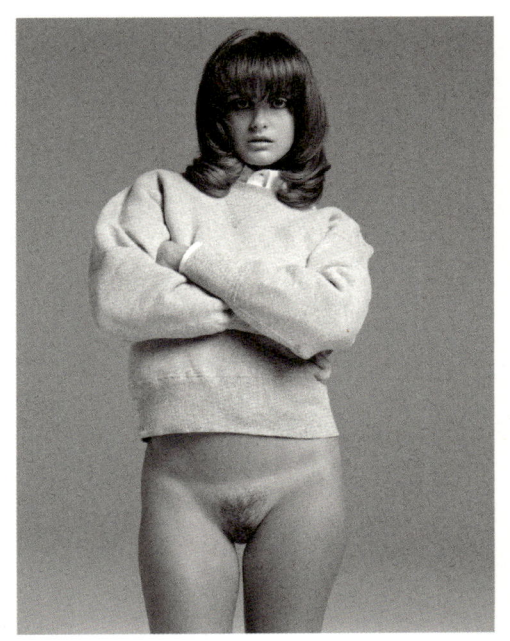
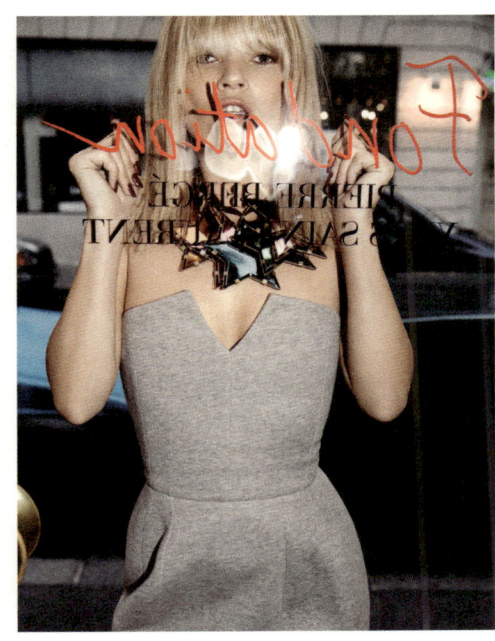
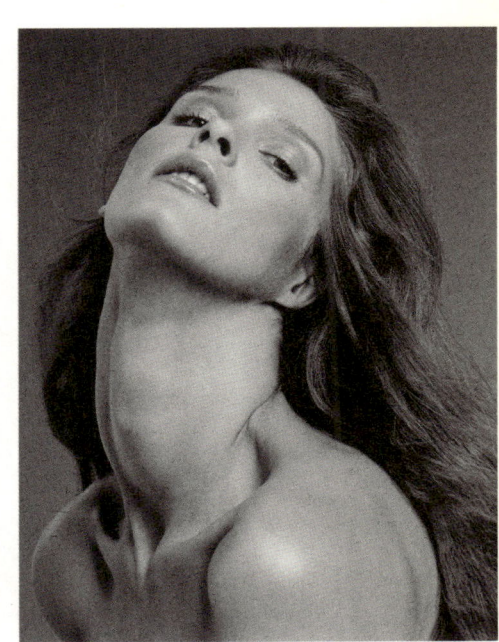
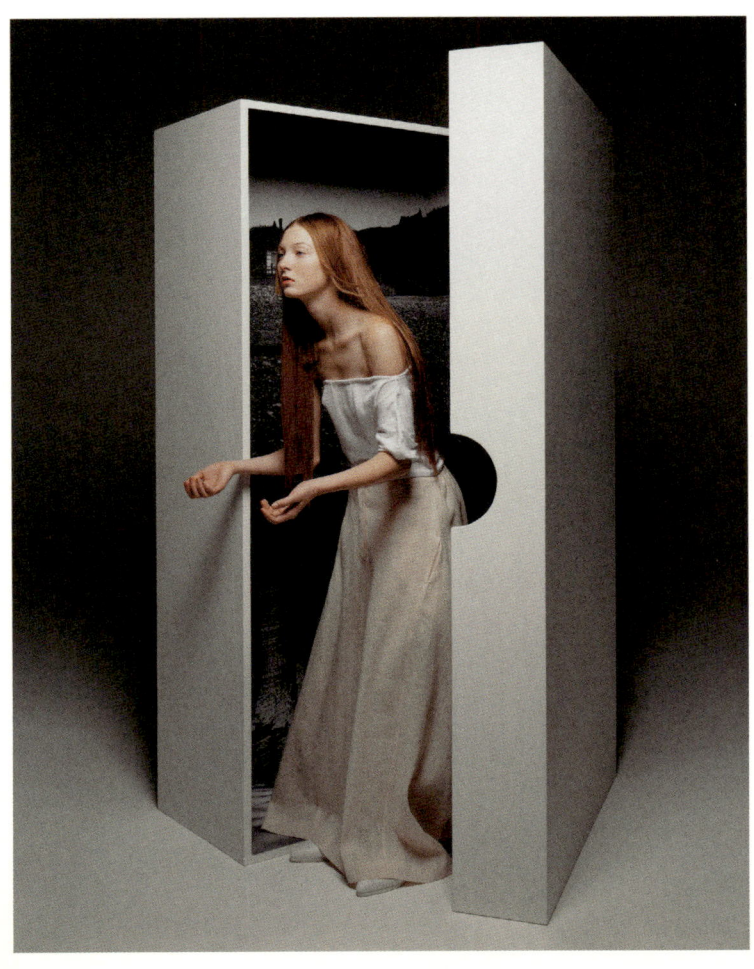
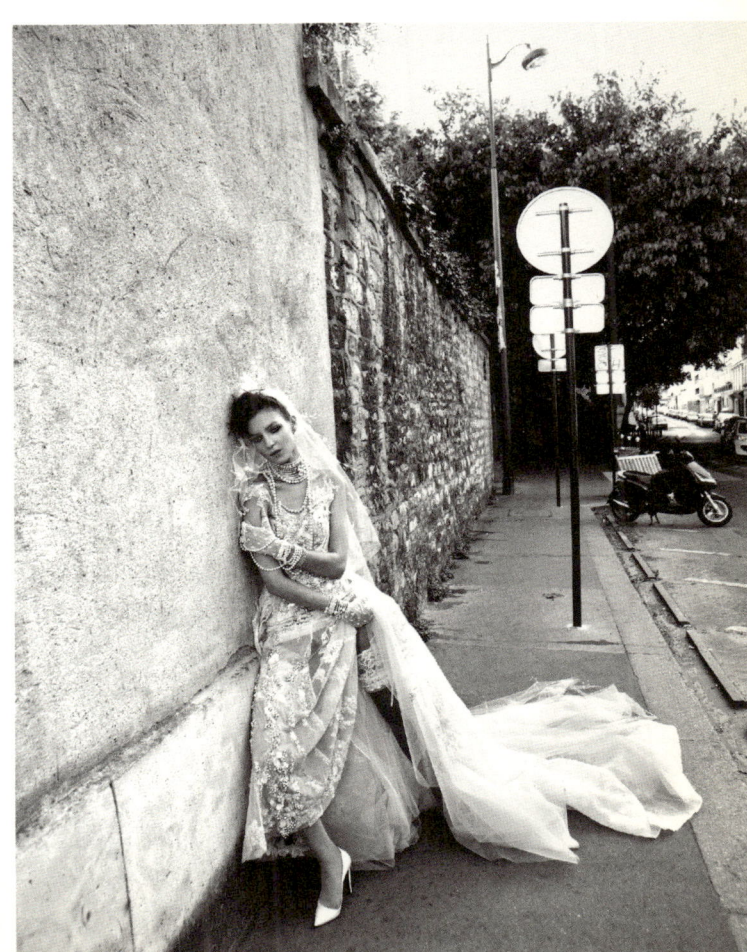

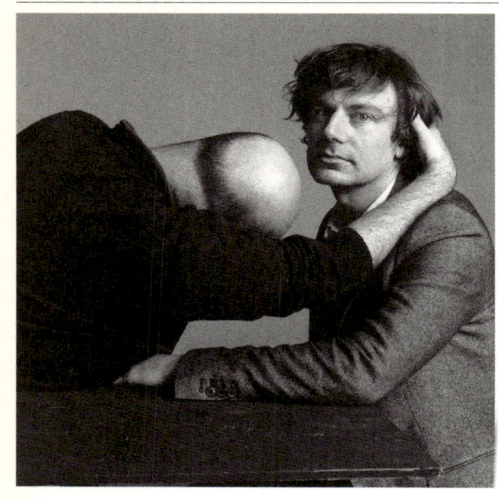
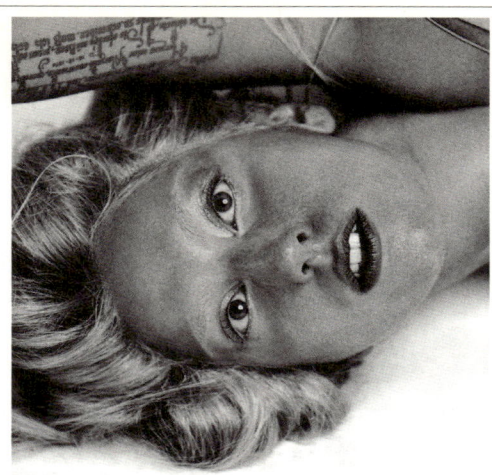
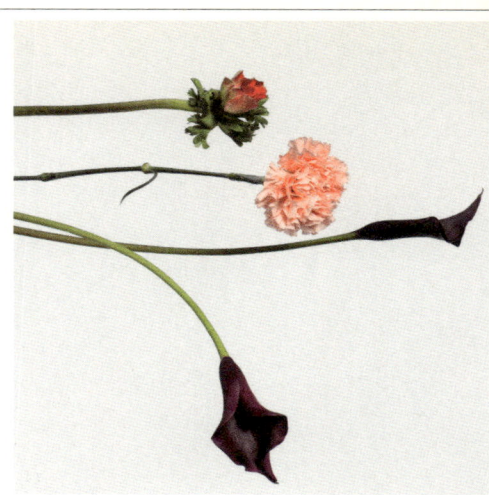
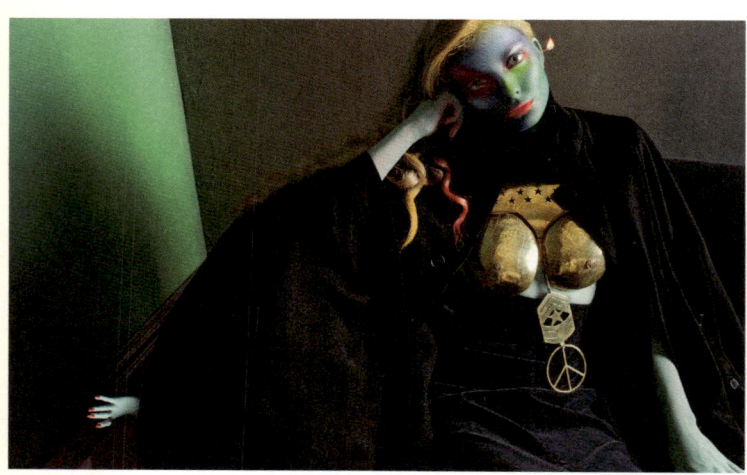
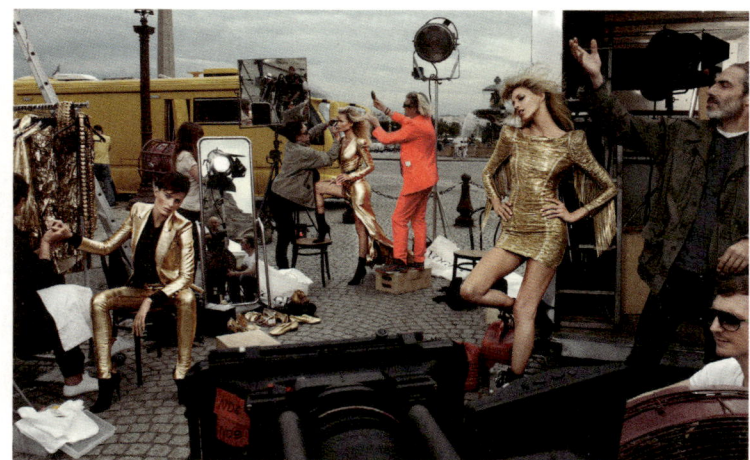
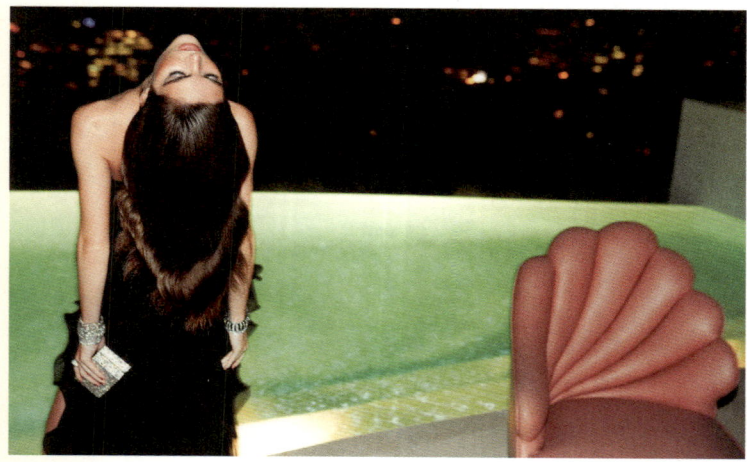
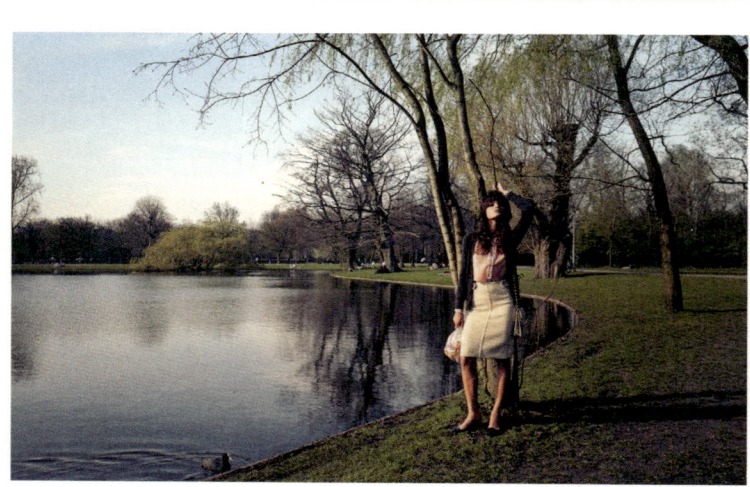
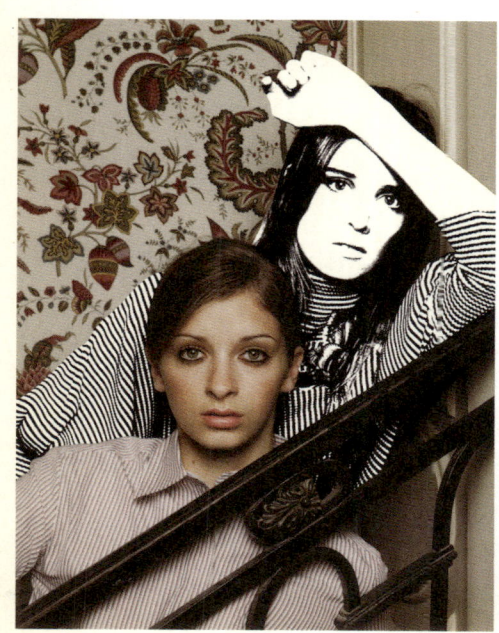
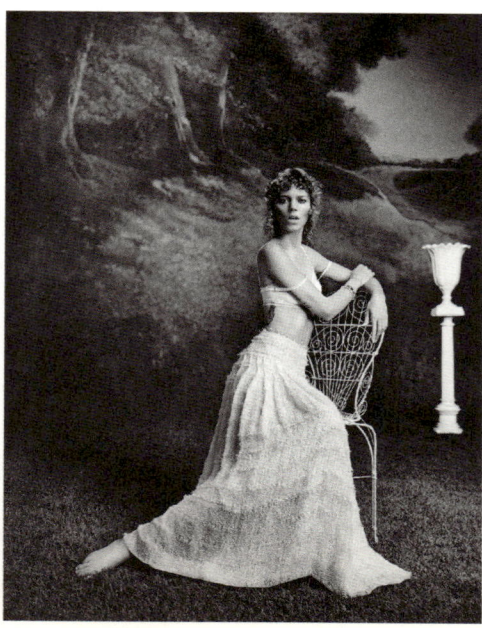
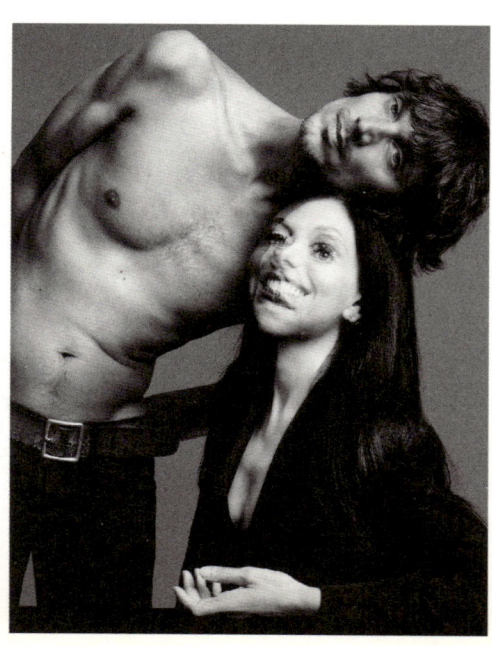

use postproduction to manipulate the shape of bodies, the acuteness of light, the intensity of colors. Other photographers of their generation wanted to engage with reality, dig deep into it, and introduce realism into fashion photography, a genre often defined by the idealization of forms. Inez & Vinoodh seek the opposite and instead play with creative patterns—they embellish, they add elements of distortion, so that the final picture is almost never a transcription of something in the real world. It is a transfiguration. They change the visual nature of reality. They create fictions.

They do not only capture the ephemeral: they also make the eternal. The models and objects present in their works—from young people to flowers—all exist as such in a specific moment of time, and then, after the picture has been taken, disappear: the young are no longer young; the flowers die. Their signature lies in the fact that they make us believe, for a second, while we look at the picture, that eternity might well exist—it exists in the fixed version that is a photograph. Even if the rest of the world rots, the picture of it will remain. The idea that they could bring all their models and subjects to eternity is a fiction, but their work, which involves transforming what their subjects actually look like, is a fiction too. These processes of fiction coincide with ethics of representation. In the same way that Lady Gaga creates a fantasy world for her followers, Inez & Vinoodh offer viewers a visual rendering of fantasy, complete with beauty, danger, and uncertainty, the longing for eternity, the ecstasy of the ephemeral. Their world carries the ethical imperative of fiction and the necessity of an underlying realism.

If you want to love the people and things that surround you, if you want love to govern your life, and life to be at least bearable, and hopefully wonderful, you need to invent the world, and make the fantasy of its eternity believable. As Giacomo Casanova once said about Nattier, "his genius lay in the fact that his portraits looked far more beautiful than the persons he portrayed; and yet, if one was to look closely and compare every inch of the painting to the face of the actual person, we could not see any difference." Photography, like Nattier's portraiture, may often be an art of the individual, but Inez & Vinoodh make photography an art of the community.

Opposite, from left to right:

Top row:
M/M (Paris), New York Times Magazine, 2007

Lady Gaga / Head, Yoü & I, 2011

One Red Anemone, One Pink Carnation, One Purple Calla Lily, 2013

Second row:
Eniko for Peace, Self Service, 2008

Girls on Film, Vogue Paris, 2010

Third row:
Hilary at Midnight, W, 2007

Isabeli in the Vondelpark, Harper's Bazaar, 2002

Bottom row:
Roos and Anne-Catherine, Balenciaga Campaign, 1999

Freja Beha Erichsen, Vogue Paris, 2014

Inez and Vinoodh, The Gentlewoman, 2010
All photographs
© Inez & Vinoodh, and courtesy Gagosian Gallery, New York, and The Collective Shift

It is difficult to think of any other photographers who would be as much at ease with the video and installation artist Philippe Parreno, a prominent figure of relational aesthetics, as with Lady Gaga or Kate Moss.

Donatien Grau is a member of New College, University of Oxford, and a contributing editor of Flash Art International, an editor of Purple, and a contributor to The Times Literary Supplement. He is the author of The Age of Creation (Sternberg Press, 2013).

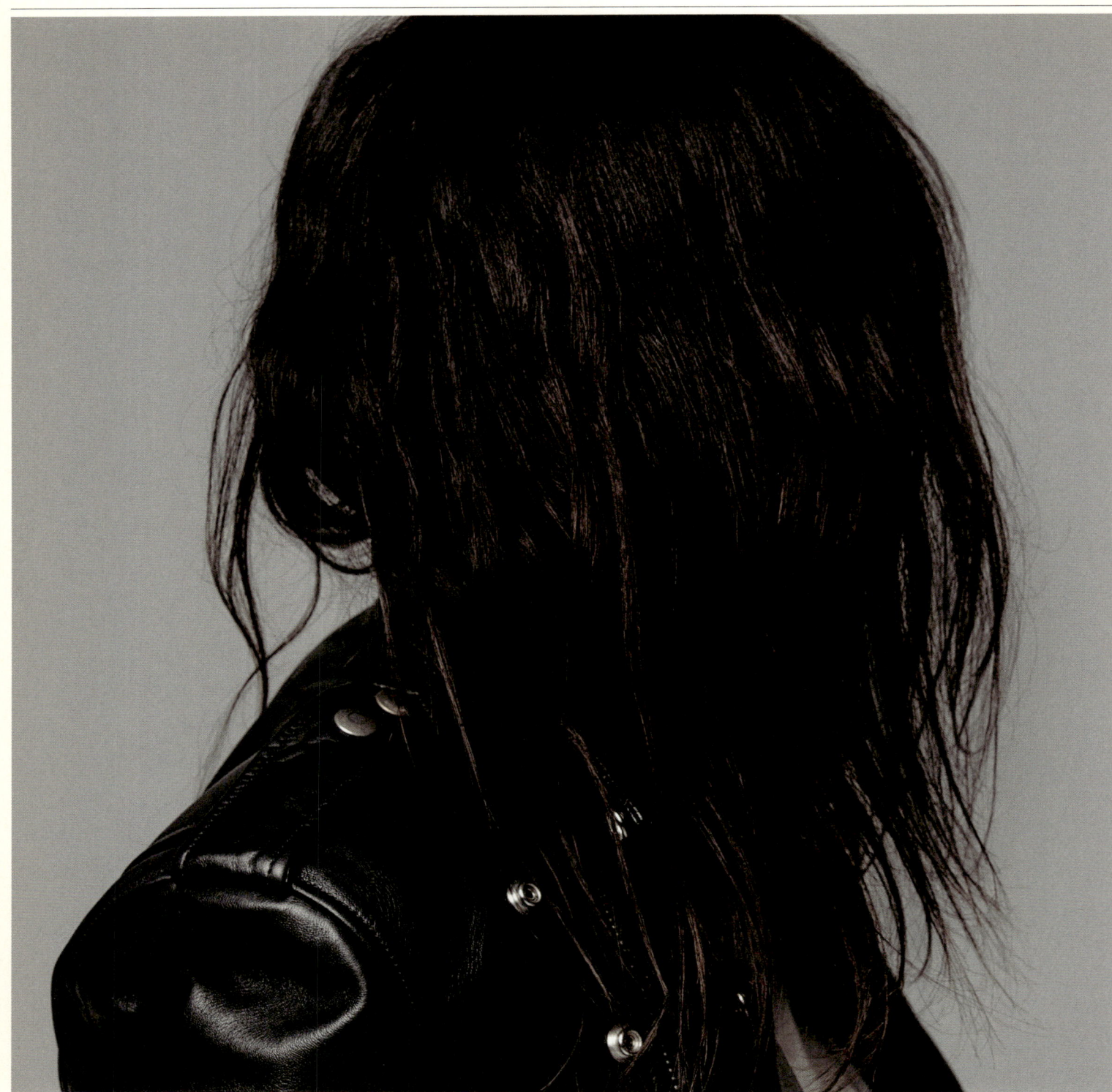

Inez & Vinoodh,
Emmanuelle Alt, 2014
© Inez & Vinoodh
and courtesy Gagosian
Gallery, New York,
and The Collective Shift

Emmanuelle Alt

Conversation with Penny Martin

Fashion photography can be a nostalgic business, but Emmanuelle Alt's appetite for the unexpected and glamorous keeps her in the vanguard of taste. A forty-seven-year-old stylist who learned her trade at French *Elle*, Alt is celebrated for reinvigorating the industry's tired '70s fashion clichés with surprising, sporty modernity since joining its most prestigious magazine, *Vogue Paris*, as fashion director in 2000.

Taking over from Carine Roitfeld as the publication's editor-in-chief three years ago has demanded a more global view of making a magazine, shifting Alt's focus away from styling and aesthetics alone. She may not now enjoy the luxury of being on set with Mario Testino, David Sims, and Inez & Vinoodh every week, but Alt still has the knack of intuiting exactly what a photographer needs to make a truly great picture. Penny Martin, editor of the women's title *The Gentlewoman*, interviewed Alt at the *Vogue Paris* offices on Rue du Faubourg Saint-Honoré this past May.

Vogue Paris,
December 2013.
Cover photograph
by Inez & Vinoodh
© Inez & Vinoodh/
Vogue Paris

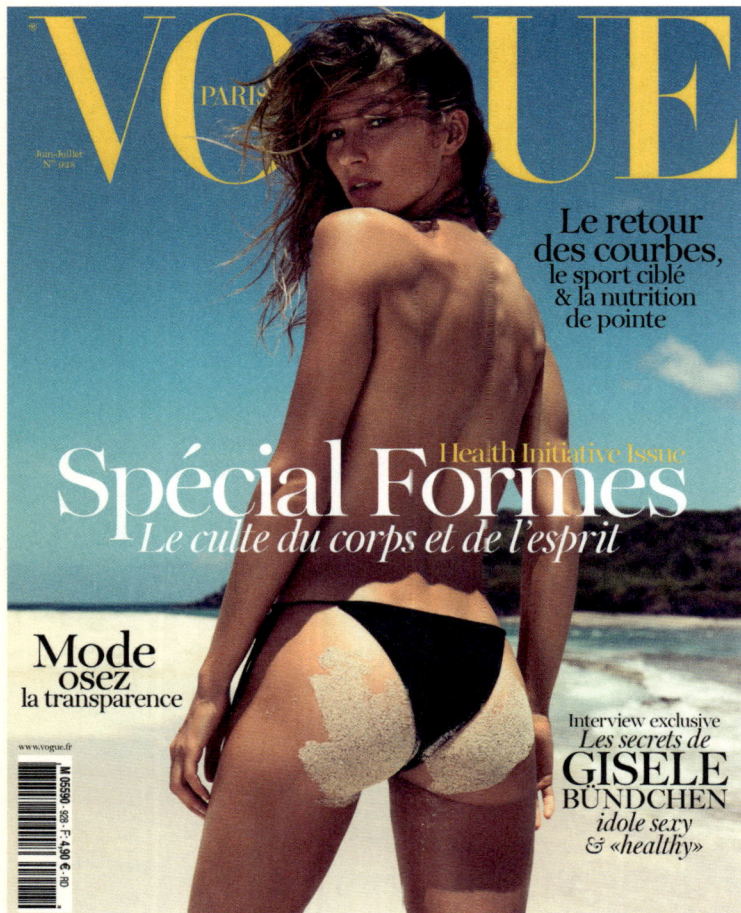

I think your first music and visual influences stay with you forever. My group all listens to Bowie; there's nothing better. You live with what was around when you first became curious.

Penny Martin: Let's start in the present. Emmanuelle, tell me about your most recent shoot—how did it come about?

Emmanuelle Alt: I was just in St. Barths with Inez & Vinoodh, shooting for our June/July issue. I've known them for about twelve years, so we've developed an easy way of working. We all love the same period of photography. And it's not only the images; it's the whole culture—a certain time of models, clothes, a certain time in music.

PM: I gather you started off in music videos?

EA: Yes, when I started styling, videos were very important. It was the era of Jean-Paul Goude and Jean-Baptiste Mondino, a totally new medium.

PM: Was this while you were at *Elle*?

EA: Yeah, I was working as a production assistant at the same time. I wasn't sure if I wanted to be a director; I was just fascinated by images, I think. I assisted on some Mondino videos; at that time he was fashion photography's God. The stylist was Ray Petri. It was a brilliant team.

PM: So that was the golden age for you?

EA: Yes, for me, probably the beginning of the '80s, the end of the '70s … I think your first music and visual influences stay with you forever. My group all listens to Bowie; there's nothing better. You live with what was around when you first became curious.

PM: When it comes to initiating a shoot, then, are those common influences even mentioned between collaborators of the same age?

EA: Well, this story began with Inez and me exchanging images by email. Sometimes it comes from almost nothing; it might just be a color. When you're shooting in the sun—you know that strong blue sky in St. Barths—you need a contrast. So I might say, "What do you think about red and white?" And Inez is like, "Oh, yeah, sure!" I'll send a picture of a red shoe and a René Gruau illustration, which is full of red, and just a silhouette or a little sketch. It's not always photographs—often it's a painting or a frame-grab from a YouTube film. Very quickly, we'll start to build up an image of a woman, and then we can discuss the casting. Some photographers will keep changing their casting or think they need a stronger idea. But Inez isn't someone who hesitates. It's like three phone calls and everything is booked.

PM: Do you ever have preproduction meetings with photographers in person?

EA: Unfortunately, everything is done over phone and e-mail since no one is in Paris. Of the bigger photographers we work with, I think Peter Lindbergh is the only one. Besides, at this time of year, we need to shoot overseas for the light. And unless photographers have made a career out of studio photography, like Penn or Avedon, I think most of them get bored if they've been stuck in there all year.

PM: The studio is all about control—leaving very little to chance so an idea can be executed exactly as imagined.

EA: Whereas outside you're looking for accidents. I'm going on a trip with David Sims in a few weeks—once a year we take him on location. For a studio photographer like him, who controls the lighting, everything, he has to face a lot of unexpected things outside. Suddenly, rain makes a fantastic picture or there's a dog in the street. The only thing is it costs a lot of money to fly photographers and their teams out there. We're far from the days of Helmut Newton traveling with one assistant, one person doing hair and makeup, the model, and a fashion editor. Five people: it was nothing.

PM: **How many people were on set with you and Inez & Vinoodh?**

EA: Oh, it's always twenty, minimum. You have the digital operator and now you have a producer … it's like a mini version of the cinema industry.

PM: **I wonder how many editors could take such a pastoral role in their photographers' careers. If you hadn't styled their shoots over the years, you wouldn't know they'd be desperate to get out into the air by now. Would you say your relationships have changed since you shifted from fashion director to editor-in-chief of *Vogue Paris*?**

EA: Before, it was probably more personal. Then, I was in charge of my shoot and had some other responsibilities. But now I have to think, okay, if I take this direction, I have to make sure that the two or three other fashion editors represent a different type of woman, clothes, and type of photography.

PM: **Are you involved in looking for young photographers to work for your magazine?**

EA: Well, I try to. I'm proud of the young photographers that we've discovered, like Lachlan Bailey—all these young guys we've pushed, who are all very successful now. As editor, my role is to take a global view—paying attention to things, like making sure we don't end up with an entirely black-and-white issue. Often it's the magic solution for photographers when there's a problem.

PM: **For a magazine like *The Gentlewoman*, in which a very small proportion of the women we photograph are models, it's crucial, though. Many of our great stories are about women over thirty, and black-and-white is a very generous means of presenting them.**

EA: Oh, of course, everyone looks better in black-and-white. And there's something about those portraits that links them to eternity.

PM: **As you say, a large body of black-and-white portraits in the issue puts a lot more pressure on the fashion stories to up the color balance elsewhere. But when I think of your work, lively color is what I see. You cut down your stories once you became editor but you still contribute one per issue, right?**

EA: I like to if I can; I was a stylist first. And when you have a woman in mind, no one else is going to imagine her exactly as you see her. It's so personal. It's like with photographers. You can give them exactly the same model and exactly the same dress but you'll get two very different pictures. It's the same for fashion editors—it's you, it's the way you see it, and you want to make it happen yourself, with your hands.

PM: **When you say, "It's you," do you mean a version of you in the picture?**

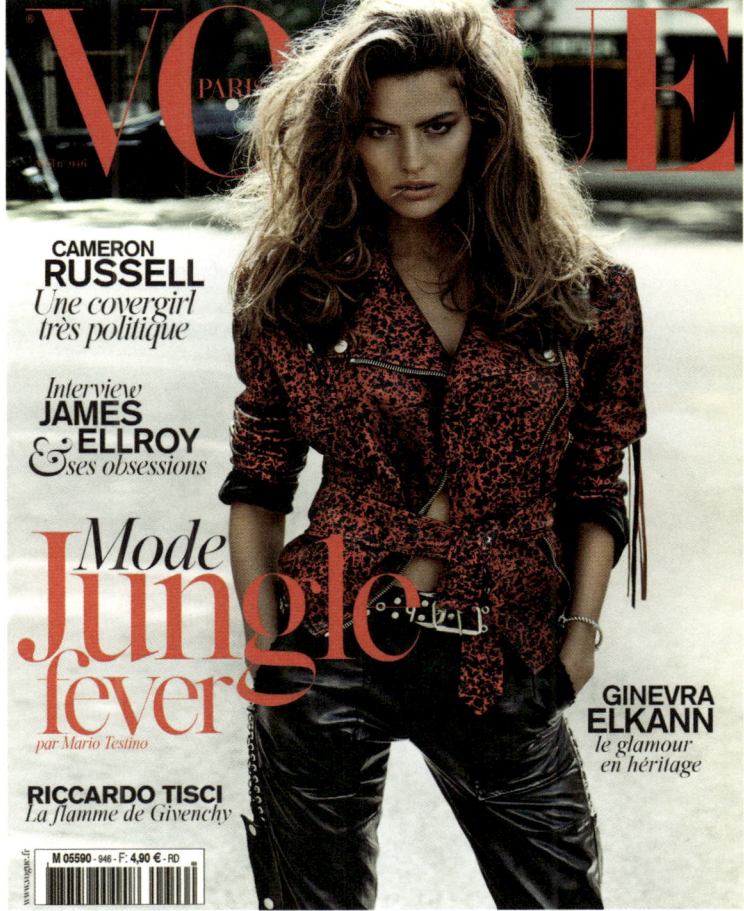

Vogue Paris, April 2014.
Cover photograph
by Mario Testino
© Mario Testino/Vogue Paris

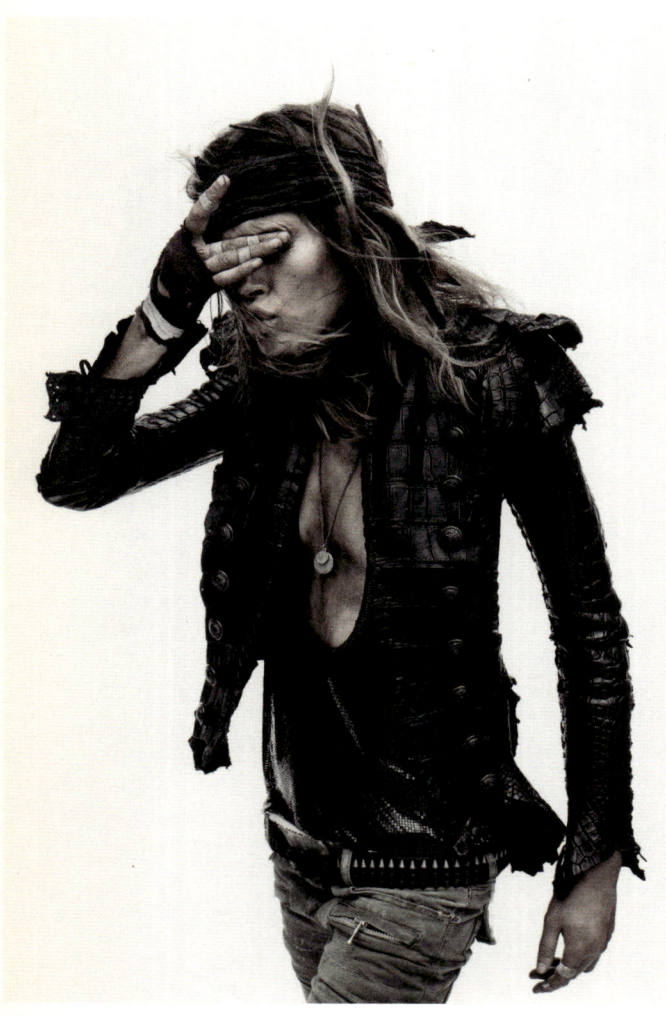

David Sims, *Commando*,
Vogue Paris, March 2010
© David Sims

EA: Yes, sometimes, though the styling will vary from photographer to photographer. If you shoot with someone like Peter Lindbergh, you're not going to bring a pink fur coat. You know that his wide shot is going to be magic because he focuses on the face, the character, and the emotions, so you have to be discreet. It's a totally different scenario from working with David Sims. His woman is very strong, masculine; she's a warrior. Oh, I love this exercise—anticipating what's going to be photogenic with each photographer's technique. With David, your styling needs to be very sure, because the white background of the studio will show everything, all the little details.

PM: You touched on the fact that portraiture has been quite dominant in fashion photography over the past decade, where head shots or three-quarter shots are common. It wasn't until I started working on the magazine that I appreciated how incredibly difficult it is to achieve a great full-length fashion image.

EA: Yeah, sometimes you have to beg photographers to get your shoe in the picture! "Can't we just try one shot?" I think often they feel that the closer they are to the face, the more emotion they'll get, which isn't necessarily true. Many of the fantastic images that were a big influence on all of us, from Newton and Bourdin to Norman Parkinson, they used to show an entire fashion landscape.

PM: People complain that so few photographic teams shoot the big stories and campaigns but it takes an enormous amount of experience to pull off a well-balanced vista. The debates about retouching and postproduction levels in fashion photography can obscure the phenomenal skill that's required on set.

EA: Actually, we've had quite a bit of criticism that our current cover of the actress Sophie Marceau has been very retouched, which isn't true. She does a lot of sport and her legs look that good in real life! Sometimes people just don't want to accept things as they are.

PM: Well, this is the new role of the editor, isn't it, to be constantly fielding assumptions about the levels of post-production on the images. But it's a difficult one, isn't it? People might ask me, "Do you retouch your images?" And the answer is yes, of course we do. We might balance the color against other shoots in the issue. We might make sure that there's not a flaw that's come through from the negative.

EA: Of course! We try to make it as perfect as possible. If she has a big spot, it's not going to make it onto the cover but that doesn't mean that we're manipulating her face—

PM: —or chopping two inches off the thigh or stretching the body out of all proportion. People forget how much a face can be distorted by lighting or in camera, after all. That said, our art department is frequently having conversations with photographers about reducing the levels of retouching: "Could we see the pores, please?"

EA: We really suffer from that. I'm saying to every photographer, "I want to see the veins!" You know, it's similar to the levels of surgery we're seeing in real life. All those older women you see in restaurants. You've no idea whether they're seventy or fifty-five but somehow, there's no illusion about their age. It's an abstraction—one face for all.

PM: Those pillowy cheeks you associate with Californian cosmetic surgery seem so far from classic Parisian beauty. How mindful do you need to be of the Frenchness of French Vogue?

EA: It's funny, I'm not sure French women see themselves in the same way as the rest of world does: those books about why French women never get fat, as if we have miraculous metabolisms. It's fantasy! What's particular to this Vogue is that whereas all the other Vogues are the name of a country—British Vogue, Spanish Vogue, American Vogue—we are the name of a city, Vogue Paris. Everyone has a clear conception of La Parisienne.

PM: One of the questions I'm frequently asked in interviews is whether I'm the gentlewoman of our magazine's title. Female editors are under a huge amount of scrutiny to personify their magazine—it must be especially the case for the editor of Condé Nast's most revered fashion title.

EA: It can be difficult, with all those pictures taken of us during the shows. We're not models: sometimes I don't feel my hair is great, I've been running between shows, or you're just coming out of a lunch and just don't feel in the mood. Especially me; it's not as if I'm doing all these crazy looks every day in order to be photographed.

PM: Which of the images you were involved in creating do you look back at—which would you say were most important in terms of establishing your signature visual language?

EA: About four years ago, my first story with David was "Commando" with Iselin Steiro—she was wearing army stuff; this was a tough, new character we created. I was very proud. And not long after I came to Vogue, I started working with Inez & Vinoodh and I think we really created something together.

PM: Do you mean all those images of Jessica Miller with the extravagant poses?

EA: Yes, that was the beginning. They were good, I think. I loved the femininity and the mystery of Inez in them.

PM: Those were published in the M/M (Paris) years, when Mathias Augustyniak and Michael Amzalag were art-directing Vogue Paris in 2002–03: for me, one of the magazine's absolute creative zeniths.

EA: Yes, it was a great time, I have to say. There was a lot of freedom. It was French people of the same generation all together, we all knew one another very well and it was fun. What M/M did was so influential, when they started painting on covers, creating captions in handwriting—especially on such an established title as ours.

PM: I remember saying to Michael and Mathias when they first got the job, "Oh my God, that archive! Having that resource downstairs is going to be great." I was so surprised when they replied that they had no intention of using it.

EA: It's a dilemma, working with an institution with such a history. "Should I look back? Should I not look back?"

PM: In our industry, a conversation about using archival references can be very nuanced. Bring it up, and people might think you're accusing them of copying someone else's work.

EA: Well, people can't say they don't work with references—I mean, they're everywhere, from advertisers' storyboards to fashion designers' mood boards. But sharing a picture in order to discuss lighting or allude to Jessica Lange's hairstyle from a particular film is different from redoing something. And what's the point of that? It's like when singers cover "La vie en rose"—you just know it's going to be a disaster since there's nothing to add.

PM: Plus, even with the best intentions, sending a photographer images of someone else's work, especially by a contemporary, is delicate.

EA: In some cases, it's better to show some people their own work than somebody else's. One of the photographers we send a lot of their own references to is Gilles Bensimon. We're like, "Oh, we want to recapture that shot of Yasmeen Ghauri or Elle Macpherson…." At the same time, nobody wants to be asked to redo something they did years ago. Sometimes I'll show David Sims those pictures he did with Linda [Evangelista] whistling in the early '90s and I'm like, "Oh wow, they're so simple," and he's like "Whoa, no!" On one hand, I think he loves that I'm acknowledging his archive, his world—his property. But at the same time, it's 2014 and that girl doesn't exist for him anymore. The result isn't going to be as strong.

PM: It must have happened to you regularly when you were still able to do consultancy before the changes at Condé Nast at the time you took over as editor. Wouldn't a client say, "Oh, Emmanuelle, remember that amazing shot you did of Kate [Moss] in the water with the bikini? Can we have that again?"

EA: Yeah, and sometimes I'd say, "Great, we haven't done that character in a long time; let's do it!" and other times, I'd be like, "I've done that too many times, and this girl's got nothing to do with that one—she's going to look stupid in this outfit."

PM: When I worked for Nick Knight, we shared an office with Peter Saville—two of the most copied image makers of our time—and it was a weekly occurrence. I'd hear people say to them, "Never mind, imitation's the sincerest form of flattery." But actually, now I'm commissioning for a magazine, I know it took six months to get that story executed, and it was so hard and you're so proud of the result, that I find it hard to take lightly. We sell ninety eight thousand copies, so not everybody in the world gets to see the images in the magazine, but more likely they do see the poorer copy since it's for a much bigger commercial client and it's with them they associate the original idea. It sounds so petty, but it hurts!

EA: Of course! It happened all the time when I was working on clothes, doing collections. You spent months doing the research and making the pants with the designer, and suddenly they're everywhere for twenty euros. But you know there is nothing you can do about it, so I try to stop myself from looking and focus instead on finding satisfaction in the fact that it was influential.

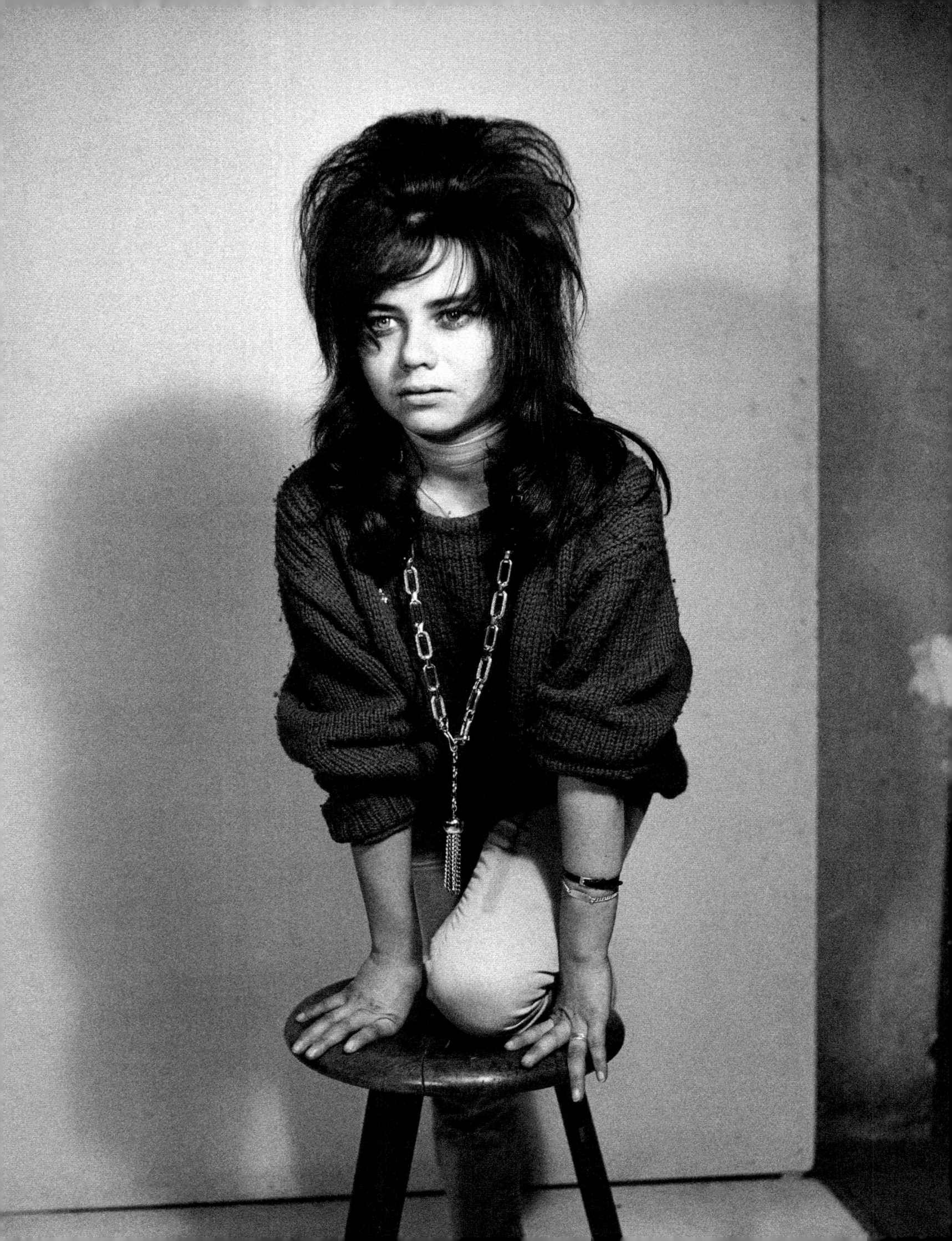

Fashion photography has been an incubator for innovation and cultural reflection, especially in the '60s, '70s, and '90s, decades of remarkable activity. What forces shaped the field in the cautious post-9/11 decade?

State of Fashion

Charlotte Cotton

In the 1990s, I interviewed many of the photographers, stylists, and art directors who shaped that decade's most creative fashion narratives. During conversations with photographers, including Corinne Day, Juergen Teller, and David Sims, as well as stylists Melanie Ward, Venetia Scott, and Simon Foxton, I would be shown a handful of photobooks from studio and home library shelves, both first editions and republished versions of Nan Goldin's *The Ballad of Sexual Dependency* (1986), Larry Clark's *Tulsa* (1971) and *Teenage Lust* (1983), Joseph Szabo's *Almost Grown* (1978), as well as examples of Karlheinz Weinberger's work on teenage rebels in postwar Switzerland. This new generation of photographers, which also included Mario Sorrenti, Glen Luchford, and Craig McDean, took root within an ecosystem nurtured by groundbreaking magazines, such as Terry Jones's *i-D* and *The Face*, then art-directed by Phil Bicker (see page 106). These influencers genuinely understood the power of fashion photography to serve as the "visuals" describing contemporary youth culture, and, as the above list suggests, the imagery they absorbed and referenced came from outside the fashion photography genre. Instead, acute and intimate representations of counterculture and independent attitudes of youth provided the map for the photographic aesthetic that came to be known as "grunge" fashion. Richard Avedon's *In the American West* (1985) as well as his 1969 frieze-like lineup of the hip, individualistic beauties of Andy Warhol's Factory would similarly provide visual prompts for these new image makers, especially as their careers took them from London to New York, the then–commercial epicenter of fashion advertising. By the twenty-first century, "grunge" fashion photography was fully absorbed into the mainstream, forming its own set of stylistic references soon felt in every delinquent shoulder shrug, folded pair of arms, yawn, and eye squint seen in the so-called "Mass Indie" style of the 2000s. The '90s, though, saw the last great critical mass of young talents to visualize a proper counterargument to current conventions of fashion photography, then a time of big hair, skirt suits, white shirts, and supermodels dressed in Azzedine Alaïa.

Fashion photography is rightly characterized by constant change, for being porous, reactive, even predictive in its visualizations and reflections of consumer society. While this has continued to be true in the twenty-first century, though with some complexity and turbulence, this century has so far failed to deliver a climate for image makers to truly innovate in the radical ways that we saw in the '60s, '70s, and '90s, decades now regarded as fashion photography high points. As a curator who is passionate about fashion photography when viewed on its own terms—as an industry and as a collaborative form of creativity—I will attempt here to pinpoint some reasons for today's stagnant state of fashion image making.

As the generation of "grunge" photographers attest, innovation in this field isn't wholly tied to the new. Fashion photography does not hide its references and influences and has always used a process akin to that of a magpie—picking

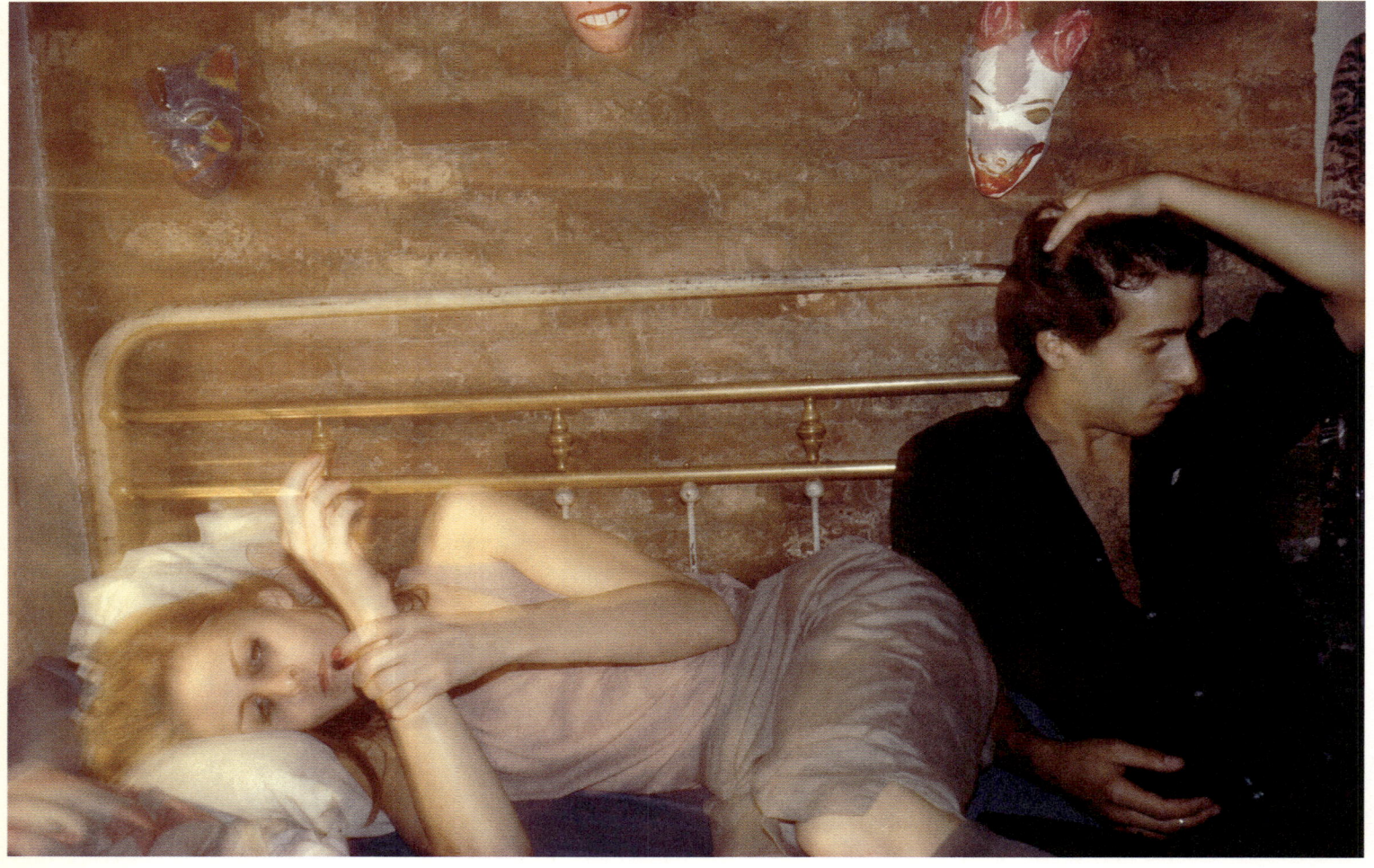

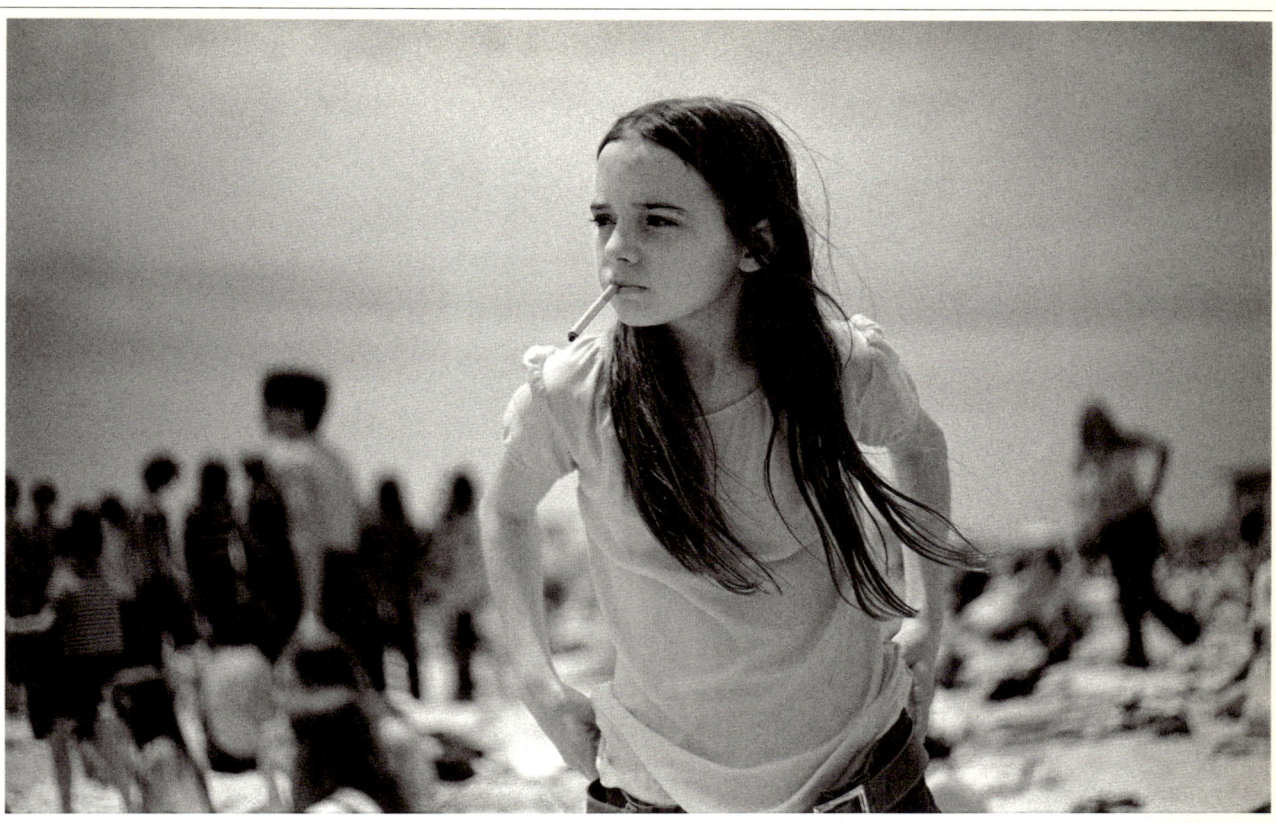

The '90s, though, saw the last great critical mass of young talents to visualize a proper counterargument to current conventions of fashion photography, then a time of big hair, skirt suits, white shirts, and supermodels dressed in Azzedine Alaïa.

out the shiniest and most timely visual trophies of culture to construct its seductive, fantastic, yet plausible story lines. Whether incorporating a new or old set of signifiers from popular culture and media or by lifting ideas from artists and film directors, fashion photography absolutely relies on its viewers' preexisting image recognition. This transparency of visual sources is one of the reasons I suspect the field has often been maligned, especially in relation to its more rarefied cousin of contemporary art photography, which operates within the same cultural and media ecologies but frames its referencing gestures as discourse and critique.

Steven Meisel is without parallel among fashion photographers who demonstrate the genre's capacity to reference, shift, and reinvent in ways that are unique and keenly focused on the idea of fashion media as a fast-paced commentary upon contemporary culture. He has been a dominant editorial presence since 1988, coinciding with the arrival of both Anna Wintour as editor-in-chief of American *Vogue* and Franca Sozzani at *Vogue Italia*, both huge supporters of his work. Meisel has created every front-cover gatefold for *Vogue Italia* as well as a lead editorial story in each issue since the beginning of Sozzani's reign. He is renowned for his towering diversity: shifting from his acknowledged talent for casting new models for nuanced studio performances, reanimating photographic and cinematic history in his references to Hollywood glamour, and channeling the legacies of Irving Penn, Hiro, Avedon, and Guy Bourdin. Once or twice each year, Meisel and *Vogue Italia* invite controversy and media traffic with stories that spin narratives both witty and sometimes downright campy that riff on contemporary issues such as terrorist security threats, the Second Gulf War, global recession, and domestic violence in ways that are pretty much unique to Meisel and his métier. Meisel has also folded contemporary media forms into the pages of the Italian glossy: mimicking paparazzi conventions on the street and endless "step and repeat" photo opportunities, webcasting, Twitpics and selfies, spoofing the pervasive, self-styled narcissism of social media.

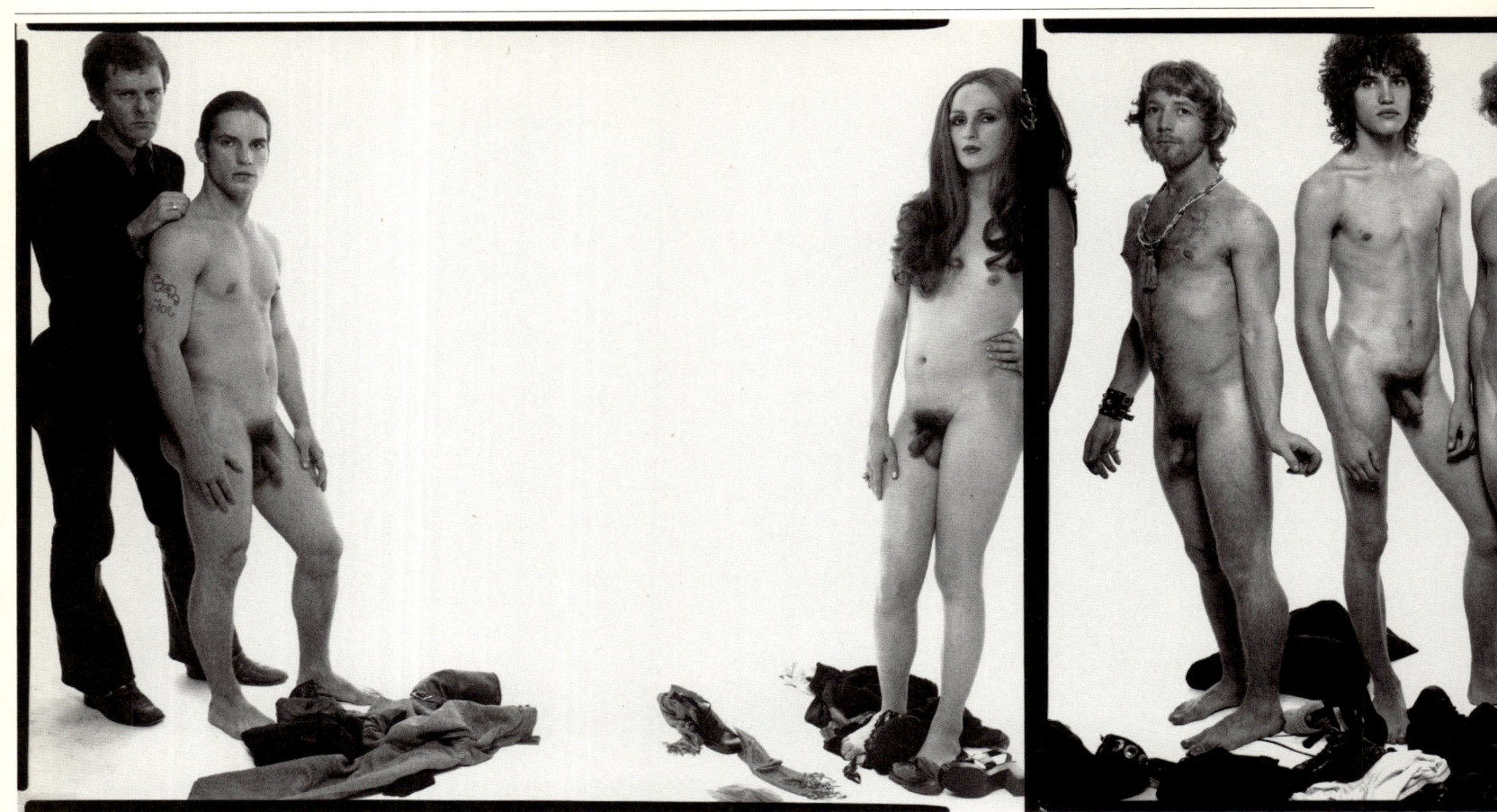

Richard Avedon,
*Andy Warhol and
members of The Factory:
Paul Morrissey, director;
Joe Dallesandro, actor;
Candy Darling, actor;
Eric Emerson, actor;
Jay Johnson, actor;
Tom Hompertz, actor;
Gerard Malanga,
poet; Viva, actress;
Paul Morrissey; Taylor
Mead, actor; Brigid Polk,
actress; Joe Dallesandro;
Andy Warhol, artist,
New York, October 30,
1969*
© The Richard Avedon
Foundation

References to digital tools in fashion narratives cropped up well before fashion photographers and magazine publishers had begun to seriously process the possibilities or consequences of digital media. Inez & Vinoodh's April 1994 editorial story "For Your Pleasure" for *The Face*, then art-directed by Lee Swillingham (see page 32), was practically prophetic of what digital would mean for the fashion photography industry, and of the shift toward the power of postproduction to render an image, and away from the in-the-moment excitement that unfolds on a fashion shoot. The duo used digital manipulation in their early 1990s art projects, and their curiosity about new imaging tools informed "For Your Pleasure," which portrayed airbrushed and Photoshop-perfect models inserted into generic stock photography backgrounds. This anticipation of the axis shift that digital postproduction would have upon fashion photography over the next twenty years was not lost on anyone who worked within the industry.

Significantly, it was a fashion photographer who created the first exploration into the possibilities for fashion on the Web. Nick Knight launched SHOWstudio.com in November 2000 and began to answer the question of what a fashion magazine that upheld an editorial vision could become in the age of the Internet. Under the creative direction of Paul Hetherington and the editorship of Penny Martin, the free website presented the practices of fashion design and image making by commissioning films, performances, interviews, and animations that both stylized and revealed the ideas and working practices of fashion creatives. Their editorial output experimented with the types of engagement asked of viewers, who became participants, collaborators, and the collective orchestrators of how ideas about fashion unfolded on the site. The project continues to hold its position as the best archive of fashion image making's potential in the twenty-first century. SHOWstudio was joined in 2010 by the online-only magazine Nowness.com, underwritten by luxury alpha brand LVMH, a more conventional yet still inventive

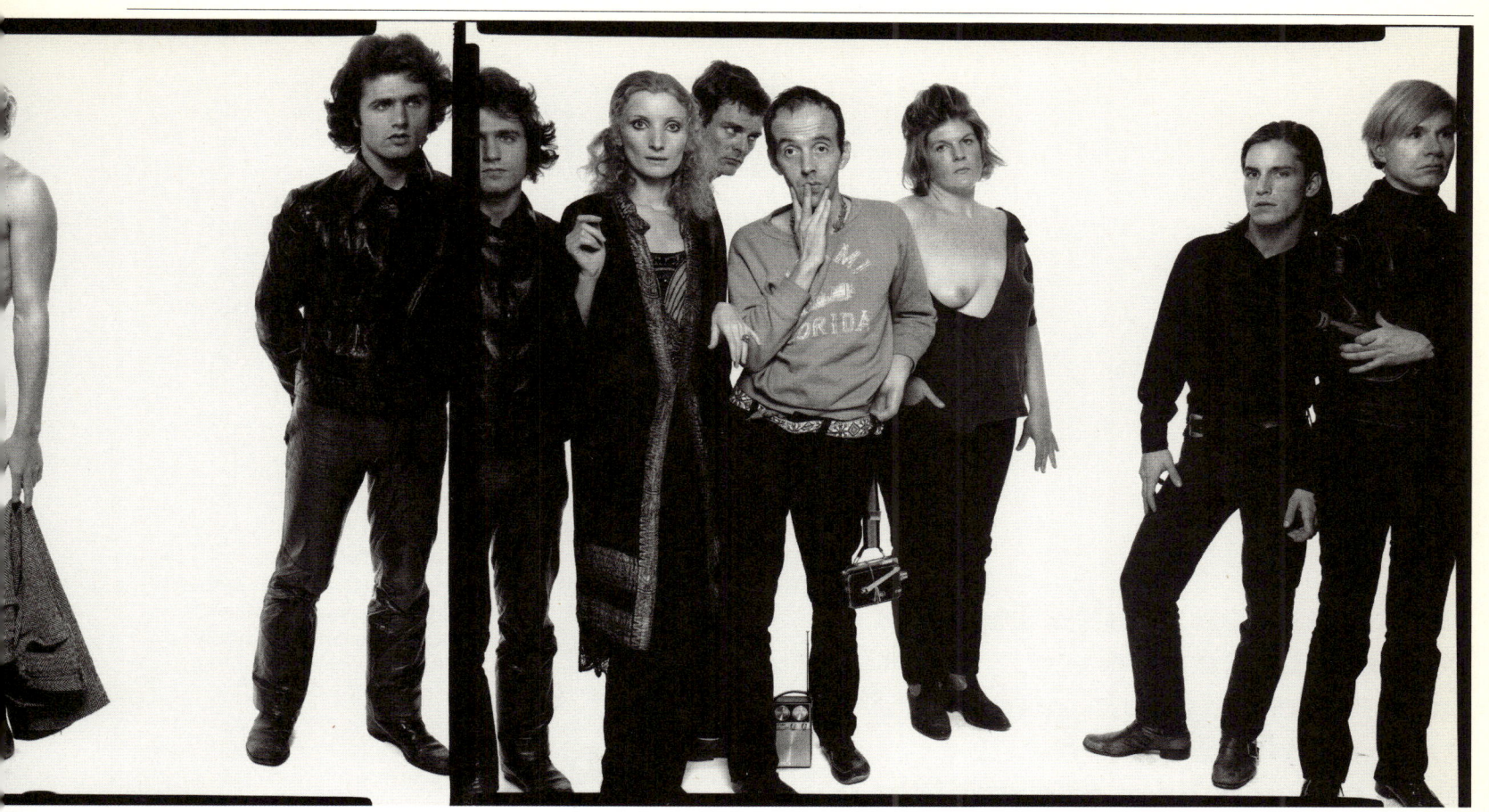

indicator of how fashion editorial translates to a paperless arena. Established magazine titles have launched tablet versions but as supplements to the printed magazine and, significantly, with no great editorial or financial investment in developing film as the new medium for fashion stories. What SHOWstudio.com proposed was a concept for how fashion photography could be usurped by fashion film, a form that allowed for innovation beyond the printed magazine page. "Fashion film," however, is an overstretched term that invariably means either a) B-roll footage of the "behind-the-scenes" of a fashion shoot, edited to suggest that its atmosphere is one of constant action and doesn't involve hours of waiting around, or b) films made by fashion photographers' assistants using a locked-off shot showing models doing something slightly goofy or durational with a banging sound track. There are exceptions to this somewhat damning statement, and the Prada Group in particular has invested in the kind of fashion films that speak in cinematic terms of luxury and style, created by (gasp) actual filmmakers. Roman Polanski, Wes Anderson, and Roman Coppola have all directed witty shorts for Prada, with Polanski's *A Therapy*, starring Sir Ben Kingsley and Helena Bonham Carter, previewing at the 2012 Cannes Film Festival. Miu Miu's *Women's Tales* series breaks new ground, with its all-women cast of film directors including Zoe Cassavetes, Hiam Abbass, and So Yong Kim, for how fashion film can offer something genuinely new.

Despite the possibilities and new technological capacities for rethinking forms and the dissemination of fashion images, the aughts won't be considered an era of innovation. The aftershocks of 9/11 and the general nervousness of fashion and luxury brands about what the consumer landscape had become was a wake-up call for fashion media. The industry gradually eroded the once sacrosanct division between advertising and editorial. Such "win-win" situations include editorial fashion photography functioning as marketing for new movies, albums, and fashion collections. This change comes at the cost of

Whether incorporating a new or old set of signifiers from popular culture and media or by lifting ideas from artists and film directors, fashion photography absolutely relies on its viewers' preexisting image recognition.

developing a new working model for a digital age that would give the final word on image creation decisions to magazine editors and creative teams; instead, the luxury brand client essentially calls the shots. In an era of risk aversion, advertisers and editors have relied on fashion photography's titans—Mario Testino, Peter Lindbergh, and Patrick Demarchelier—for recognizably "aspirational" and pre-"grunge" narratives for fashion. Most advertising campaigns in the mid-2000s were created by the fashion image elite, including Steven Meisel, Steven Klein, Inez & Vinoodh, Juergen Teller, David Sims, Craig McDean, and Mario Sorrenti—the same photographers whom editors would have turned to ten years previously. It is not that the history of fashion photography doesn't have its precedents for incredible careers extending over multiple decades, but this is the first time that it feels as if there are few opportunities, in such a heavily prescribed environment, for new voices.

This is an era when most major fashion and beauty advertising campaigns favor leading actors and performers. Almost every cover of American *Vogue* since the early 2000s has featured an actor or pop star. Brand alignments—of fashion labels, celebrities, and powerful figures in the fashion industry—have become the underpinning of fashion photography in the twenty-first century. One important precedent-setting shift in the business of fashion happened in 1994 with the appointment of Tom Ford as creative director of the then-declining luxury brand Gucci. Ford's role as creative director placed significant emphasis upon his astute talent for shaping the *image* of fashion and his creation of an ideogram of luxury. He diversified the fashion brand (through ready-to-wear collections, perfume, and beauty lines, the all-important handbags, and so on), and cultivated a lucrative desire for its wares. The success of the Ford model brought about concerted and irreversible change in the image identity of fashion brands, epitomized at its best by Marc Jacobs's creative direction of Louis Vuitton and his commercially successful collaborations with artists Richard Prince, Yayoi Kusama, and "Superflat" founder Takashi Murakami. For many, the appointment in 2012 of Hedi Slimane

In the fashion publishing context there is space for interesting things to happen, where the mantle of photographers and stylists can be taken over by younger talents.

Tyrone Lebon,
Adwoa for Stussy Deluxe Advertising, **2011**
© Tyrone Lebon

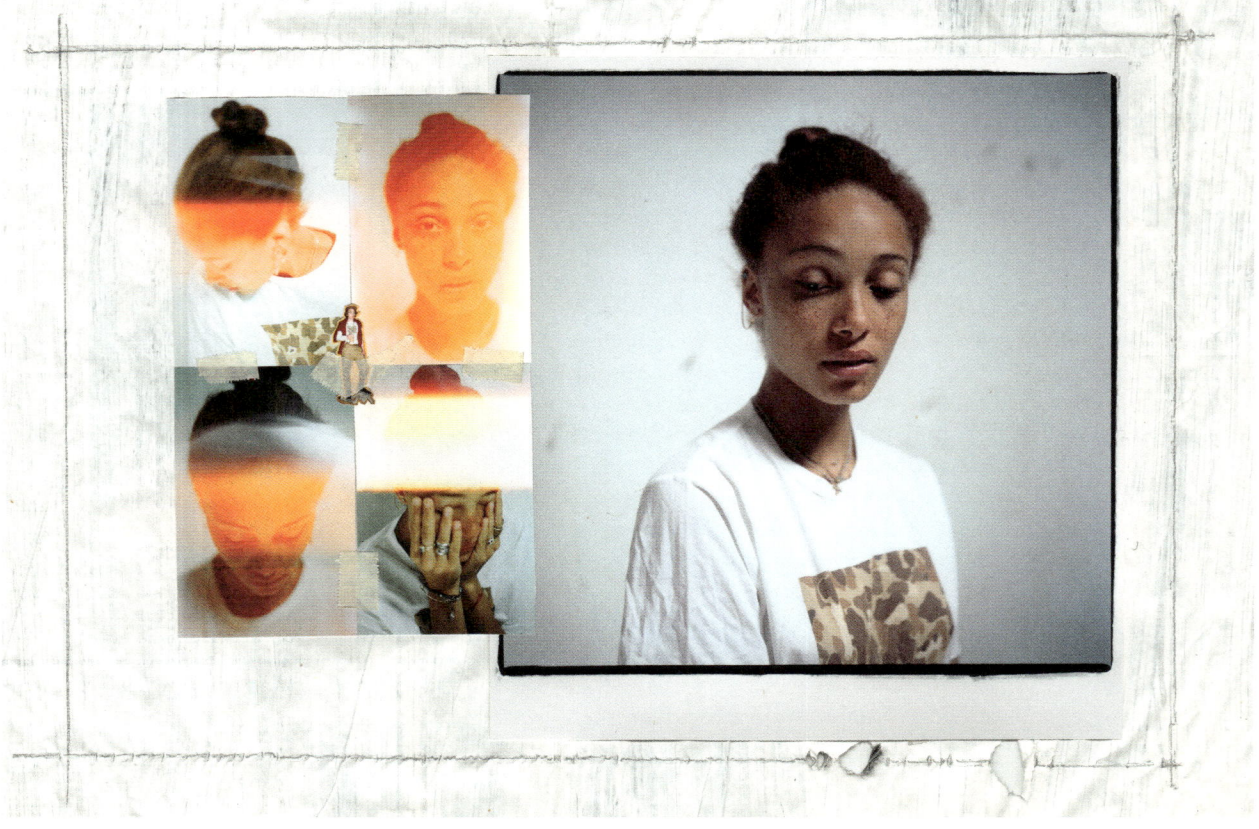

to head up Yves Saint Laurent marked the logical conclusion to the pervasive control of creative directors, with Slimane styling the runway shows and shooting the advertising campaigns himself and, controversially, moving his creative studio from the couture center of Paris to Los Angeles and dropping "Yves" from his design of the new "Saint Laurent" logo.

Practically the only fashion photographers in recent years to compete with the field's well-established figures are Mert Alas and Marcus Piggott. The duo have a long-established collaboration with fashion editor Katie Grand, starting at *Dazed & Confused* (which Grand cofounded in 1992), and continuing with her launch of *POP* in 2000 and *LOVE* in 2009. The potency of Mert & Marcus's approach to fashion is its absolute reinforcement of fashion as a world of its own. Their visual references are hermetically focused on the history of fashion and advertising photography, with a bent toward the gorgeous pop-coloration and ring-flash aesthetic of the '70s and early '80s, mixed with pore-less Photoshop perfection and a seeming belief in the quite unreconstructed idea that if you bring a great team of creatives together on a shoot, something "aspirational" can happen. Looking at their work, I am reminded of a John Berger quote from *Ways of Seeing* (1972), "glamour cannot exist without personal social envy being a common and widespread emotion," and it prompts me to think that we always get the fashion photography that we deserve.

There is some good news to close these notes on contemporary fashion photography that centers on the rejuvenation of the printed fashion magazine. Publications including *Tank* (founded in 1998), *V* (1999), *POP* (2000), *AnOther Magazine* (2001), *Purple Fashion* (2004), *Acne Paper* (2005), *Dossier Journal* (2008), *LOVE* (2009), and *CR Fashion Book* (2012) are just a handful of the most editorially precise titles released biannually and quarterly for the shelves of specialist newsstands and fashion boutiques. *Fantastic Man*, founded in 2005 by Jop van Bennekom and Gert Jonkers, and its sister magazine *The Gentlewoman*, launched in 2010 by editor Penny Martin, have been especially influential on the fashion publishing landscape because of their design, photographic, and editorial positions that are timely reminders of the thoughtfulness of the "slow read" magazine form. It is in this context that there is space for interesting things to happen, where the mantle of photographers and stylists, including Jason Evans and Simon Foxton, can be taken over by younger photographic talents such as Tyrone Lebon and Mel Bles, creating the visuals for our epoch. It is great to see artists such as Viviane Sassen use the mass-distribution mode of style magazines with an acuity parallel to Wolfgang Tillmans in the late 1980s, and for established figures such as Sims, Teller, and Alasdair McLellan to continue to make their proposals for the editorial direction of fashion photography. Such visual confirmation of contemporary fashion photography's authenticity and vitality is now the hard-won exception rather than the genre's enduring rule. Thanks to the behavior of photography's biggest industry—its inaction in the face of social and commercial change and a new digital media ecology—this delightful niche of independent magazines is left to burn a candle for the once-innovative capacities of fashion image making.

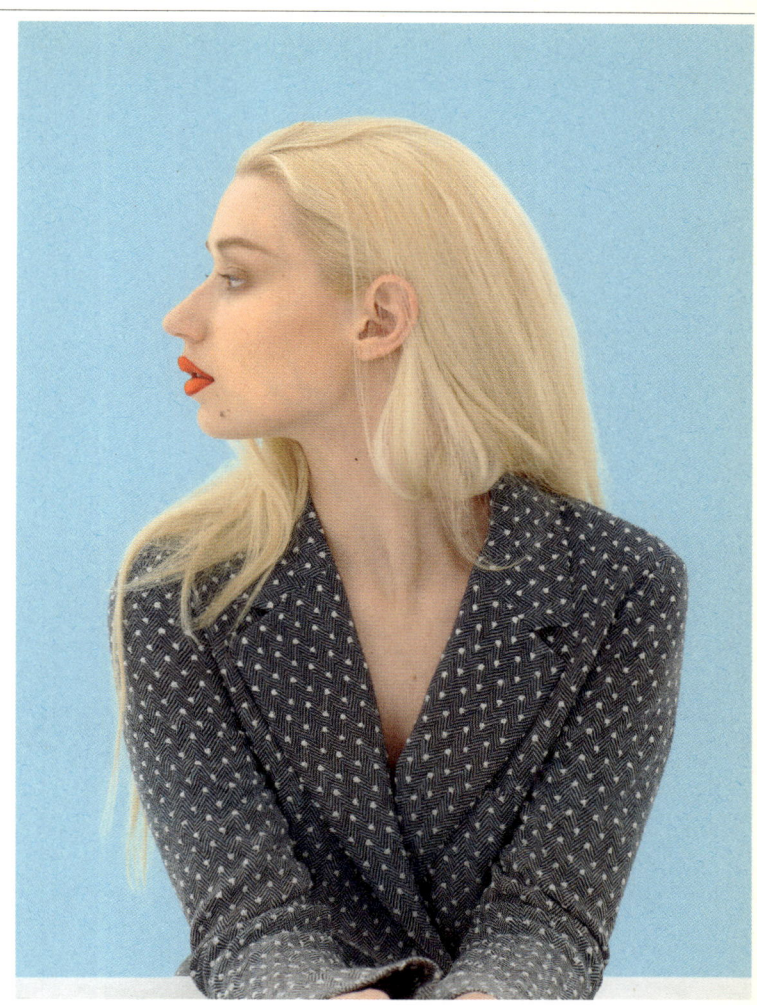

Mel Bles, *Iggy Azalea for POP*, 2013
© Mel Bles

Charlotte Cotton is a curator and writer. Her writing about fashion photography includes *Imperfect Beauty: The making of contemporary fashion photographs* (V&A, 2000), "Process, Content and Dissemination: Photography and Music" in *Words Without Pictures* (Aperture, 2010), and essays surveying the past twenty years of fashion photography to be published by Rizzoli in *Louis Vuitton Fashion Photographs* in October 2014.

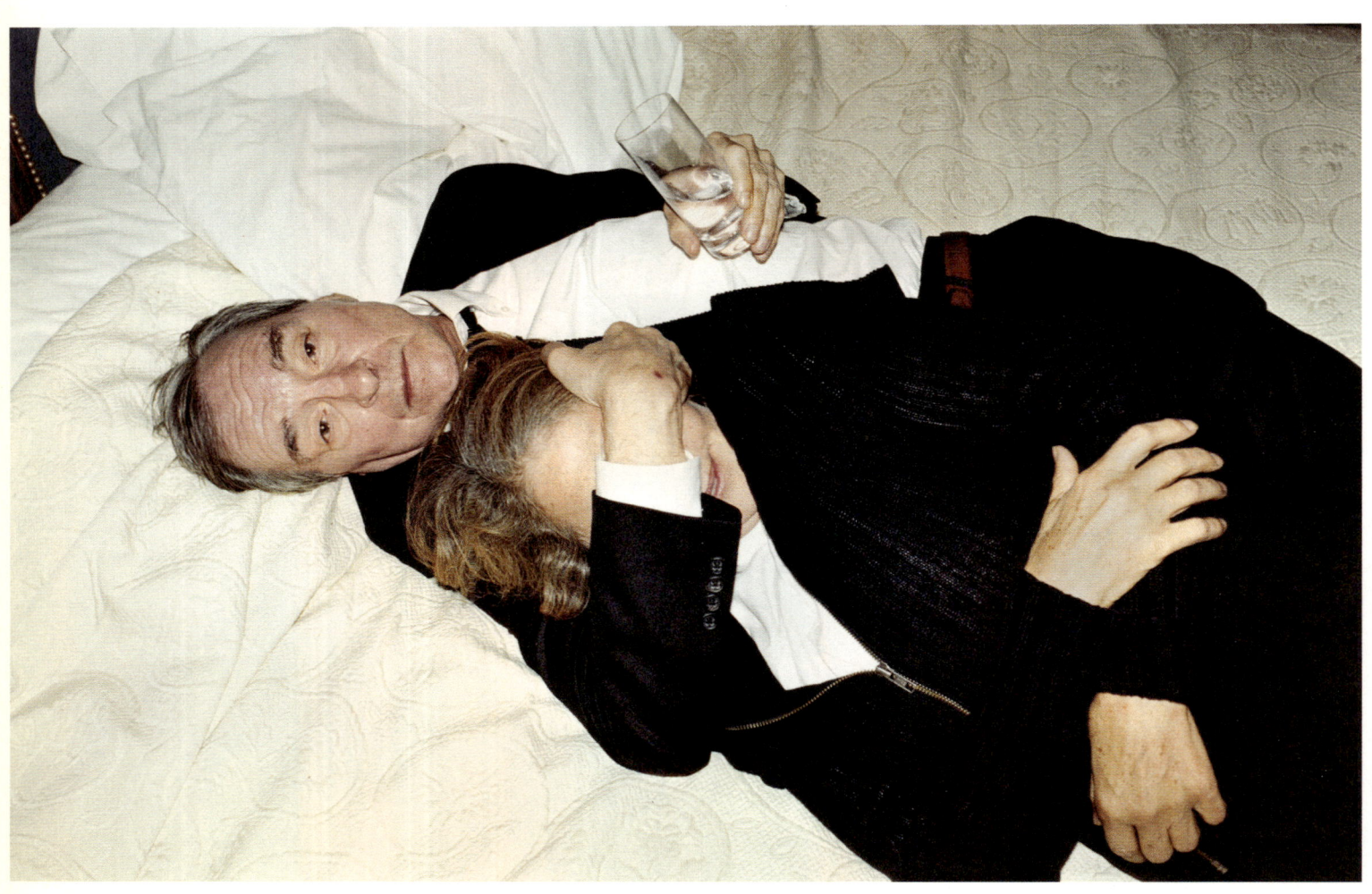

Juergen Teller,
William Eggleston with
Charlotte Rampling,
Marc Jacobs advertising
campaign S/S 07, 2007
© and courtesy Juergen
Teller Ltd.

The documentary tradition has influenced the work of many fashion photographers, but the interaction between the two fields is far from simple.

Uneasy Bedfellows

Alistair O'Neill

Documentary photography has long been mined by fashion photography as an antidote to glamorous, fantasy-driven imagery. Documentary photographs convey imperfection that jars with the conventional polish and exactness of fashion photographs. The codified means through which documentary is expressed by fashion photography is usually far from its origins in social awareness. British society and fashion photographer Cecil Beaton once claimed, "I want to make photographs of very elegant women taking the lipstick off their teeth." He never pulled it off, but the statement captures the scope of fashion photography's investment in documentary, and the extent of its power for change.

The idea that fashion photography assimilates the style of documentary is simplistic; their histories are more intertwined than many would care to admit. In a recent Marc Jacobs advertising campaign by Juergen Teller, Charlotte Rampling reclines on a bed with William Eggleston. Part of the ad's charge is how it revels in being a distasteful signing of documentary for the purposes of fashion. And yet, for a number of postwar American documentary photographers, climbing into bed with fashion was a means of establishing an early career.

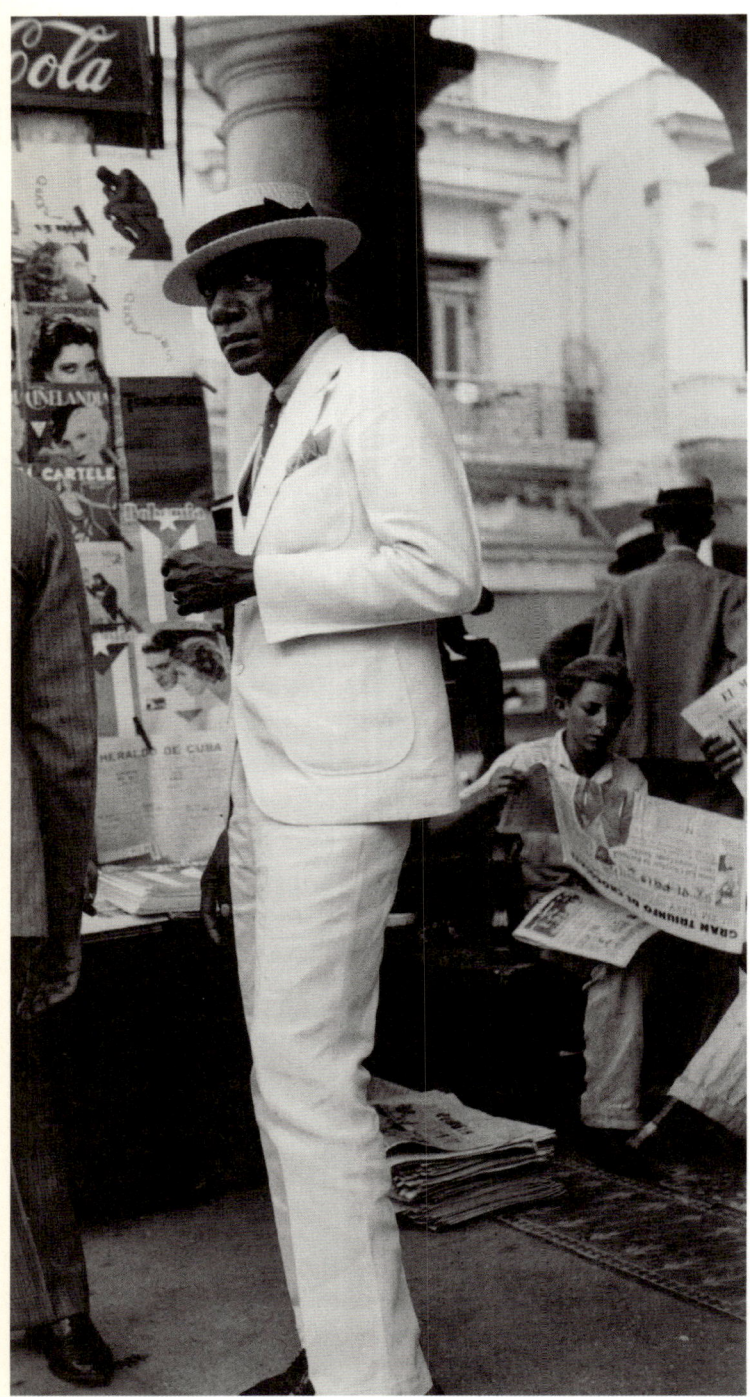

The informal art schools and cooperatives they attended, such as the Design Laboratory, the Photo League, and the Camera Club of New York, were taught by practitioners who included the likes of Alexey Brodovitch, then *Harper's Bazaar*'s art director. These connections often led to work for Midtown fashion magazines, Fifth Avenue department stores, and the wholesalers of the city's garment district. And while this work was informed by the sense of experimentation fostered by these societies and schools, the photographers considered what they produced of little worth beyond the money it paid, in contrast to the personal work it funded.

Arriving in New York in March 1947, the young photographer Robert Frank wrote to his Swiss parents: "Never before have I experienced so much in one week as here. I feel as if I am in a film." He was yet to learn that Brodovitch had already formulated a cinematic vision for print, deploying it in the art direction of double-page fashion-magazine spreads as if syncopated to the rhythm of the city. Frank soon gained an introduction to the Russian émigré who employed him as a staff photographer, first working on product shots of accessories for the back pages of *Harper*'s and its sister title, *Junior Bazaar*.

Evidence of Frank formatively exploring the idea of the documentary snapshot can be found in one of his first pieces of fashion editorial, published in *Junior Bazaar*. Titled "New York Was Never Like This," it takes the theme of a young person arriving in the city, so it is likely to have been informed by Frank's own experience.

> When a girl leaves home for a job in New York City, she automatically acquires, unknown to herself, a multiple personality. In the mind of her friends and relations, she is suddenly a glamorous figure living in a glamorous world. Each person has a different vision of her, but all are equally improbable and unshakable. On these two pages we see Amy, 23, who came to New York six months ago, as the people back home visualize her, and as she really is.

The photo-story charts the inconsistencies between the projection of lived experience in the city and its actuality: for example, Amy's younger sister imagines her as a fashion model, but the only time she is in front of a camera is on a cheap date with a man from the office. The slippage between expectation and reality is heightened by the style of photography employed. Rather than polished studio photography, the look alternates between documentary and domestic.

The inclusion of work by Frank and other documentary photographers in *Junior Bazaar*, such as Lisette Model, Herman Landshoff, Louis Faurer, and Paul Himmel, helped define the short-lived fashion magazine as directional and innovative, but not by all: Himmel and Frank became firm friends united in their disdain for fashion photography and the people who worked in the fashion world.

This view was redressed in 1989 when Frank's work was reappraised in the promotional magazine *Six*, published by the Japanese fashion line Comme des Garçons. It featured the work of a range of documentary photographers such as Frank and Saul Leiter, showcasing work taken in New York in the 1940s and complemented by the more recent work of fashion photographers Arthur Elgort and Peter Lindbergh, some of it editorial for Comme. Looking at the magazine as a whole reveals that the separation between documentary work and fashion photography is indistinct; one segues into the other with the turn of a page. More importantly, the magazine documents how fashion helped revive interest in the early work of Frank and Leiter, qualifying portfolios

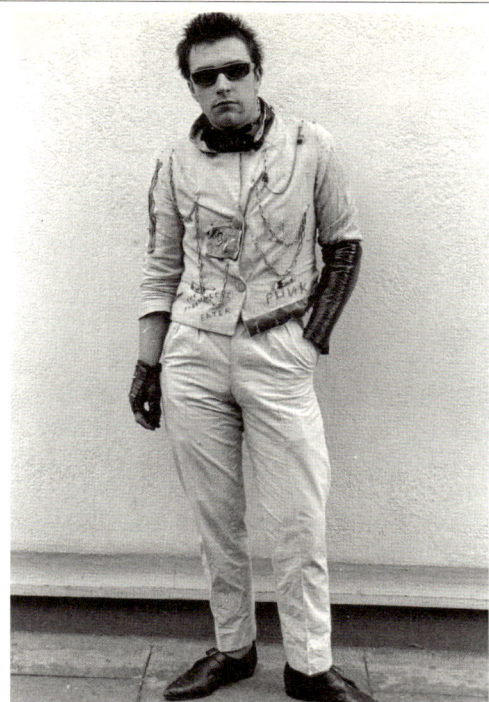
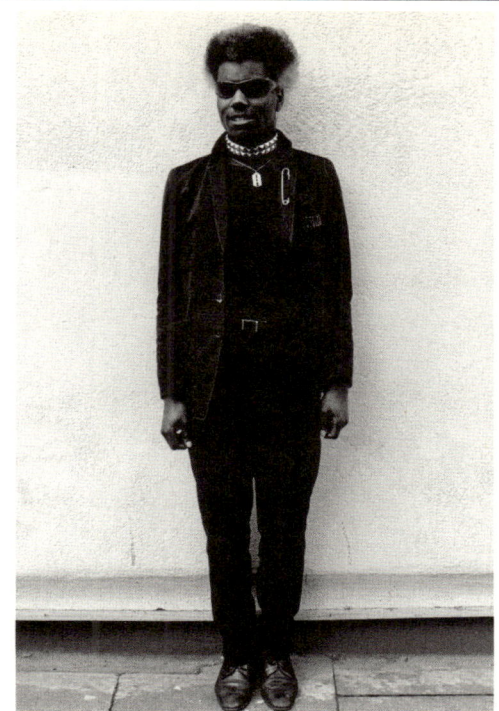

Steve Johnston,
"Straight-Ups,"
King's Road, London
ca. 1977
© Steve Johnston

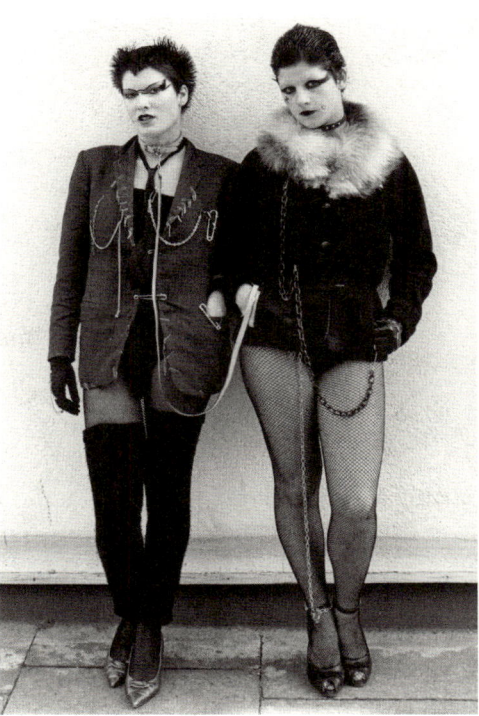
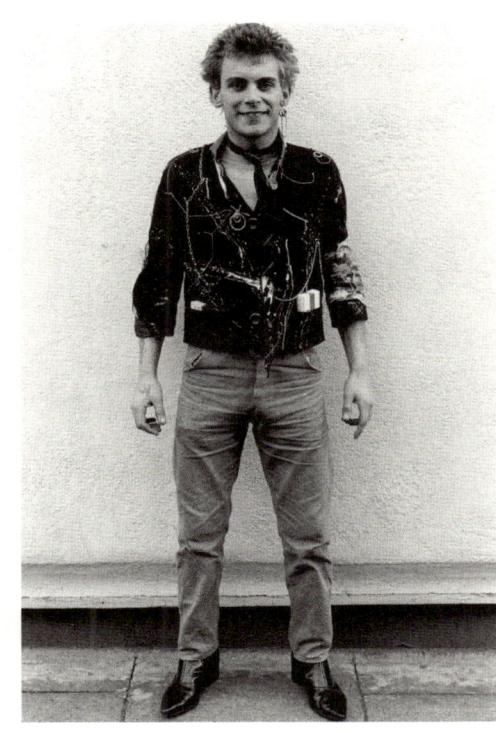

of work not through the usual forms of exhibition or acquisition but through their select circulation via a high-end promotional fashion magazine that is now, in turn, a collector's item.

Frank maintains that he was "never any good at fashion photography," but this didn't stand in the way of his surprising return to commercial fashion work in 1989, producing the first of three promotional catalogs for the Italian clothing brand Alberto Aspesi, shot in and around Frank's studio on the Bowery, in New York, where a number of the shirts worn were notably creased. Frank's fashion work is hardly easily classified as fashion photography—yet that very tension makes the photographs expressions of style rather than documents of fashion.

As art director of *Vogue* in the late '40s and '50s, Alexander Liberman often referred to the example of a photograph taken by Walker Evans in Havana in the '30s of a black man wearing a white suit. He used it to illustrate a particular quality he was after, and he used it to convey the idea to the photographer he was commissioning. To look at the photograph is to see a man smartly dressed in a white linen suit and straw boater at a newsstand—but a man who averts the camera's eye by glancing upward to express unconcern but also awareness. The art director said of this photograph: "While not a fashion photograph, I believe this is a statement essentially about style."

Liberman pointed out how a documentary photographer might see clothing—not as a product for marketing but a surface that transforms the wearer or their situation. His suggestion that style could be expressed as a pictorial statement beyond the genre of fashion photography was prophetic.

In the postwar period, street photography gained in popularity. Though different from fashion photography, such work established what we now term "street style." In line with 1970s documentary photography, which swung away from social awareness to explore more personal interests, street-style photography started to adopt a less conscious handling of subject matter.

Liberman pointed out how a documentary photographer might see clothing—not as a product for marketing but a surface that transforms the wearer or their situation.

An example of this is the work of Al Vandenberg, an American photographer who trained at the Design Laboratory before beginning a career in commercial photography, including fashion. From the 1950s, Vandenberg amassed a personal portfolio of street portraits often conscious of style expressed by dress and demeanor. If there is something that characterizes this kind of outdoor portrait photography, it is an undirected pose: mindful of a teenager's sensitivity to appearance, and alert to what it might disclose. The development of the "Straight-Up," a type of straightforward fashion photograph with minimal staging that was pioneered in the British style magazine *i-D*, arguably stems from this kind of modest address.

Prior to establishing *i-D* in 1980, Terry Jones art-directed British *Vogue*. In the space between the two jobs he designed *Not Another Punk Book!* (1978), by Isabelle Anscombe, which responded to the emergence of the youth subculture and its presence on London's streets, particularly King's Road in Chelsea. One spread is a composite contact sheet of negatives, overlaid with a handwritten narrative outlining a walk the photographer Steve Johnston took with a group of punks down King's Road before the police intervened. Another is a series of street portraits of the same punks, in which the white plaster of an exterior wall serves as backdrop for full-length shots of the subjects, who face the camera. The difference between the two kinds of photographs in the book—one essentially a wide shot and the other a mid shot—is startling: if the former documents a parade of collective belief, then the latter expresses the needs of the individual. While one stresses sociability and the mentality of the pack, the other is by contrast antisocial and insular. When translated into the opening issue of *i-D*, captions were added citing the names of the subjects, where they bought their clothes (unless they were handmade), and a short statement on musical tastes and beliefs.

In the same era, the art director and photographer Jean-Paul Goude was documenting similar kinds of youth culture in New York; like Jones, he also had connections to high-end fashion magazines, but in his case they were from Paris:

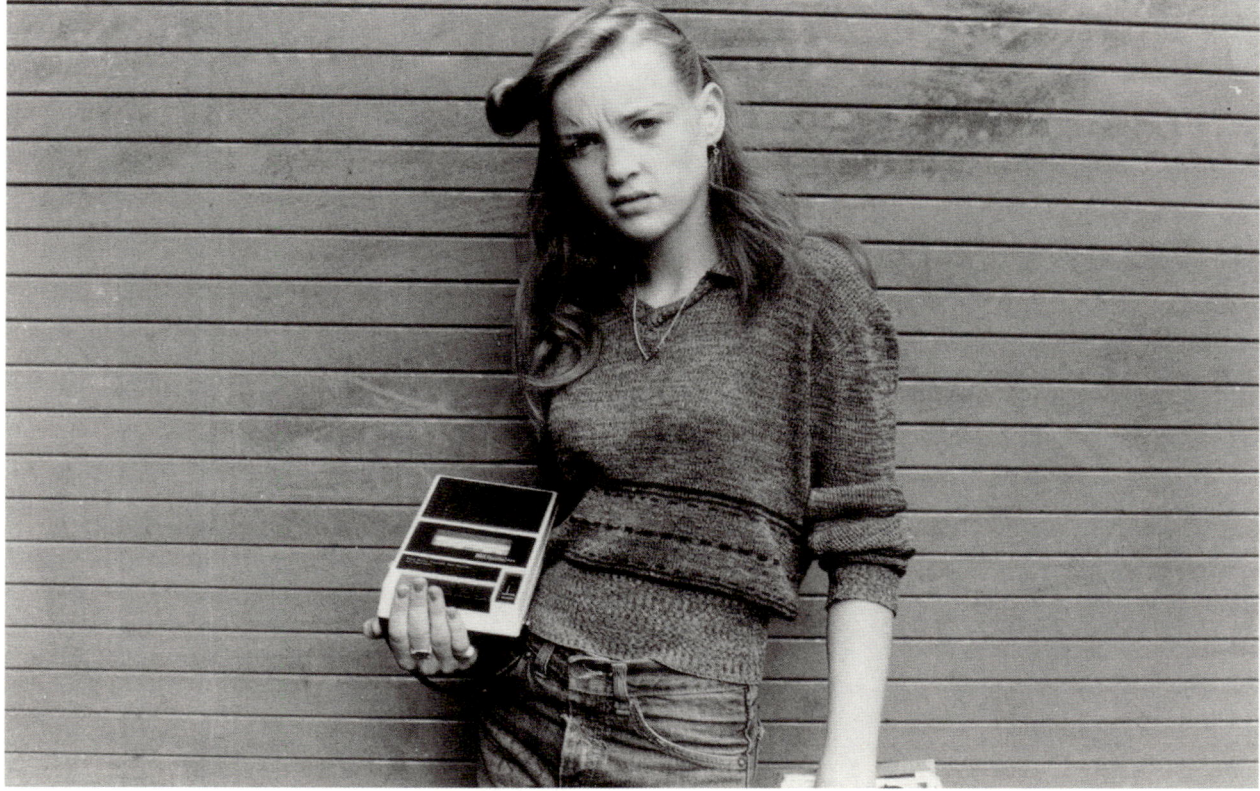

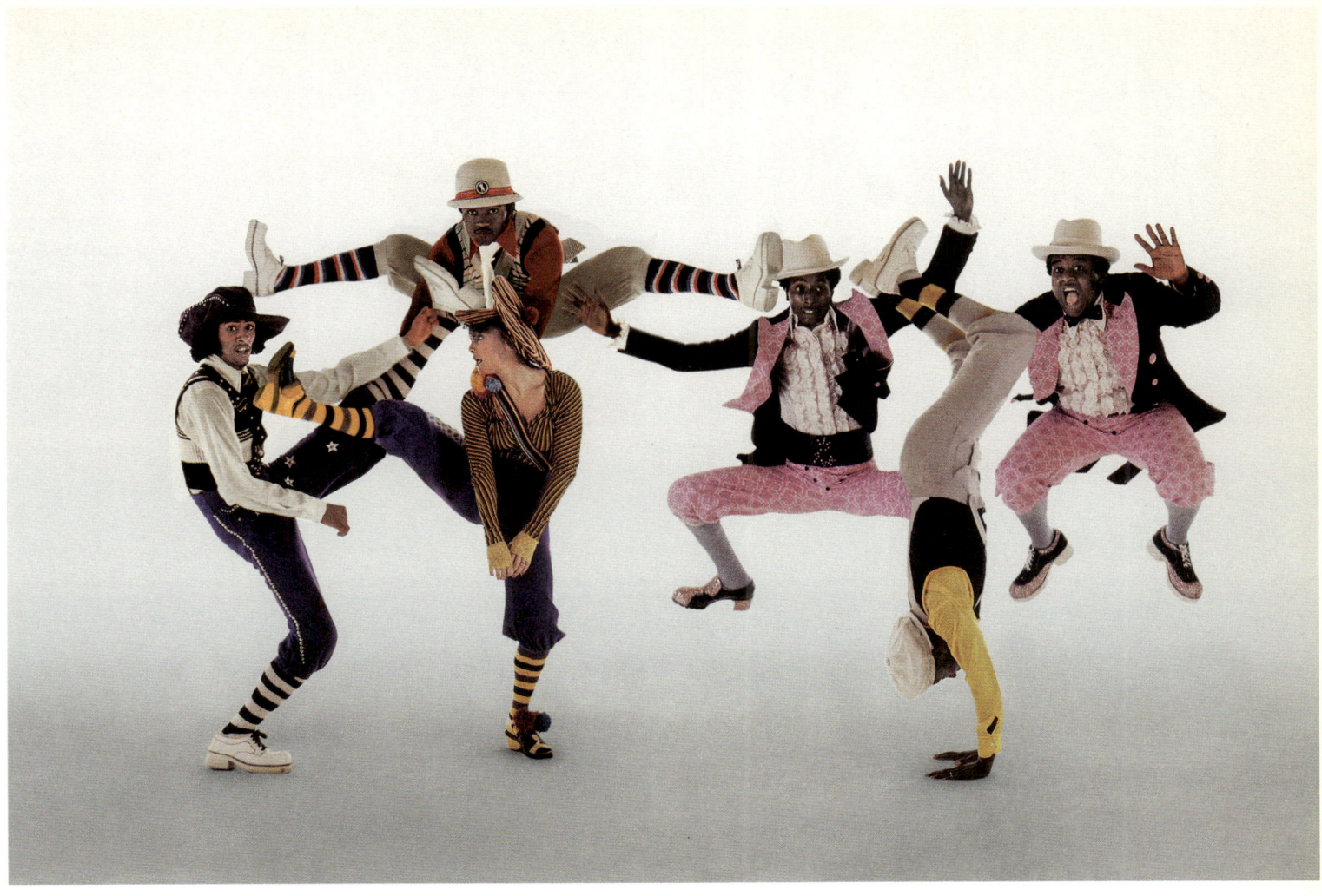

One time the editors of French fashion magazine *Elle* asked me what was interesting in New York then, and I said, "To a French reader, I don't think it's skyscrapers anymore, or yellow cabs, or Broadway. It's the barrio." And I took all those fashion editors out there and they thought they were going on some crazy safari. They were scared, so naturally they loved it. "Darling, *c'est fabuleux!*" They loved it because foreigners see such things with such fresh eyes, and because they were so scared. They were in the heart of Williamsburg where all the murders are committed.

Goude was ingratiating himself with a group of young Puerto Ricans in Brooklyn who dressed in vintage Ivy League college clothes from the '50s and wide suits with broad-brimmed Panama hats. Goude's approach toward documenting subcultures—in a series on dancers from 1975 he included black people, gay tea dancers, Latino and white ballroom dancers—was much more studio-oriented than the "Straight-Up." Goude was already known for altering photographs through elaborate retouching by airbrush, or through the use of multiple transparency film composites in his work for *Esquire* magazine and a range of fashion titles.

Jones and Goude were essentially limelighting sections of urban communities who had little currency in fashion culture but who compensated for this through the verve of their personal style. They were motivated to document the sartorial aspirations of such dispossessed groups for their visual pull, but it was the sense of transgression that clung to the images that made their consumption by a fashion-literate readership more borderline, and therefore pleasurable, if problematic.

The assimilation of documentary photography and the "Straight-Up" continues to inform contemporary fashion imagery: the work of photographers such as Walter Pfeiffer and Nan Goldin, who have been less critical about the role of fashion commissions in their professional portfolios, have inspired a generation of photographers invested in fashion work such as Ryan McGinley, Collier Schorr, and Jack Pierson; the influence of the "Straight-Up" is manifest in fashion blogs such as *The Sartorialist* or *Face Hunter*, and its infiltration into mainstream fashion publishing both in print and online is now unquestionable.

But this accommodation of documentary remains provisional, and it would be foolish to regard its connection to fashion as anything nearing a relationship, as a number of surveys of fashion photography have attempted to do. Like Eggleston's stiff embrace of Rampling, they remain entwined yet uneasy bedfellows.

Alistair O'Neill is a reader in fashion history and theory at Central Saint Martins, University of the Arts, London. He recently curated *Isabella Blow: Fashion Galore!*, at Somerset House, London.

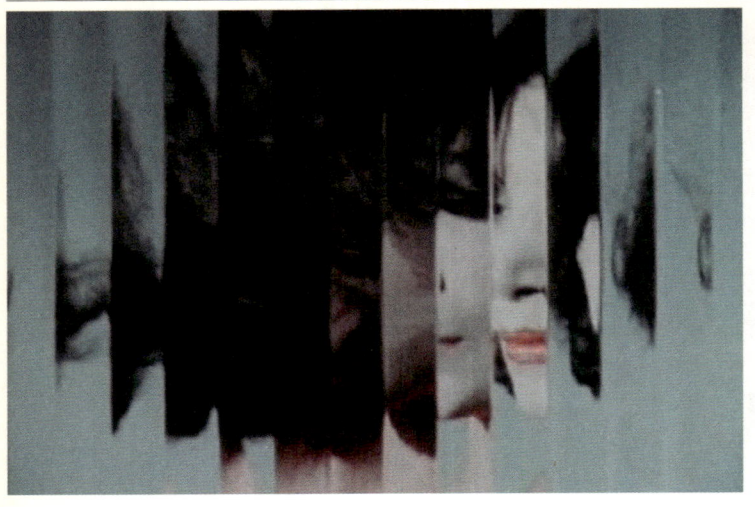
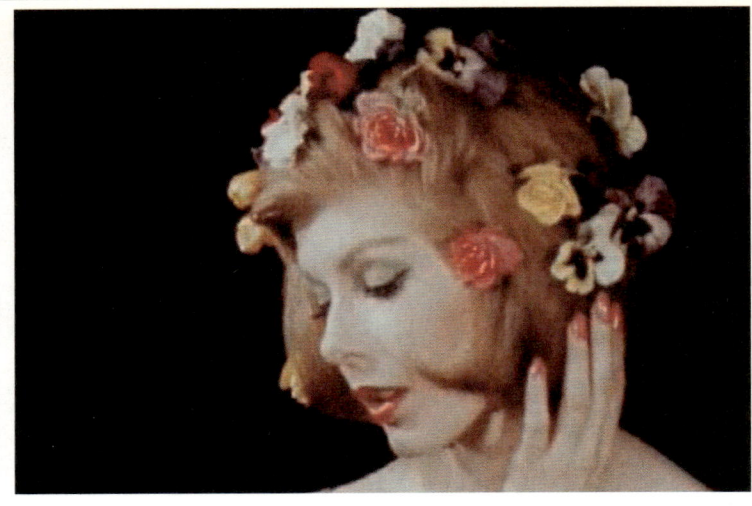
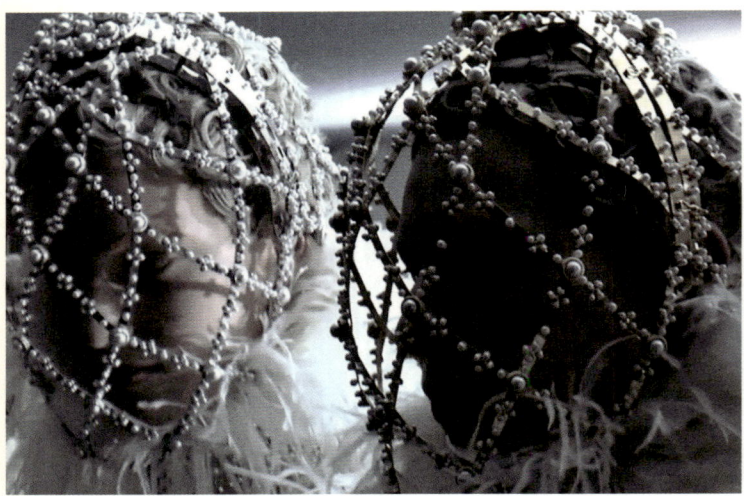
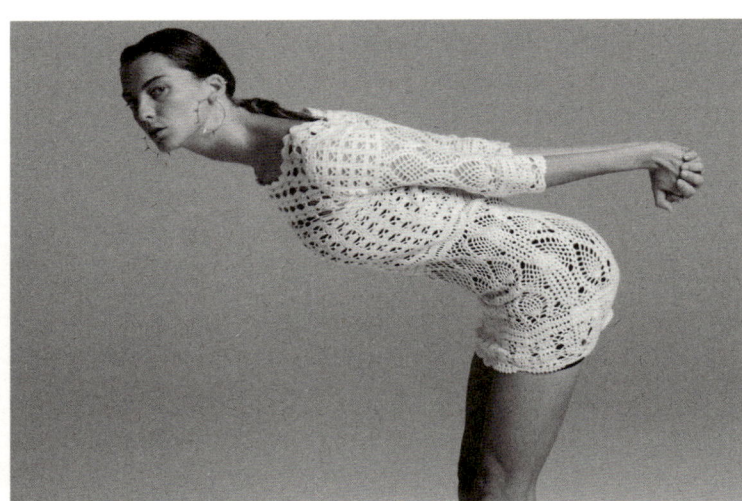
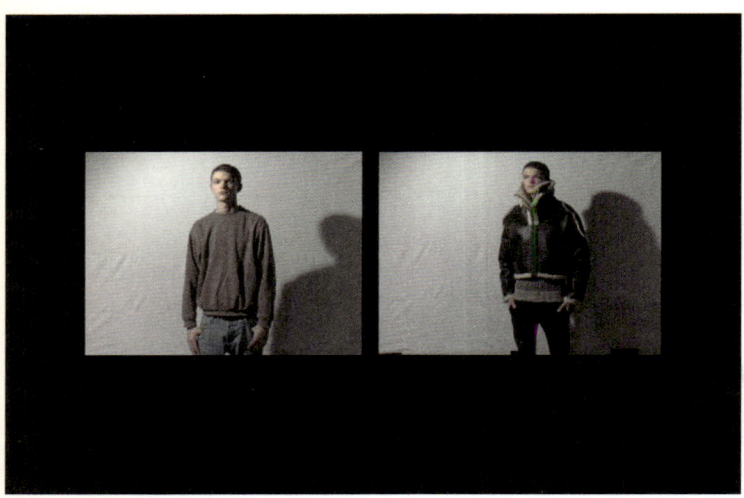
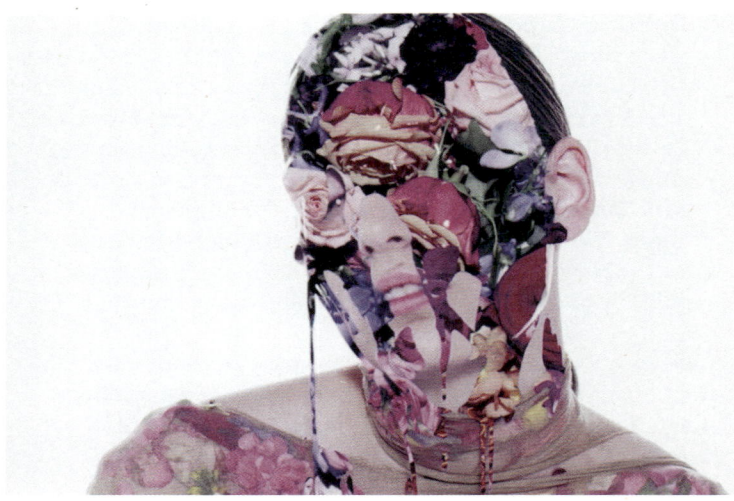

Top row:
Stills from *Experiments in Advertising: The Films of Erwin Blumenfeld* (1958–64), edited by filmmaker Adam Mufti and sound designer Olivier Alary, 2006

Middle row, from left:
Still from John Maybury film for Alexander McQueen Autumn/Winter 2013 collection, 2013; still from Inez & Vinoodh fashion film with Daria Werbowy for *Vogue Paris*, 2012

Bottom row, from left:
Still from Jean-François Carly, *I Feel* for Raf Simons, 2005; still from Pierre Debusschere, *Holy Flowers*, 2012

Blumenfeld: © Yorick Blumenfeld and courtesy SHOWstudio; Maybury: courtesy John Maybury; Inez & Vinoodh: © Inez & Vinoodh and courtesy Gagosian Gallery, New York, and The Collective Shift; Carly: courtesy Jean-François Carly; Debusschere: © Pierre Debusschere and courtesy Art + Commerce films, New York

Brief, non-narrative films make up a burgeoning area of fashion image making today. How do these films reference the conventions of their sister form, still photography?

Fashion Film & the Photographic

Marketa Uhlirova

From Bob Richardson, Helmut Newton, Guy Bourdin, and Deborah Turbeville to Steven Meisel, Glen Luchford, and others, fashion photographers in the past few decades have often emulated the aesthetics of cinema. They have pictured carefully constructed and dramatically lit scenes that brim with narrative potential or, more directly, quote mise-en-scène drawn from the vast reservoir of the movies. This type of photography is, not surprisingly, described as "cinematic." But what if we flip this familiar concept of the "cinematic" fashion photograph to make a reverse claim: that some recent fashion film, a newly prominent type of fashion image, has curiously dwelled on the "photographic"? In fact, could it be that the fashion film has, more than any other form of the moving image, a proclivity to reside in, gravitate toward, or at least somehow hover around photography?

This may sound odd because, surely, the initial stimulus of its makers was the opposite—to escape the confines of the photographic medium. Take Erwin Blumenfeld, who, in the late 1950s, began to experiment with film chiefly to extend the scope of his work in fashion photography. His desire was to set into motion the traditionally static form—very much in an echo of the primary impulse of early cinema to "animate photographs"—and outline a new visual language for fashion by introducing movement and time. While the recent fashion filmmakers were spurred on by such motivations, it is worth stressing that, like Blumenfeld, they have also transposed onto film what were essentially photographic problems and conventions, by holding onto processes, structures, and concerns specific to fashion photography.

Alhough fashion film assimilates a number of diverse film genres and forms, for the most part it evokes short, intense, non-narrative spectacles dedicated to the display and promotion of fashion. It is perhaps best characterized as a rhythmic fusion of visual and aural effects, somewhat similar to the music video. As a form of moving image, it is certainly not new, for it had appeared in different mutations since the beginnings of cinema (consider fashion commercials, newsreel and cine-magazine pieces, or various hybrids of promotional and documentary films). Yet, it had until recently been a form strangely overlooked, even displaced: an unclaimed ground half-lost somewhere between fashion and cinema—two industries with different demands. So it makes sense that when it reemerged from within the fashion community during the aughts, it "arrived" with unprecedented vigor. This rejuvenation has evidently been enabled by the "digital revolution," especially in the new millennium, which has seen an intensified encounter between new media and technologies on the one hand, and fashion image makers and clients keen to explore them on the other.

Fashion film has shared photography's clients, settings, budgets, and, progressively, imaging tools. And it has replicated—at least to a degree—its crews and cast. Many of today's fashion filmmakers have backgrounds in photography but little or no formal knowledge of film or animation techniques and have generally continued with their previous practice of producing editorials and advertising for print magazines. This hybridization between photography and film has increasingly manifested itself through specific projects. Nick Knight and Tell No One's *Dynamic Blooms* (*AnOther* magazine/SHOWstudio, 2011), Pierre Debusschere's *Holy Flowers* (*Dazed Digital*, 2012), or Sølve Sundsbø's *The Ever Changing Face of Beauty* (*W*, 2012), for example, all treat the material generated in a single "shoot" as the basis for a published fashion editorial and an online fashion film, simultaneously and with no obvious hierarchy between them. In the same vein, recent advertising campaigns such as Inez & Vinoodh for Yves Saint Laurent's Autumn/Winter 2010–11 and Steven Meisel for Lanvin's Spring/Summer 2013 present a seamless continuity between photography and film. This intermedial coexistence feels very real as it has also found its platforms in museum exhibitions, retail and public spaces, and, above all, online fashion magazines and websites. The most important of these has been Nick Knight and Peter Saville's SHOWstudio, which has since its conception been very specific about the "studio" as a physical space that can amalgamate various creative practices (photography, filmmaking, and so on), while also being a broadcasting station.

Alongside these material and functional connections, there is another way to consider this close alliance between film and photography. It is through fashion's vital preoccupation with the pose—something that has in fact been a recurrent source of fascination for the cinema. Stanley Donen's *Funny Face* (USA, 1957), and Věra Chytilová's *Strop* (Ceiling, Czechoslovakia, 1962) are two fiction films about fashion that in their portrayal of photo shoots use the freeze-frame or photographic still to provoke a tension between the models' pose as a process, a choreography unraveling in time, and a final product—a privileged fashion image. By highlighting the moment of the holding of a pose, both expose its intrinsic paradox whereby one must become an immobilized image prior to the fact. (Both films did so with a different purpose: *Funny Face* elevates the frozen moment as the ideal image whereas *Strop* draws attention to its falsity.)

In a similar, if less ideological, manner, a distinct group of early fashion films associated with SHOWstudio explore the deceptive borderline between photographic stillness and filmic illusion of stillness. For example, *Shelley Fox 14* (Shelley Fox and SHOWstudio, 2002) and *Maison Martin Margiela A/W 2004–05* (Nigel Bennett, 2004) both arrange sets or sequences of still photographs into a temporal experience. Two other early SHOWstudio films, Jean-François Carly's *I Feel* (2005) and Knight's *Sleep* (2001) approximate photographs in the way their subjects are statically framed and portrayed as ostensibly inactive. Carly's film shows a string of young male subjects standing in front of a white sheet, facing the camera in a way that is reminiscent of Warhol's *Screen Tests*. The screen is split into two, with each pair of portraits showing the same boy, one dressed in his own clothes, the other in Raf Simons. The juxtapositions are accompanied by sparse comments in which the boys state how they feel as their newly fashioned selves, bringing into focus the transformative potential of clothes. In another nod to Warhol, Knight's *Sleep* was first staged as a "live photo shoot" portraying nine models while they slept in their hotel rooms. Initially filmed by webcams and streamed via SHOWstudio, the footage of *Sleep* was subsequently turned into nine short films that speed up the non-action by applying a time-lapse effect. The edited films reintroduce movement, spotlighting the lyrically mutating draperies of the models' flimsy dresses.

The attachment to the photographic seen in SHOWstudio's early films also permeates a number of other, different strands of the fashion film: Inez & Vinoodh's campaign for Yves Saint Laurent Autumn/Winter 2010–11 shows a simple event of a model descending a staircase and walking past the camera, very much in the style of early Lumière films. The model's descent is not, however, captured as fluid motion but rather as a broken and disjointed sequence of slow-motion shots displaying an array of outfits. Yang Fudong's campaign *First Spring* for Prada Spring/Summer 2010 inserts deliberately stilled or decelerated shots into otherwise dynamic street and interior scenes. Steven Klein's *Time Capsule* series (2011) are pared-down filmic continuations (in black-and-white) of the very (color) images that make up the photographer's editorial for *W*.

Why, then, this insistence on stillness and restricted expression in so many fashion films? Perhaps there is a sense (articulated by many, most famously Roland Barthes and Susan Sontag) that photographs are ultimately more memorable and impactful than moving images. Or perhaps the prolonged static shots allow for a closer study of shapes, colors, textures, and detail, something that industry clients and consumers may like to see. What is certain, though, is that the growing entanglement of the two media has naturally pushed for a new level of aesthetic and conceptual dialogue between them. In this relation, film is not necessarily an extension of photography, but rather, each medium is an extension of the other.

Marketa Uhlirova is director and curator of the Fashion in Film festival and a research fellow at Central Saint Martins, University of the Arts, London. She is the editor, most recently, of *Birds of Paradise: Costume as Cinematic Spectacle* (Koenig Books, 2013).

Pictures

Ed van der Elsken,
*The Fair on the Nieuwmarkt,
Amsterdam*, 1961

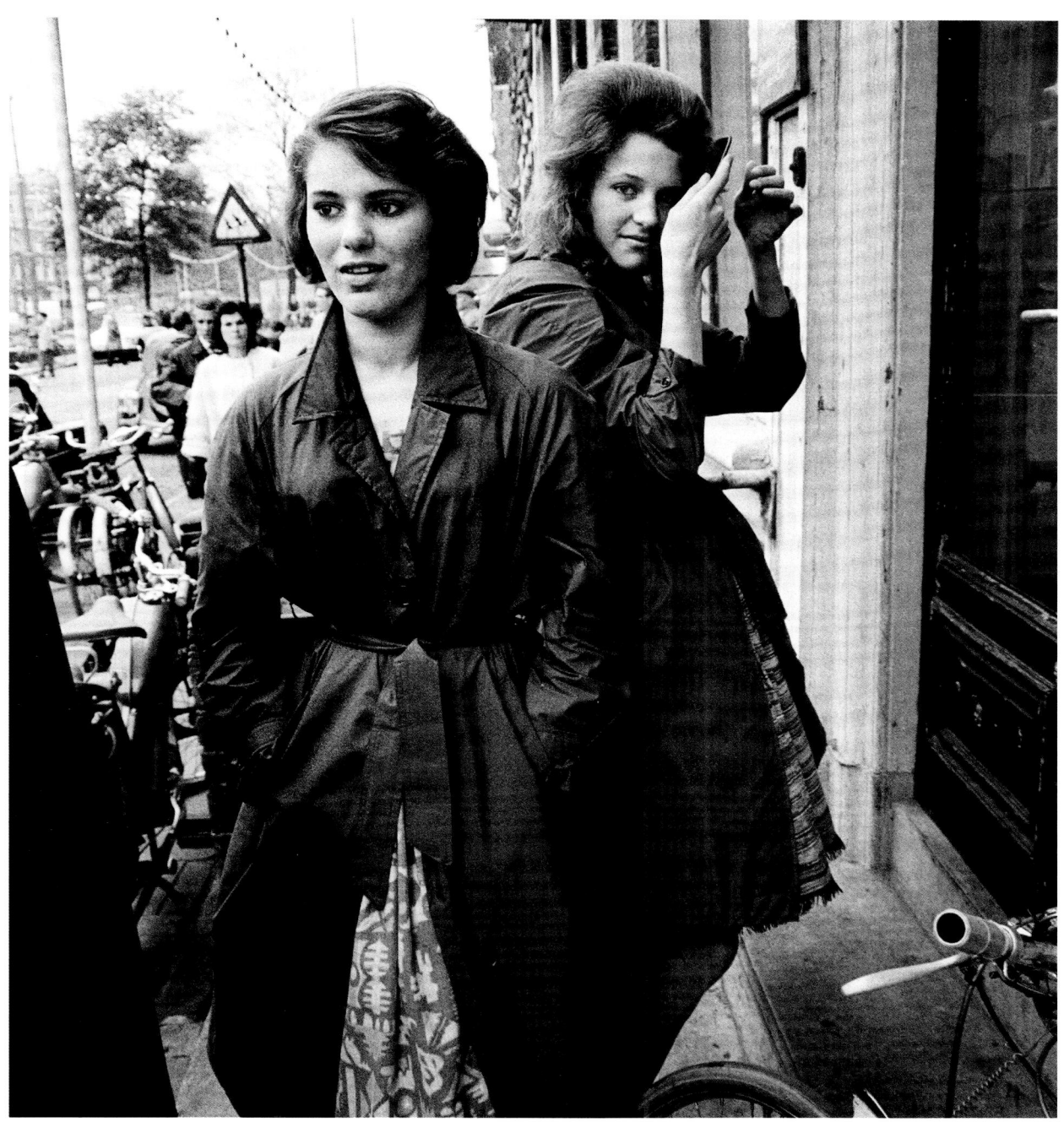

The Dutch photographer and filmmaker Ed van der Elsken (1925–90) photographed people. He was drawn from the beginning to characterful individuals, and he roamed the streets of his native Amsterdam and, later, Paris, Hong Kong, and Tokyo, seeking them out; over the course of his forty-year career he made dozens of photobooks and films in which his personal and professional lives were inextricably intertwined. Along with Robert Frank and William Klein, van der Elsken belonged to a new generation of photographers who, each in their own way after the atrocities of World War II, recorded a world of drama, somberness, and gloom. Today, van der Elsken's influence is felt in the work of later photographers such as Nobuyoshi Araki, Nan Goldin, and Larry Clark, who took a similar interest in subcultures and adopted the street-style portrait in their diaristic approaches.

In 1947, van der Elsken's father gave him a plate camera; three years later, the photographer went to Paris, where he would photograph bohemians in Saint-Germain-des-Prés for his first photobook, *Love on the Left Bank* (1956). The resulting images are sometimes emotive, sometimes seductive—nobody ever smiles in his photographs; expressions are grave, sultry, or drugged. Van der Elsken depicts people on the edges of society as proud individuals rather than as pitiable figures, and his images reflect his admiration for their refusal to conform. The central character in these is the striking, redheaded beauty Vali Myers, who with her wild hair and her dark, kohl-ringed eyes epitomized the bohemian for van der Elsken: she represented freedom and personal expression.

Initially van der Elsken worked with a Rolleicord, later also with a Leica. He preferred to use available light because he sought to capture reality as he found it. He was not a purist: he cropped his images and loved contrast. By the end of the 1950s, van der Elsken also began to work in color, in photographs that were often commissioned and published in magazines. Although he is known for his pictures of nightlife, the red-light district, and the counterculture, the majority of his photographs focus on the everyday. In his portraits he captures, beautifully, a sense of optimism, vitality, and love. More so than his contemporaries, he revealed himself and his surroundings; he was always present in his own work. Take, for example, his self-portrait with his girlfriend, later wife, Ata Kando, made in 1952 while doing housework in Paris, or his final film, *Bye* (1990), in which he confronts his own mortality.

As a photographer, van der Elsken was notorious for the way he provoked people, pranced around them, challenged them. He was a charismatic figure. Some called him a genius; others saw him as a loudmouth, a provocateur. Photographing or filming meant an intense interaction between artist and subject. He was always demanding eye contact; the expressions, the glances exchanged between photographer and subject, are never neutral. Van der Elsken never got bored with people. He wandered the city, fascinated by its dark side and its neglected inhabitants: those who resolutely rejected the deeply entrenched middle-class society. Van der Elsken compellingly captures this mentality in his photographs. He succeeded in doing so because it reflected his own.

Ed van der Elsken

Tamara Berghmans

Tamara Berghmans is a curator at the FotoMuseum Antwerp.

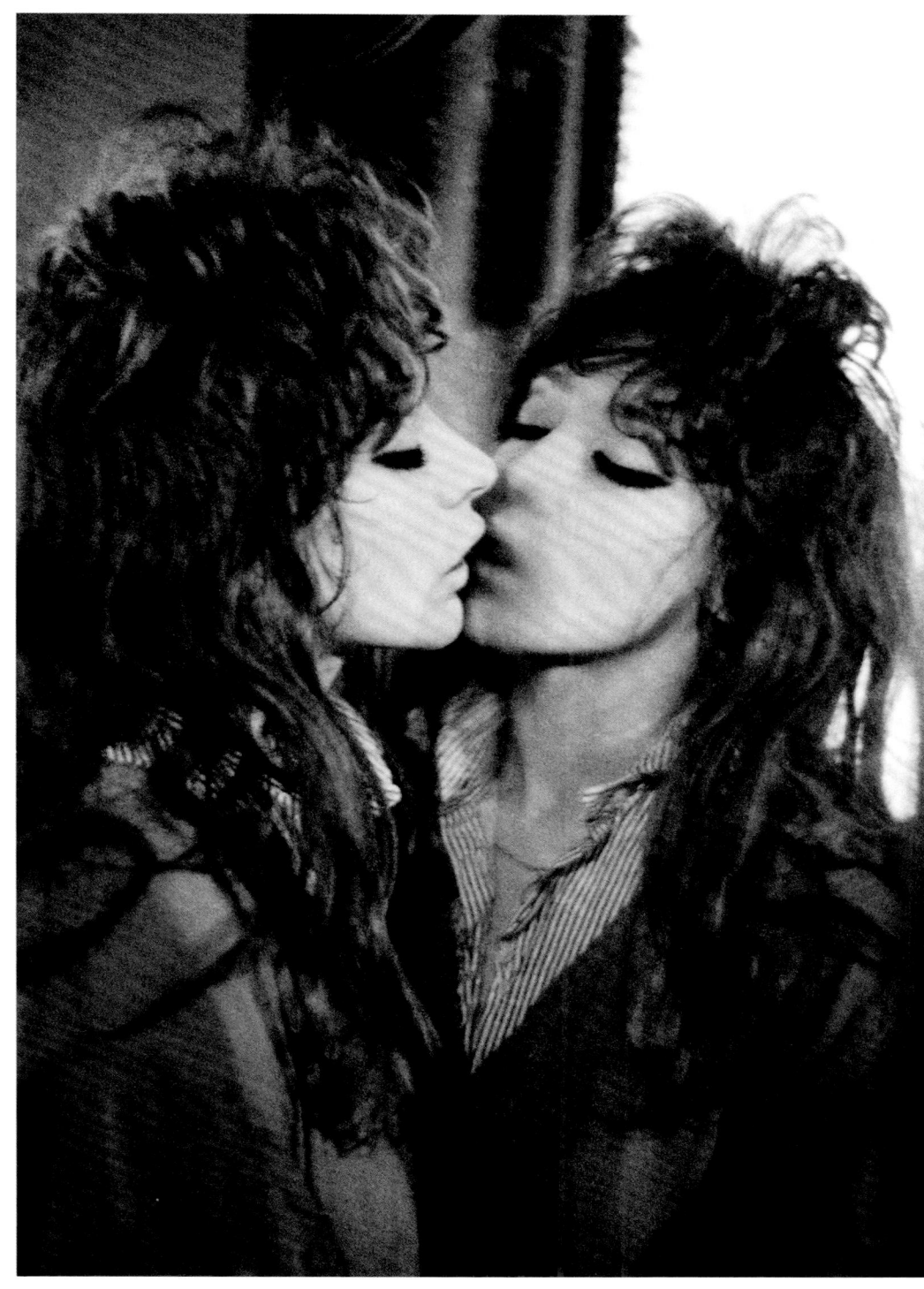

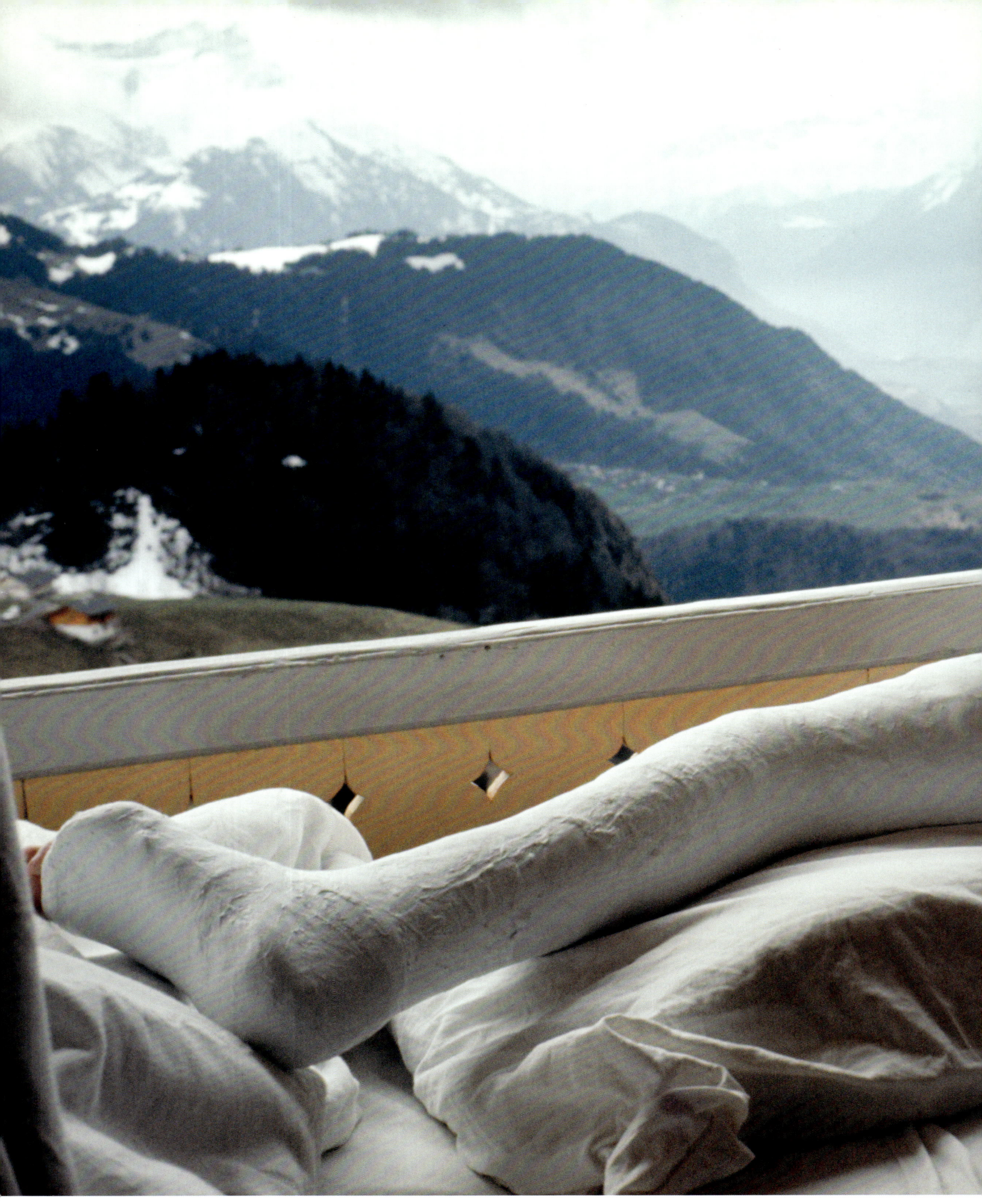

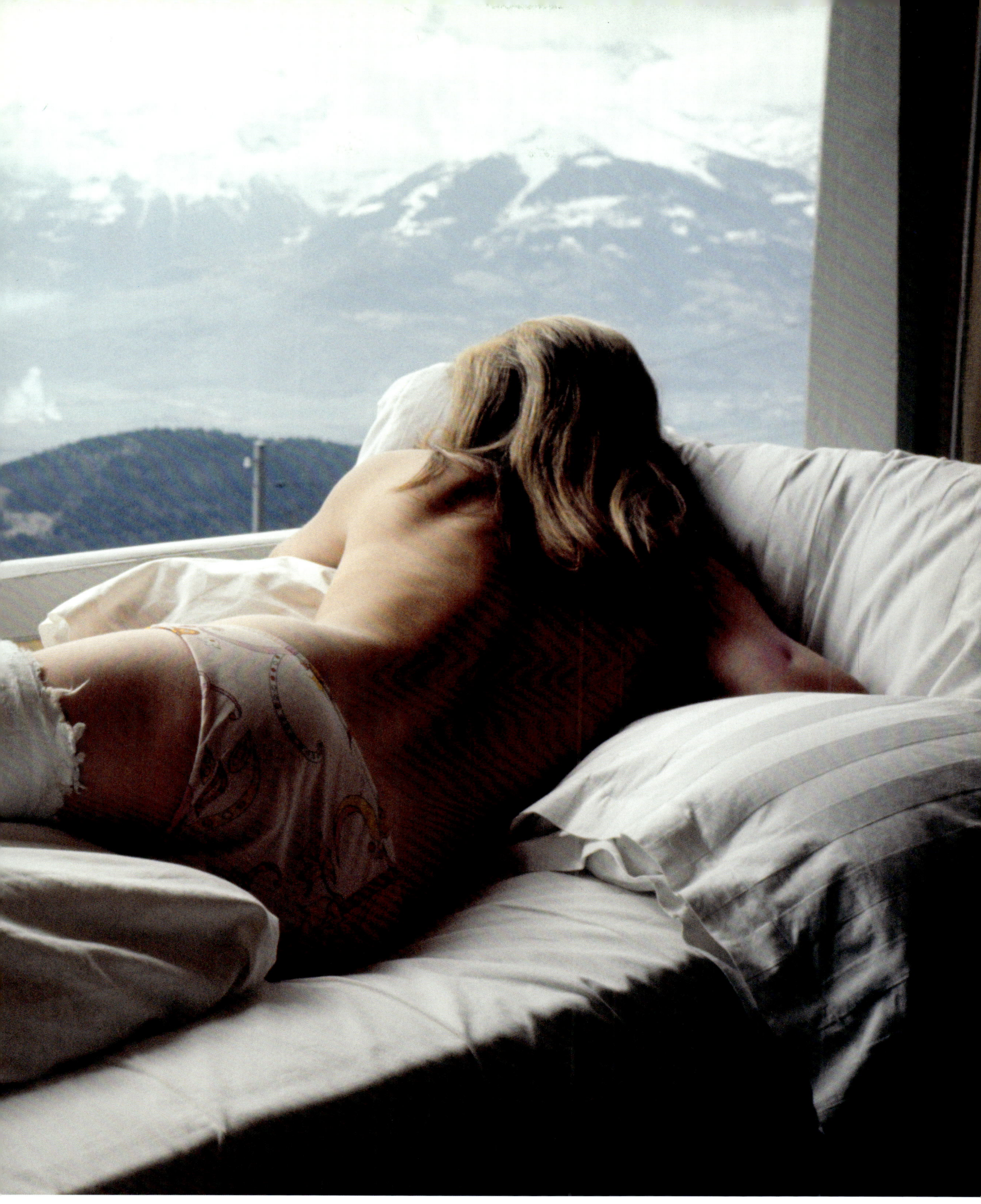

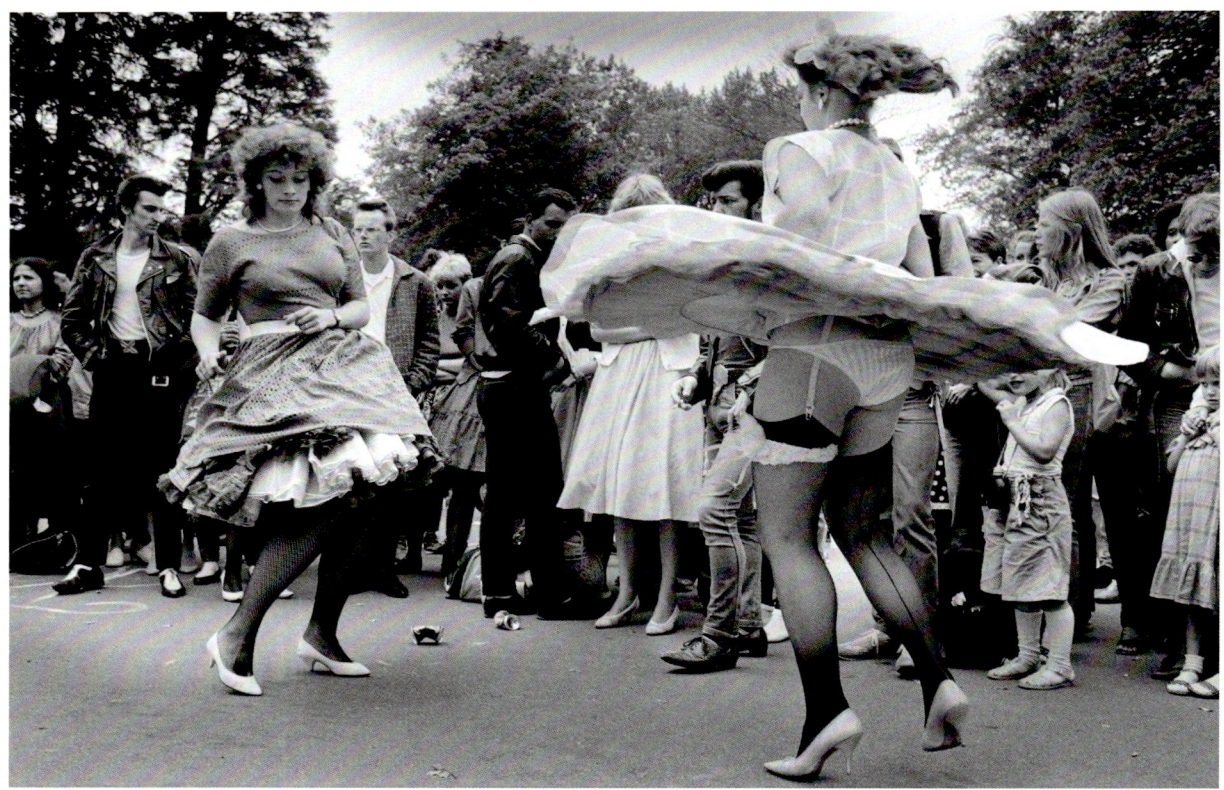

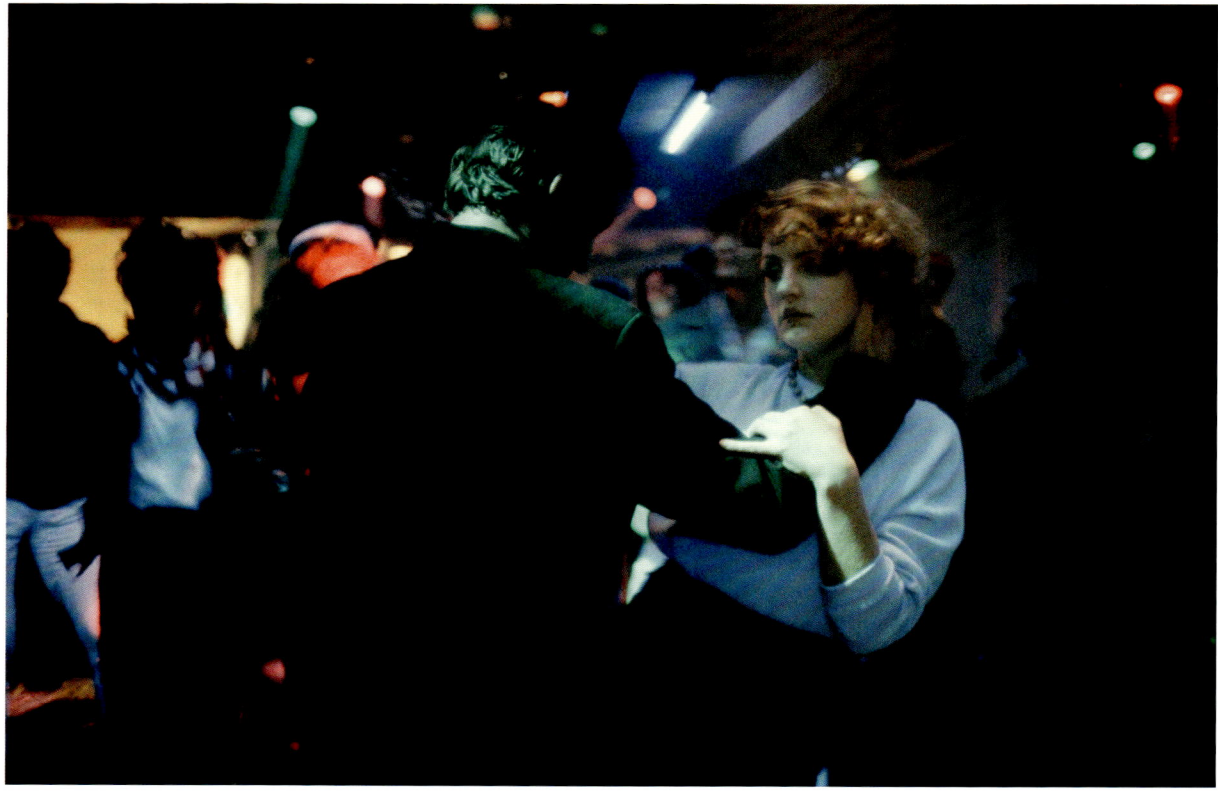

This page:
Gerda van der Veen,
Amsterdam, ca. 1957

Following pages:
Couple making love, Edam,
1970

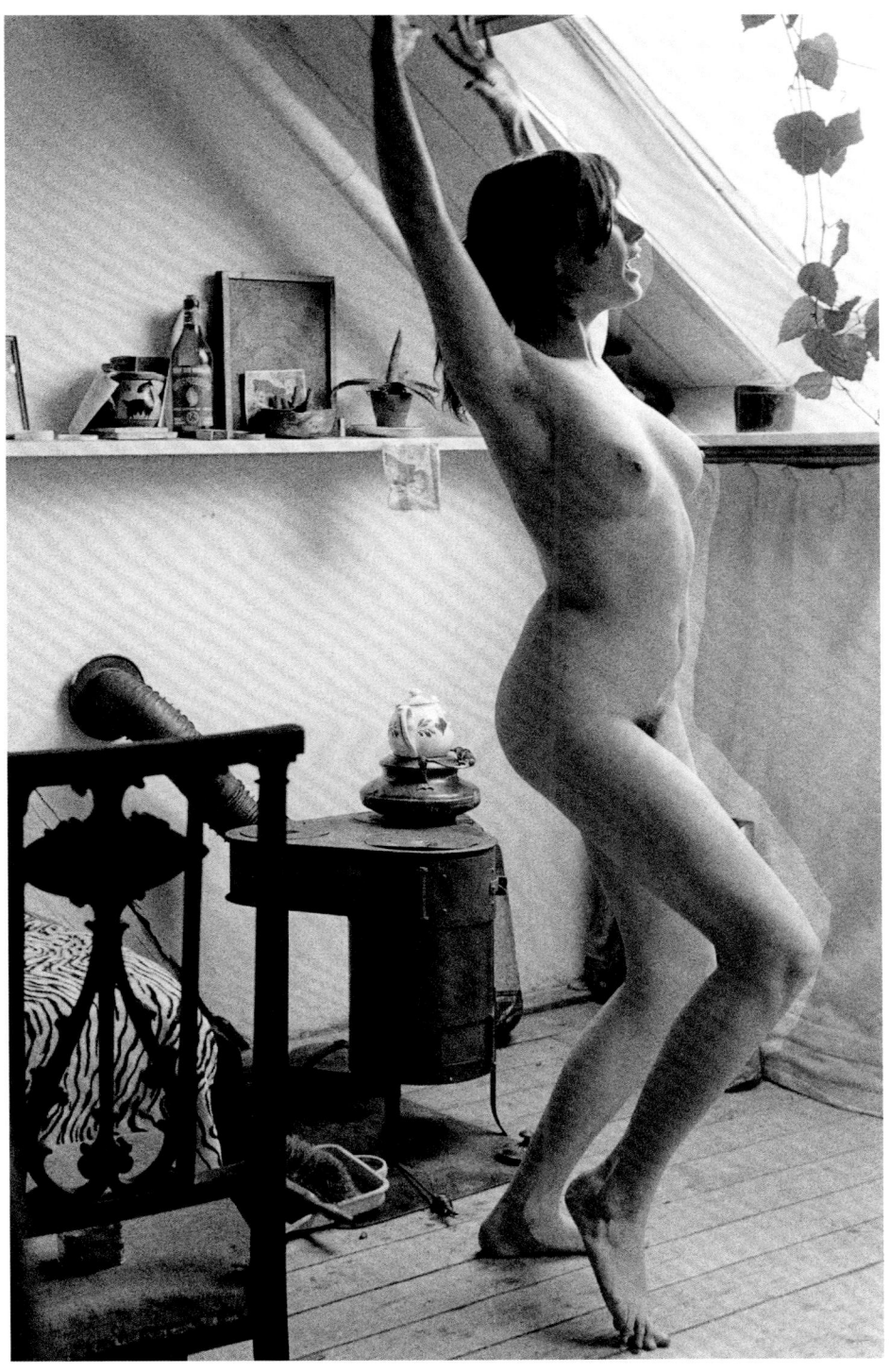

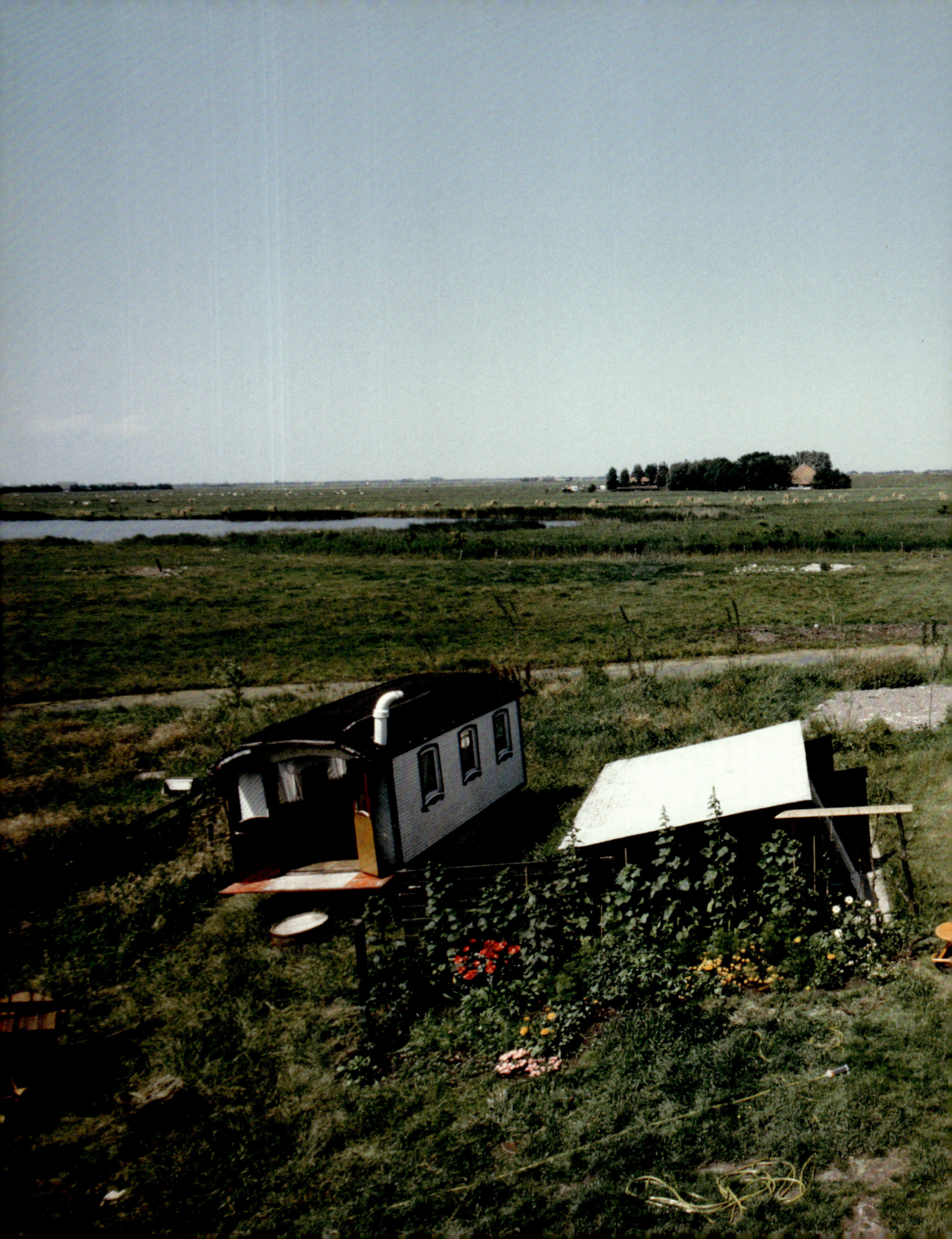

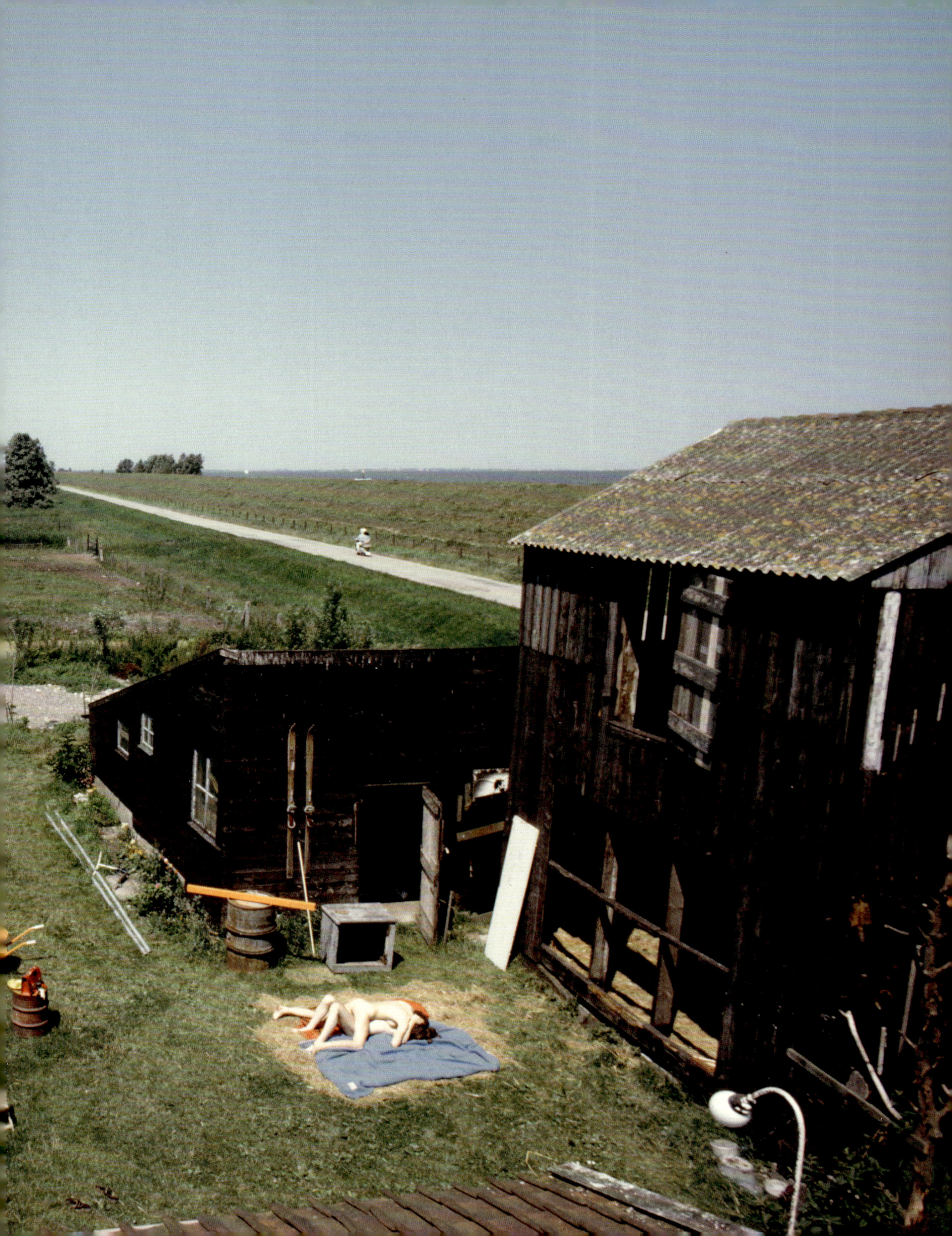

Top:
*Kees and Franulka,
Amsterdam,* 1969

Bottom:
*Self-portrait with
Ata Kandó, Paris,* 1953

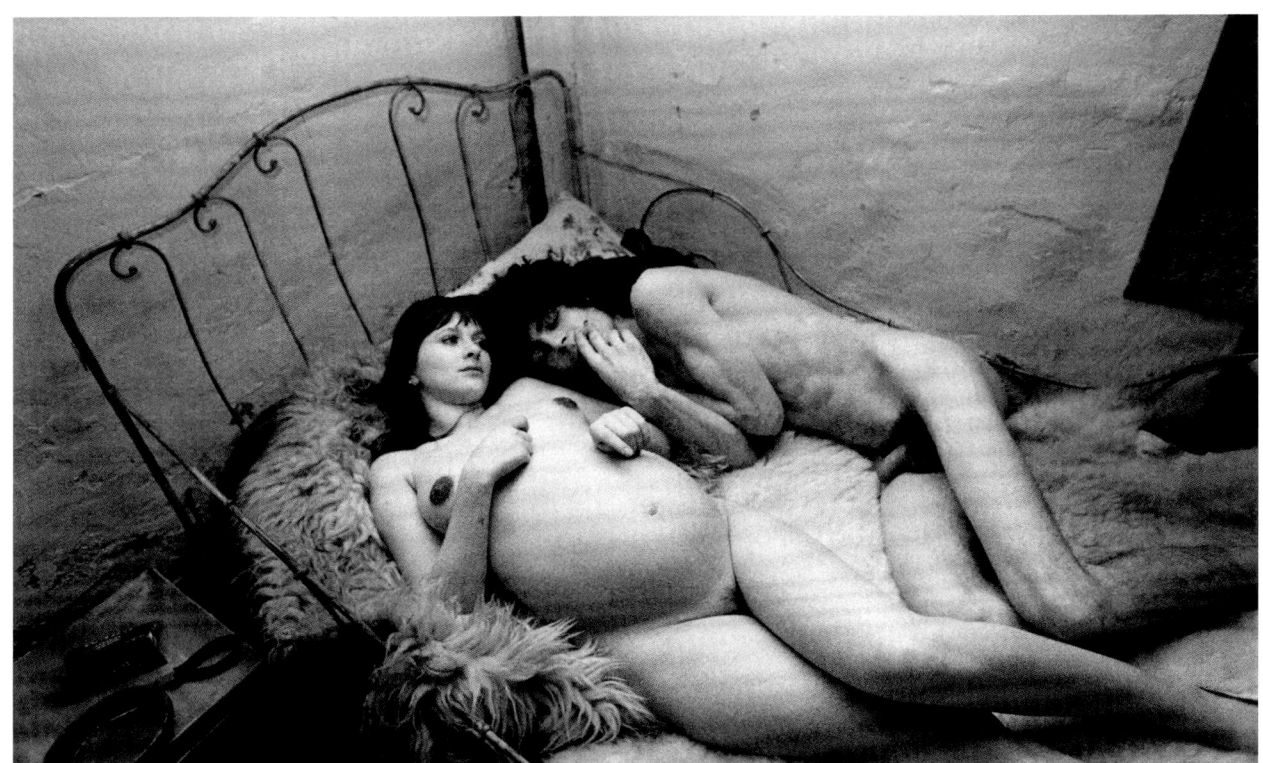

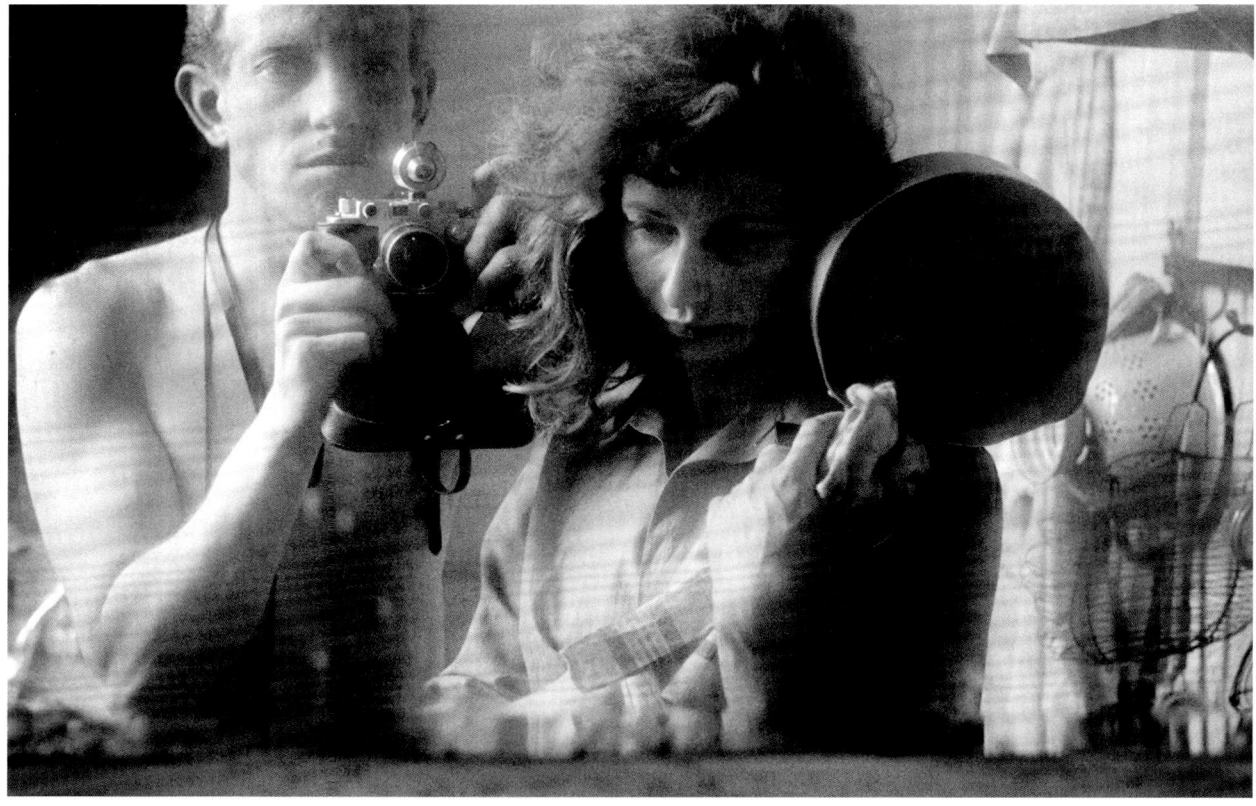

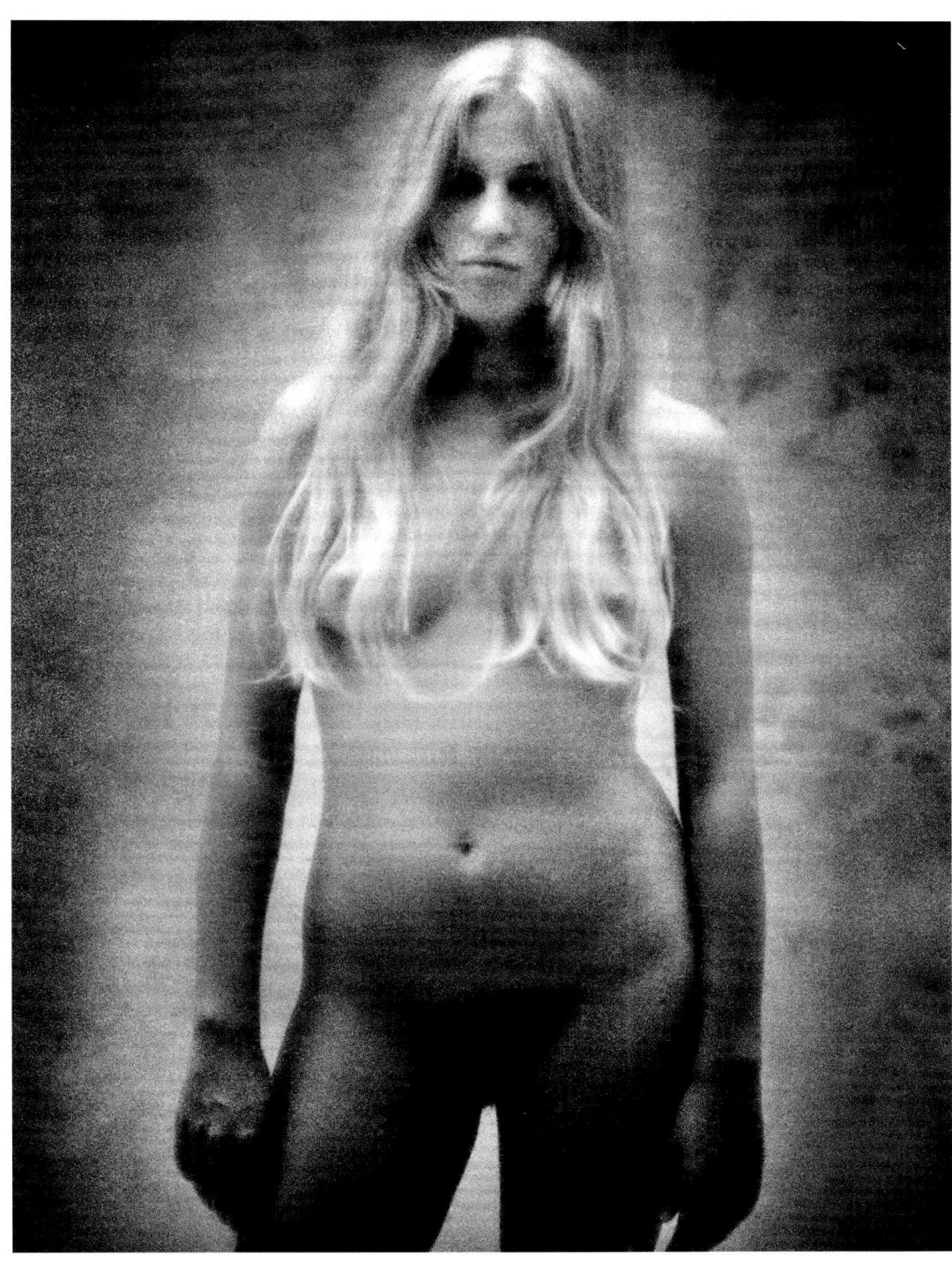

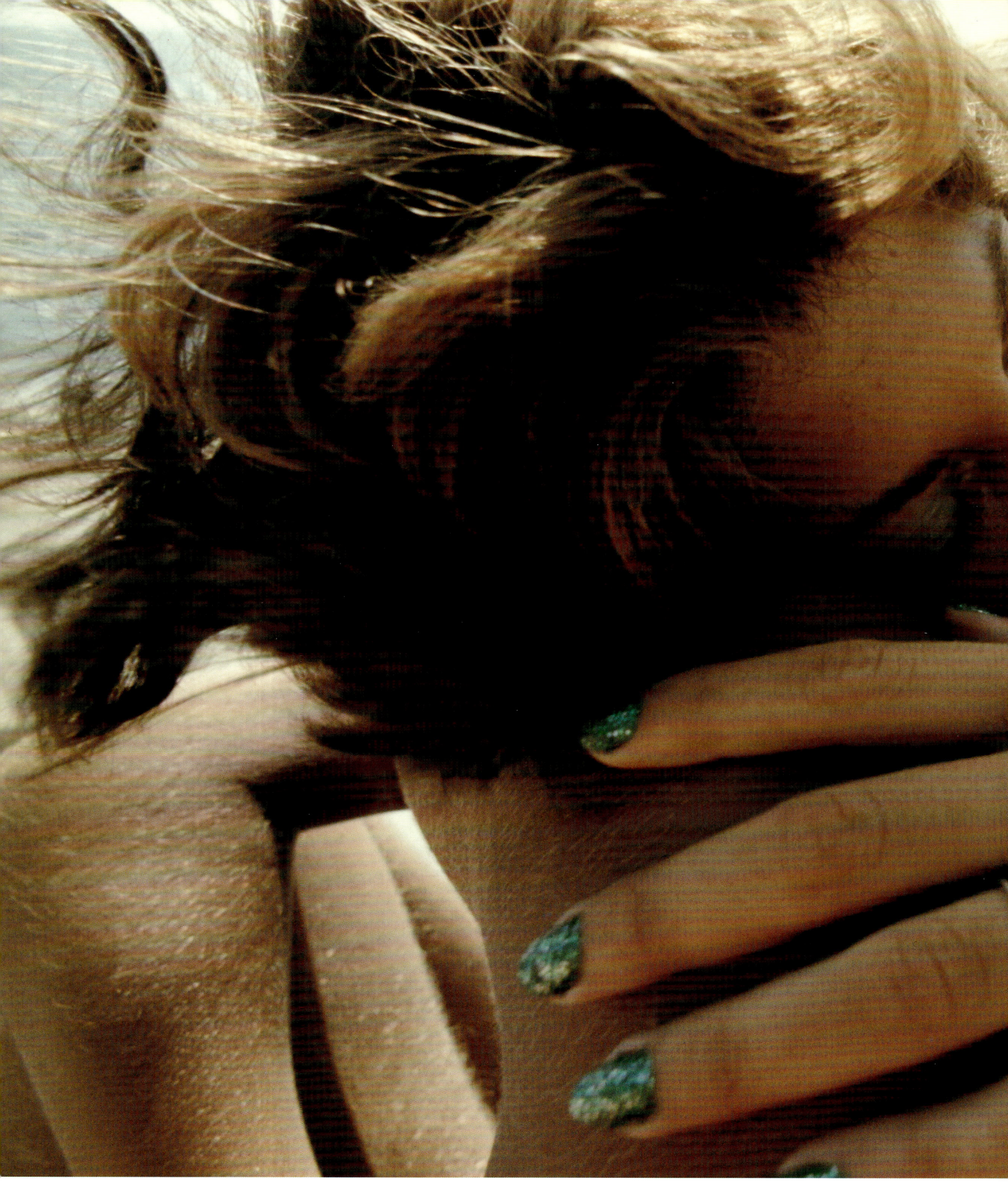

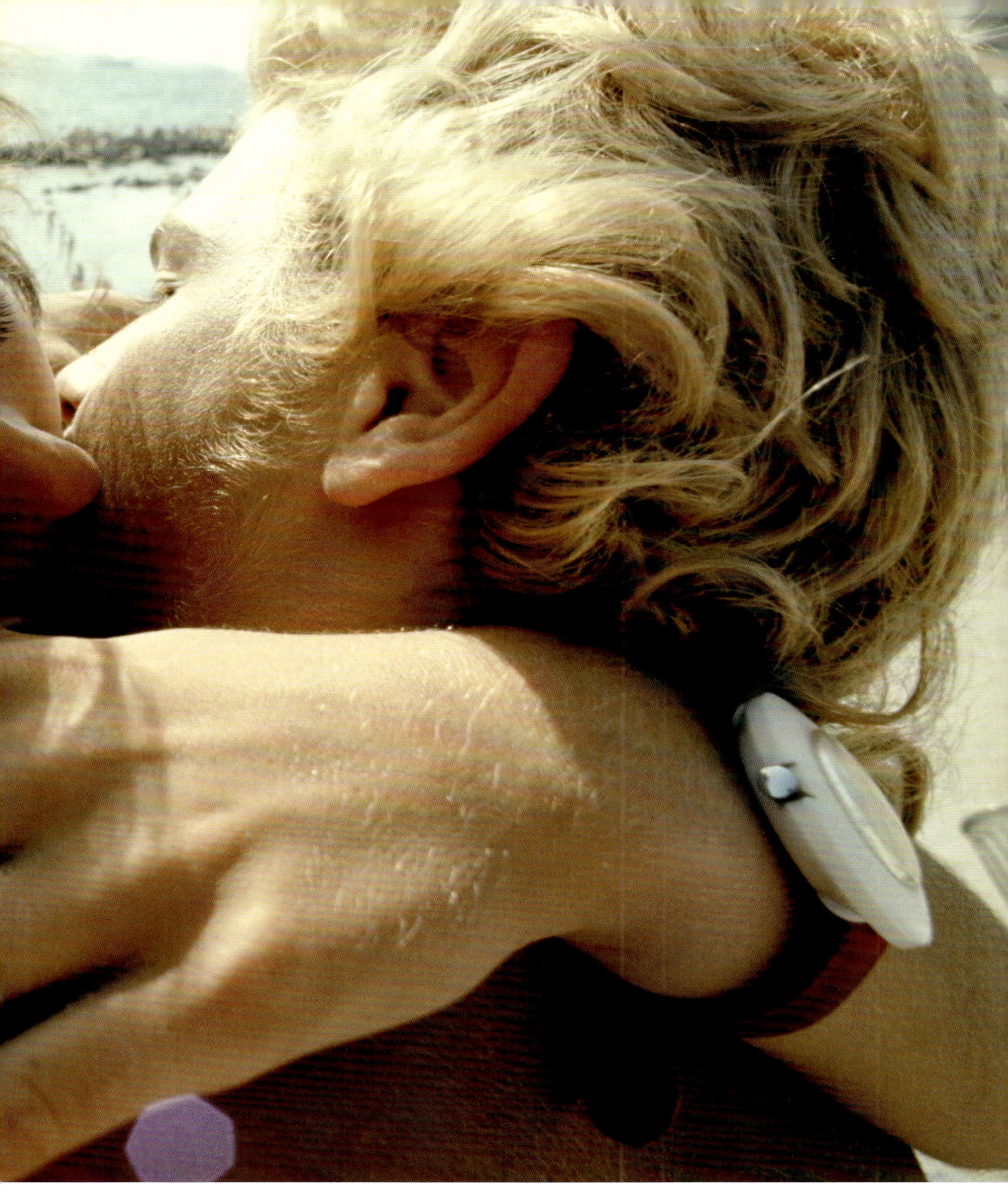

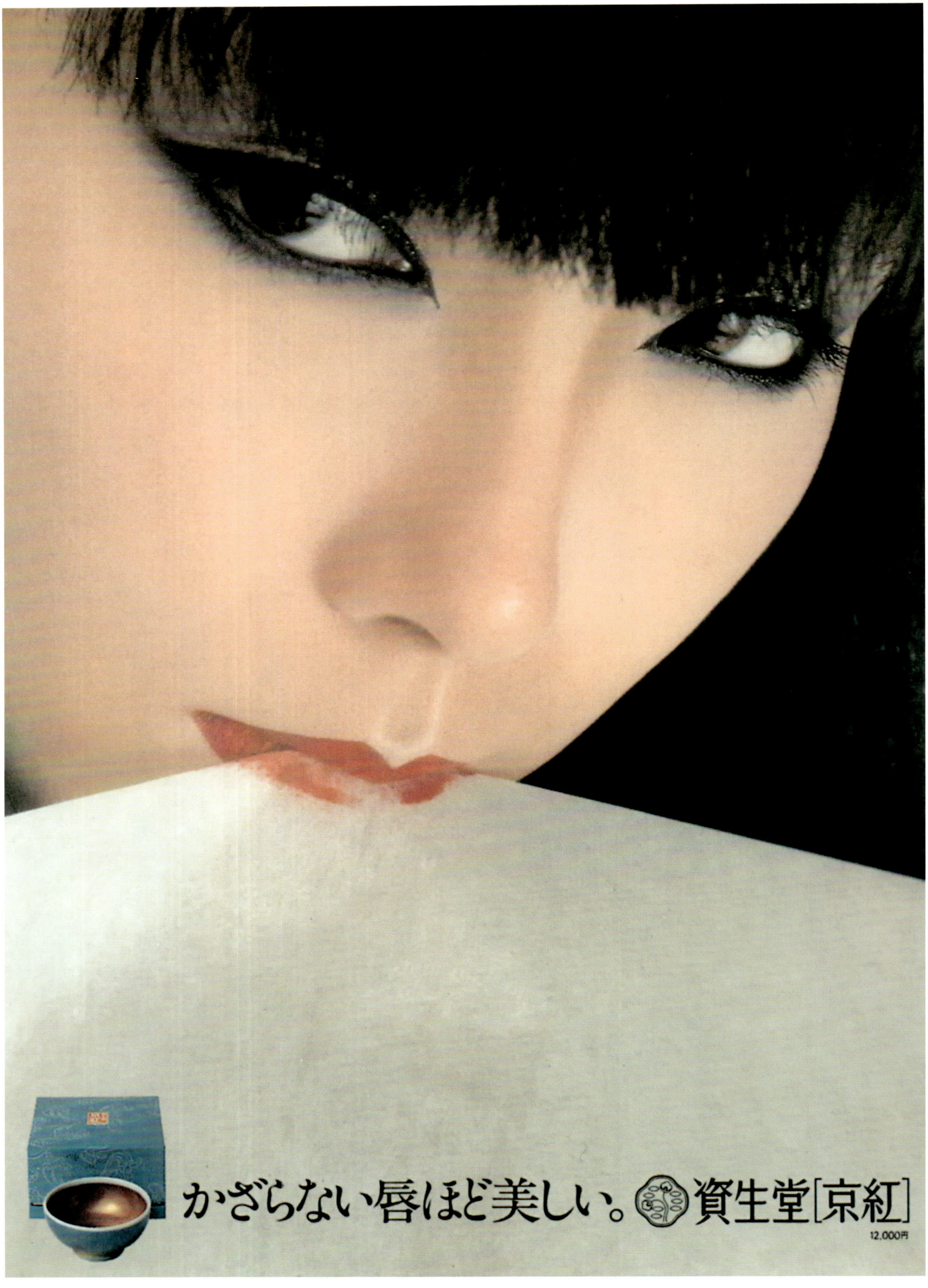

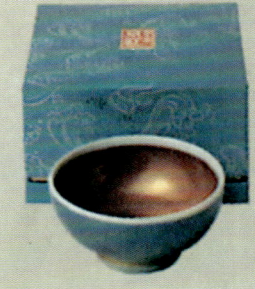

かざらない唇ほど美しい。　資生堂［京紅］

12,000円

**Makeup products
("As fair as unadorned
skin"), 1978**
Makoto Nakamura
(art direction and design),
Noriaki Yokosuka
(photography),
Kesao Uchida (copy)

The images in these pages comprise a tiny selection of the extraordinary visual culture produced by Shiseido, the Japanese purveyor of beauty products. Founded as a pharmacy in Tokyo's fashionable Ginza district in 1872 by Arinobu Fukuhara, and now the fourth largest cosmetics company in the world, Shiseido has always had a strong relationship with photography. Fukuhara's sons published monographs of their own modernist-inspired work and established the Japan Photographic Society in 1924. Arinobu's grandson, Yoshiharu Fukuhara, is the director of the Tokyo Metropolitan Museum of Photography. Alongside the company's innovative use of imagery, the design of their products, packaging, and retail outlets contributed to a seductive brand identity based on a "stateless, universal" ideal.

Shiseido is responsible for bringing many Western concepts to Japan, including toothpaste, ice cream, and carbonated drinks. They also opened the first free public art gallery, still in Ginza today, albeit in a smart, new tower. Their most important activity, though, was educating customers about overseas grooming trends and practices, which the company did through their corporate magazine *Hanatsubaki*, launched in 1937. Despite its primary purpose of cultivating demand for Shiseido products, the publication deserves to be ranked alongside other radical postwar titles, such as the German youth magazine *twen* or the British women's magazine *Nova*, for its dizzying photographic layouts and challenging design.

Shiseido's innovative, enigmatic visuals transformed their products into fetish objects; it was not enough simply to introduce the long-isolated Japanese public to foreign fancies. As with most applied photography, advertising work is often overlooked or disregarded as "commercial," a disingenuous distinction that anyone who has visited a recent photo-art fair will contest. A look through the Shiseido archives reveals a tacit commentary on the powerful changes affecting Japanese society, particularly in the postwar years when Japan's economy boomed. The company's marketing materials underscore how art directors, photographers, typographers, fashion designers, and makeup artists reconciled traditional values and aesthetics with twentieth-century sensibilities, resulting in the gorgeous hybrids that can make a visit to Japan so beguiling for outsiders.

For some Western observers, part of the intrigue of Japanese photography may stem from a lack of context, for we are often unable to read the copy on the ads, the titles of the books, or the names of the authors. That said, to ignore the machinations of product photography is to uncritically digest corporate promotional materials. Beautiful as these Shiseido ads may be, they were designed with the sole purpose of encouraging consumption. Yet unlike most of their Western counterparts, they did so not by reinforcing stereotypes and promoting existing ideals of beauty but by championing new trends through a tireless output of class-A eye candy. The sophistication of these images often lies in a reconciliation of both new, European influences and local sensibilities. Consider the use of space and perspective, which could be seen in relation to traditional Japanese woodcut illustration. Flat colors abound while textures lack specific detail. Facial expressions feel mimed and frozen. Objects become magic talismans in oblique narratives divorced from any sense of realism. A floating dream world beckons.

Shiseido Magic

Jason Evans

**Jason Evans is a
photographer based
in Ramsgate, England.
He created numerous
editorials and covers for**
Hanatsubaki (working
with legendary art director
Masayoshi Nakajo)
between 2006 and 2012.

**Summer Color Promotion
("Winds from the south-
southwest, in living color"),
1976**
Isamu Hanauchi
(art direction),
Reikichi Nakayama (design),
Noriaki Yokosuka
(photography),
Takao Onoda (copy)

**Men's product "MG5"
line ("The era of men,
the era of MG5"), 1968**
Takushi Mizuno
(art direction),
Jyosuke Kubo (design),
Yojiro Adachi
(photography),
Takuichiro Hosokawa (copy)

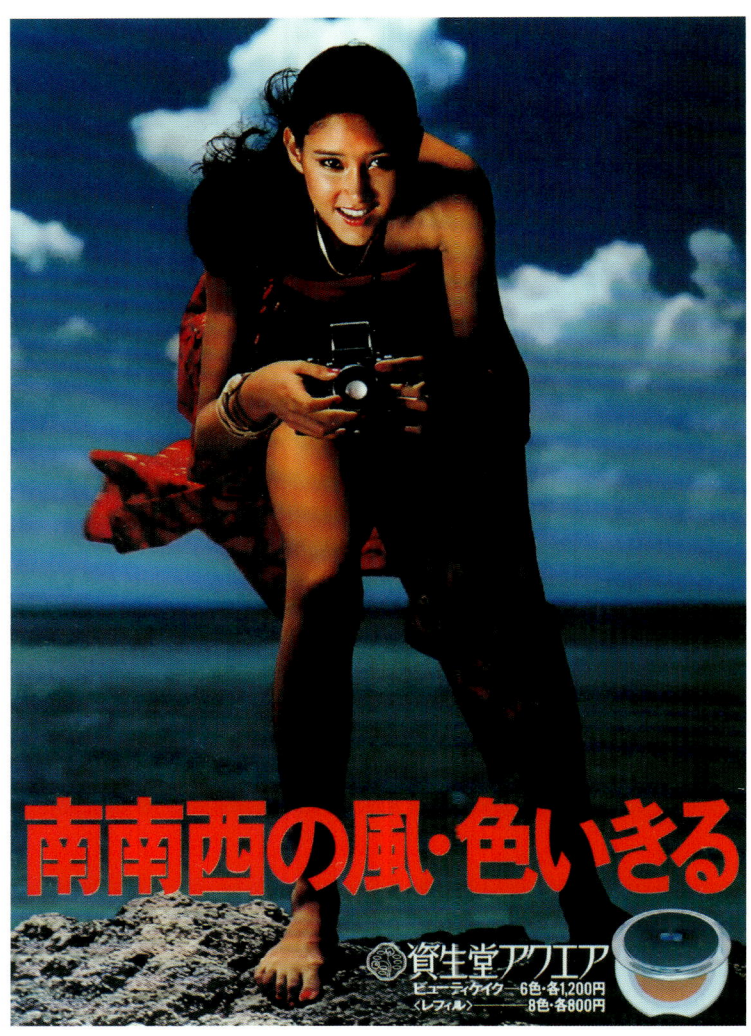

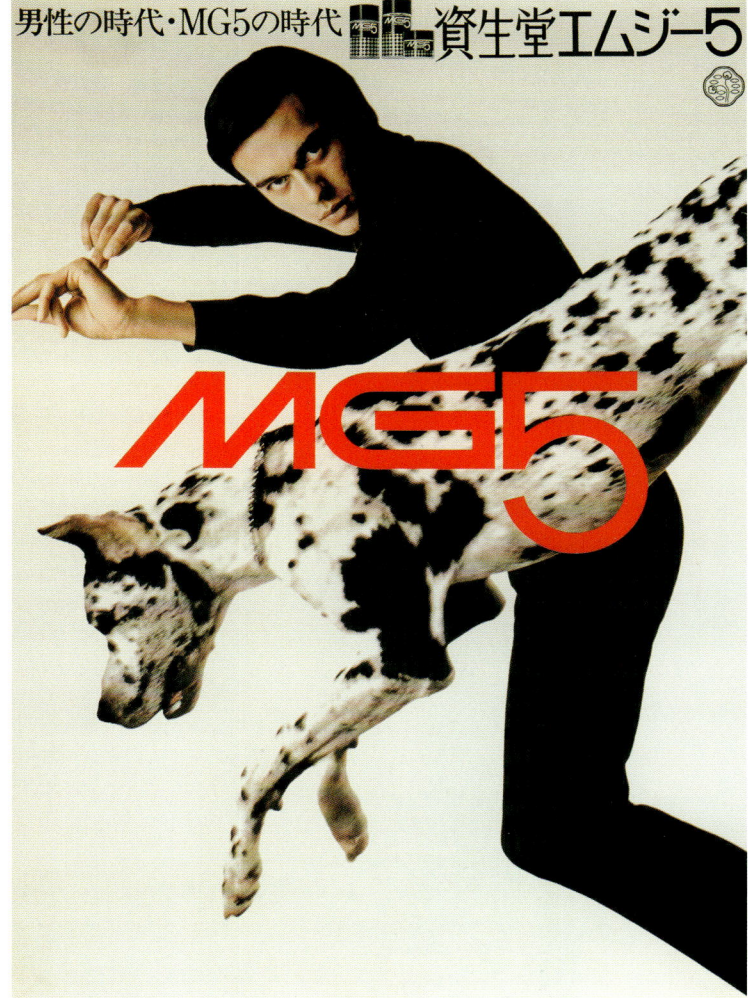

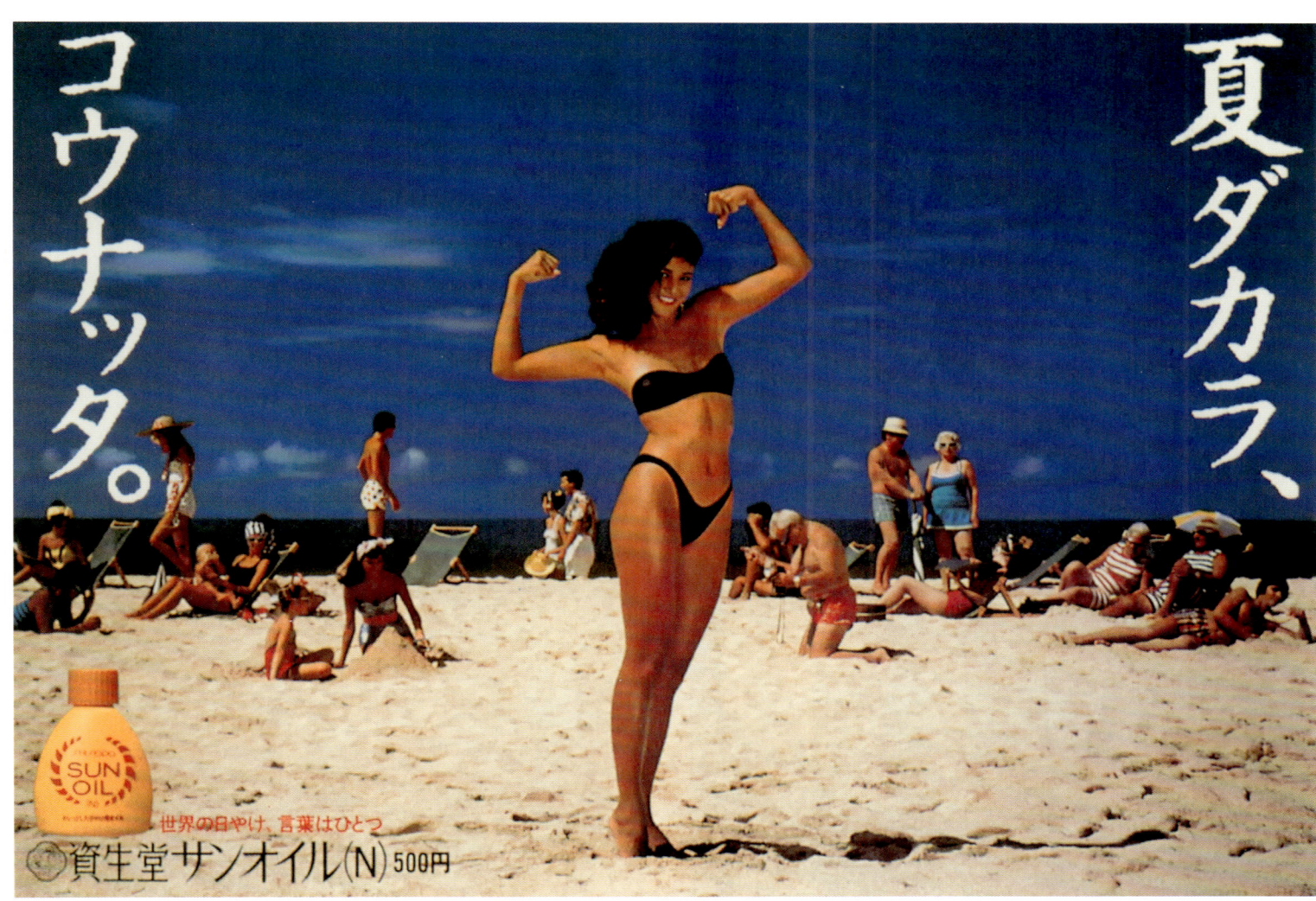

"Koto" Perfume ("White,
autumn, thoughts"), 1982
Makoto Nakamura
(art direction and design),
Noriaki Yokosuka
(photography),
Takao Onoda (copy)

"Zen" Perfume
("As enchanting as
a pure scent"), 1978
Makoto Nakamura
(art direction and design),
Noriaki Yokosuka
(photography),
Kesao Uchida (copy)

Opposite:
Nail enamel
("Make a wish and throw
a romantic curveball
to your fingertips"), 1978
Makoto Nakamura
(art direction and design),
Noriaki Yokosuka
(photography),
Kesao Uchida (copy)

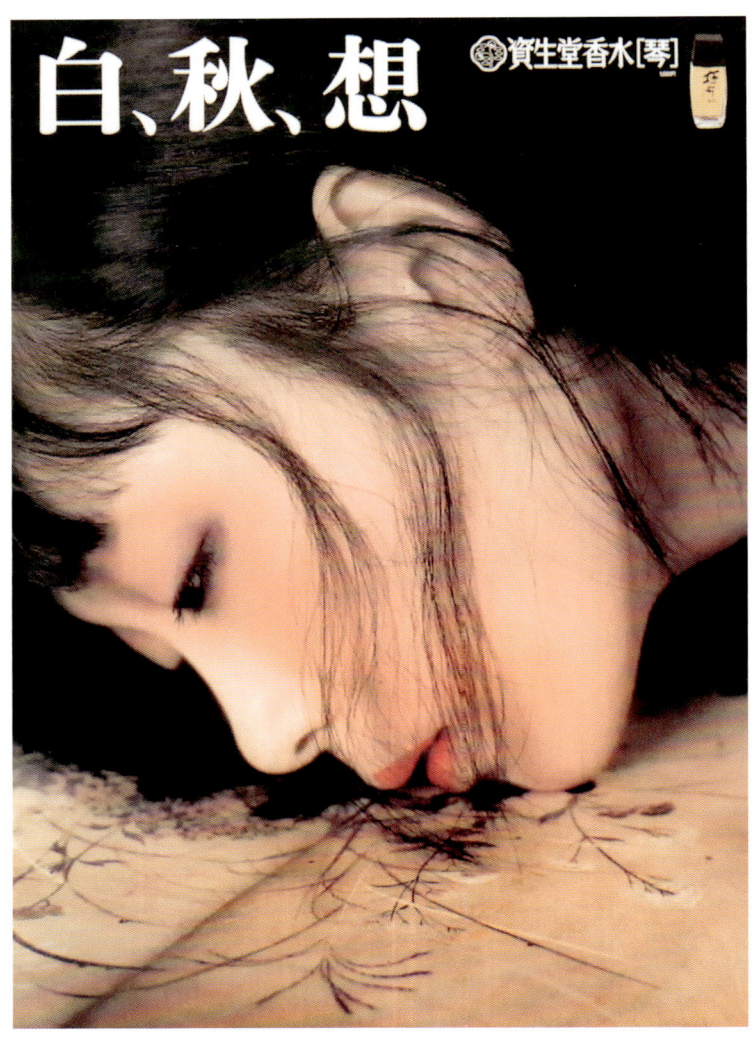

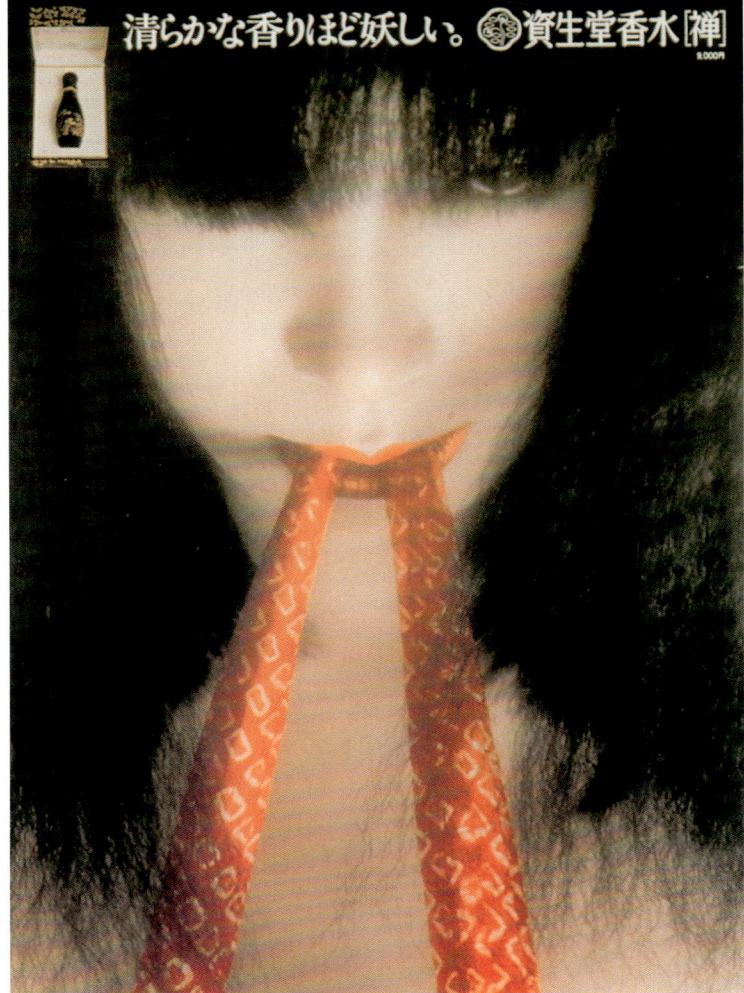

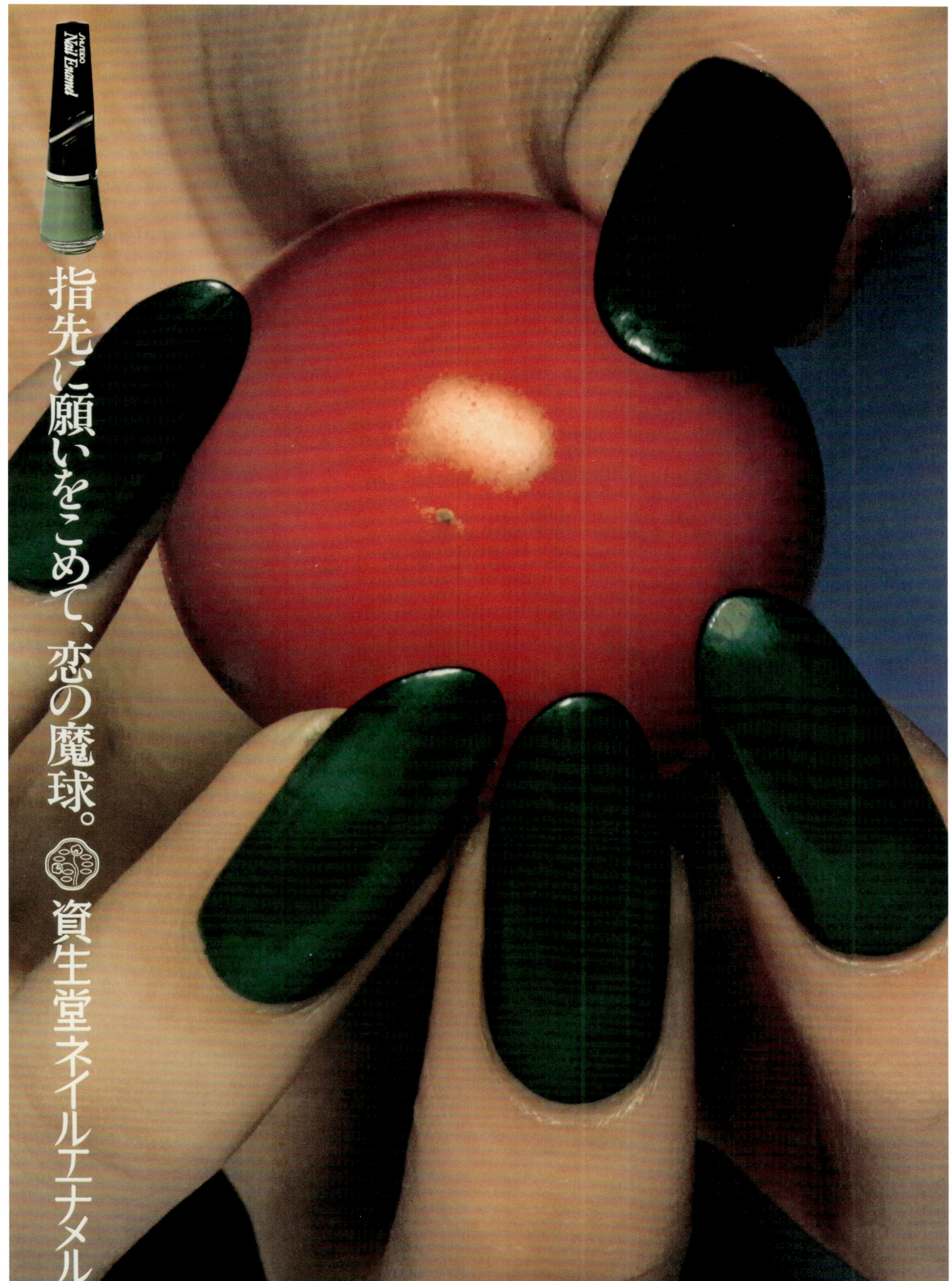

指先に願いをこめて、恋の魔球。 資生堂ネイルエナメル

Nail color and makeup products ("A new sensation at your fingertips… and around your eyes"), 1973
Makoto Nakamura
(art direction and design),
Noriaki Yokosuka
(photography),
Takuichiro Hosokawa (copy)

Nail color product ("The dreams of your childhood are now at your fingertips"), 1980
Makoto Nakamura
(art direction and design),
Noriaki Yokosuka
(photography),
Kesao Uchida (copy)

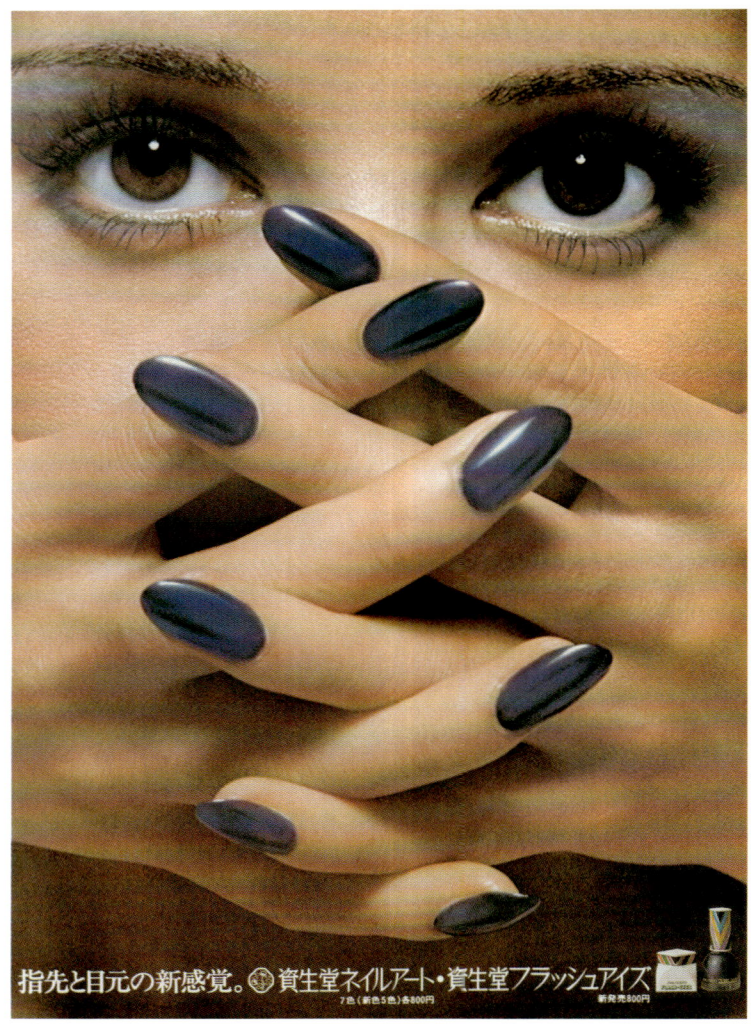

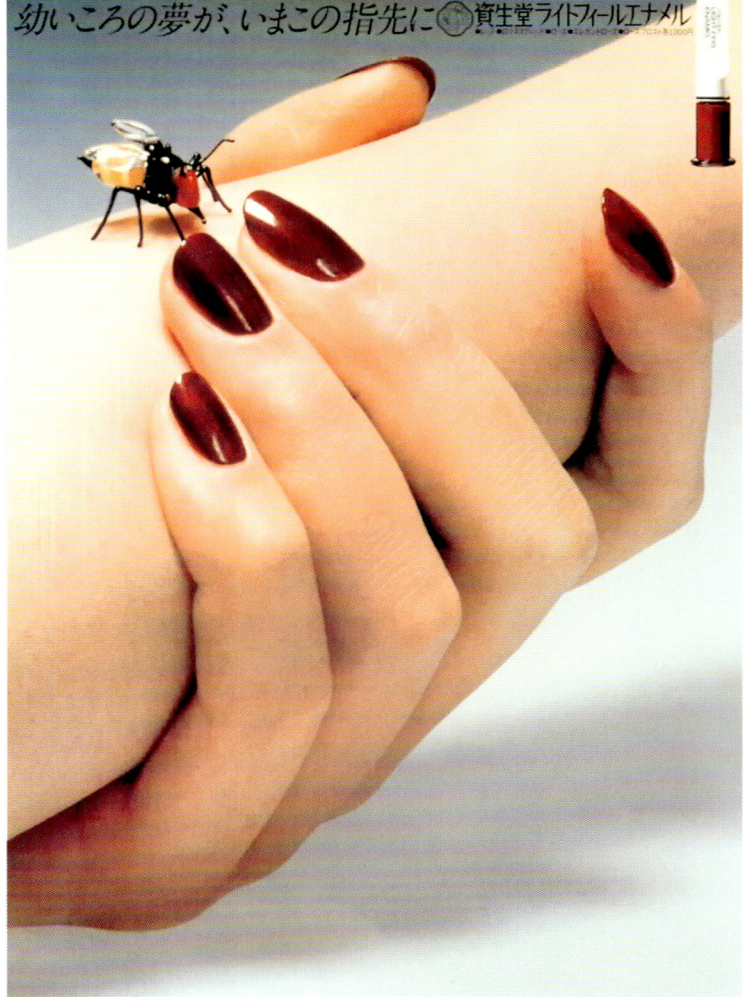

**Skin care promotion
("A beautiful woman, even
without makeup"), 1978**
Takao Onoda (art direction),
Kuni Kizawa (design),
Koichi Inakoshi (photography),
Takao Onoda (copy)

**Skin care product
("The gentle moisture of
the early morning hours"),
1970**
Takushi Mizuno
(art direction),
Kuni Kizawa (design),
Yojiro Adachi (photography),
Takao Onoda (copy)

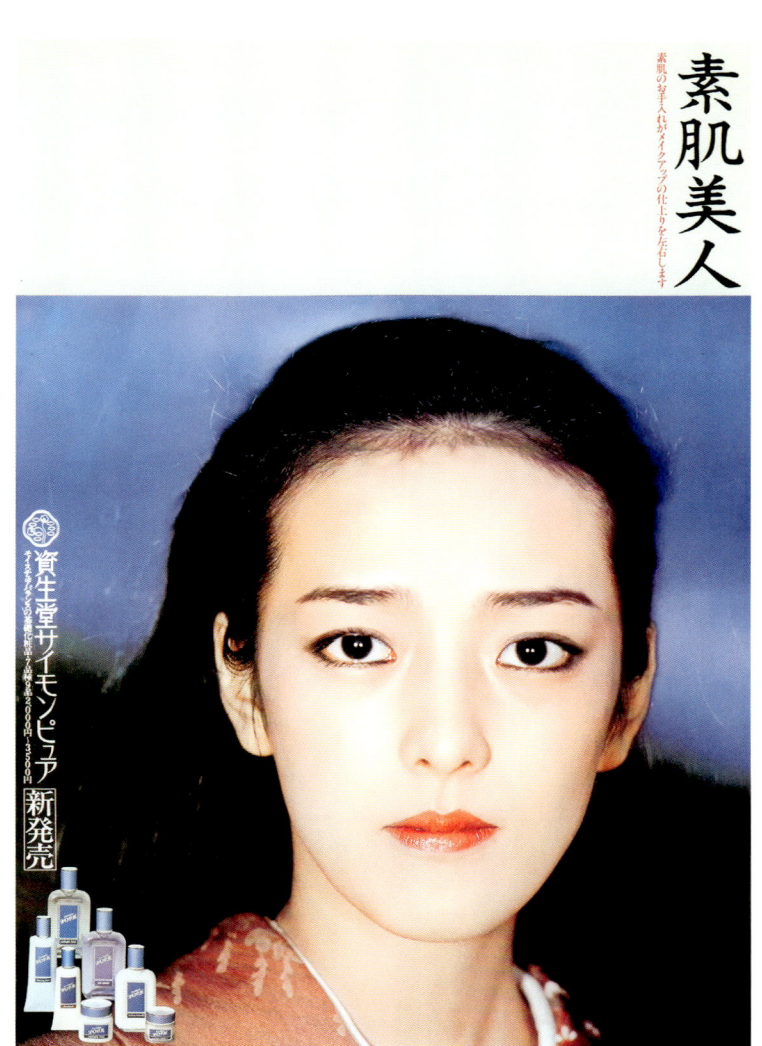

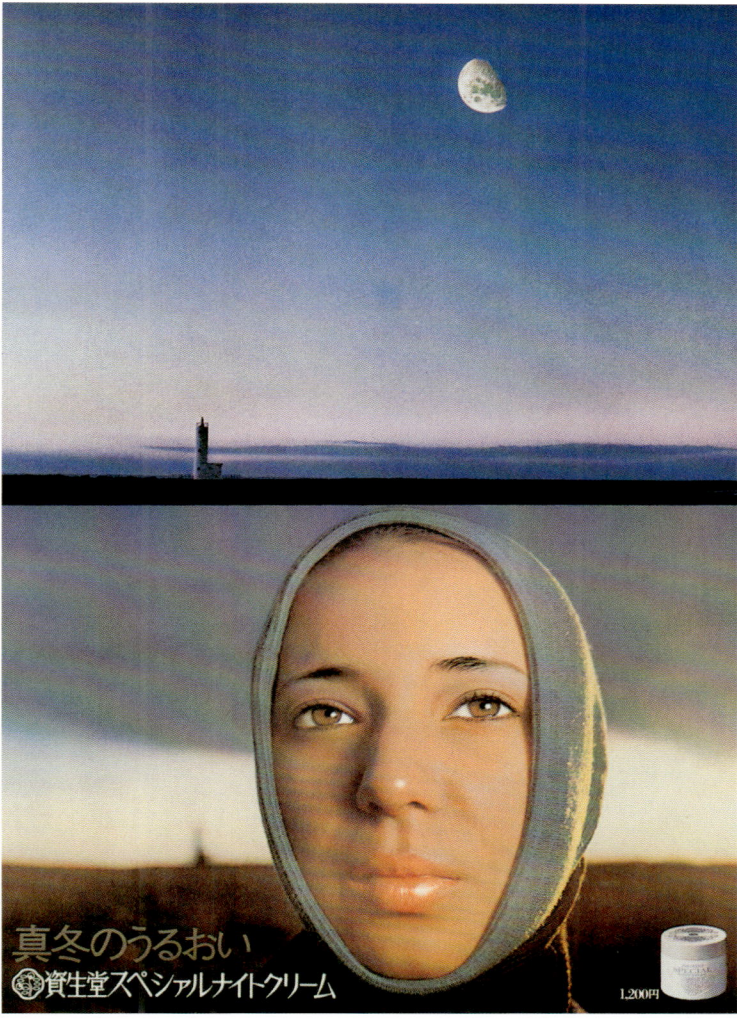

We would have never thought that Balthus used Polaroids as studies for his paintings, and were blown away by the show of them last year at Gagosian Gallery. These photographs show his way of working on composition and on the body language of the girls he painted. He had a way of showing an unspoken, complicated story in each of his paintings but with an innocence that draws you in before a certain underlying darkness hits you. In this Polaroid, which we own, we love the girl's Victorian-style dress and how she is sitting, so childlike, seemingly unconscious of Balthus's camera.

Several years ago, a friend of ours, a makeup artist, gave us a book on the German painter Paul Wunderlich. She found it at a flea market and was obsessed with how the faces were painted. Wunderlich's paintings were based on photographs taken by his wife, Karin Székessy. The photographs, shot with a wide-angle lens that distorted the bodies of the women, are as incredible as the paintings and weren't simply studies: they probably inspired Wunderlich to depict a more surreal world, especially in the way he dealt with bodies, colors, and fantastical elements such as burning matches sticking out of ears and floating hands. What was going on in their heads? What did this husband and wife talk about? How did they come to make these photographs?

We discovered the Swiss painter Franz Gertsch in Zürich in the mid-1990s, when we had a show there. What impressed us was that he makes snapshots of his friends and then takes a year to delicately paint a photo-realistic version of the photograph, as big as an entire wall. We were drawn to the style of the subjects and the way he treats their hair and skin. He carefully builds these features out of bright colors. The work with Patti Smith posed with her back to us is a favorite; Gertsch spent ages painting a fashion and rock icon from behind and turned a quick moment into an everlasting experience.

While Gertsch is hyper-realistic, David Hockney, a hungry experimenter, created different versions of reality though collage. What he does with the distortion of one's eye is almost unfathomable. The nude in this portfolio comes very close to how Willem de Kooning looked at women. There is beauty, but there's also a giddy ferociousness and sense of the grotesque that is exciting.

British Pop artist Richard Hamilton also played with the dualistic tensions between the elegant and the grotesque. Sometimes, in our work, it's not about choosing the most beautiful picture of someone but rather an image that shows another side. In Hamilton's *Fashion-plate* collages, art and fashion are combined into a single image—it's both photography and painting. It's old school yet anticipates the digital. At some point, everything in the fashion industry became so perfect; people started using the computer and making people's faces and bodies so perfect that we decided, "Okay, we've got to destroy this idea of only perfection through the computer." Hamilton's work is about cutting through notions of what's real and what's not in a photograph, and what's special in the *Fashion-plate* works is how you see the light and the stand: the typical photography studio setup. The faces are so big, proportionally, and distorted through the use of different images taken from fashion magazines—it's fantastic. Pop art has been a big inspiration for us; you might say fashion photography is the ultimate Pop art.

Photography into Painting

Notes and selection by Inez & Vinoodh

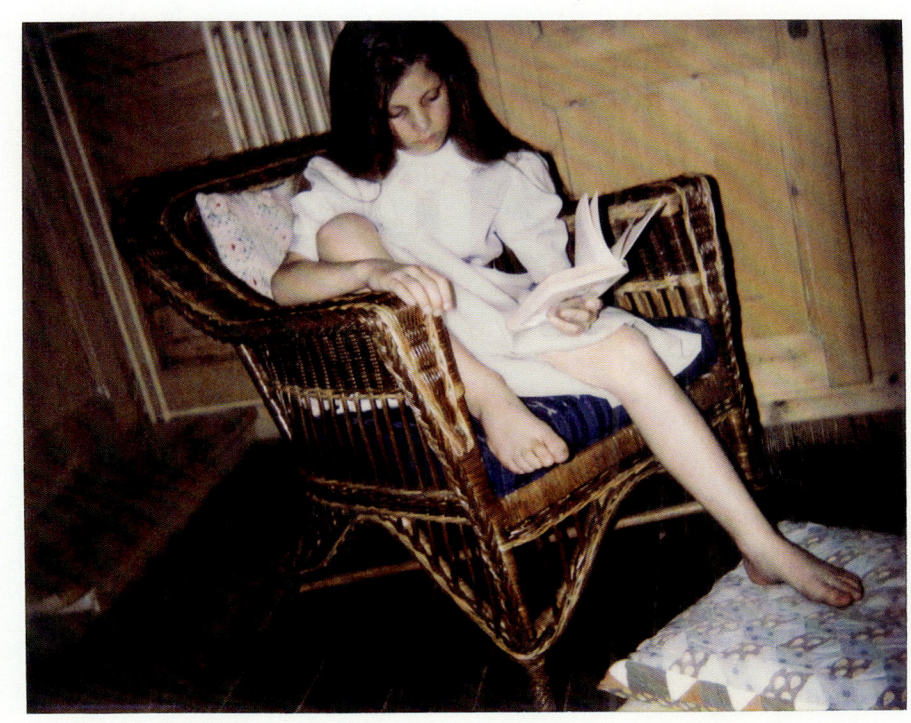

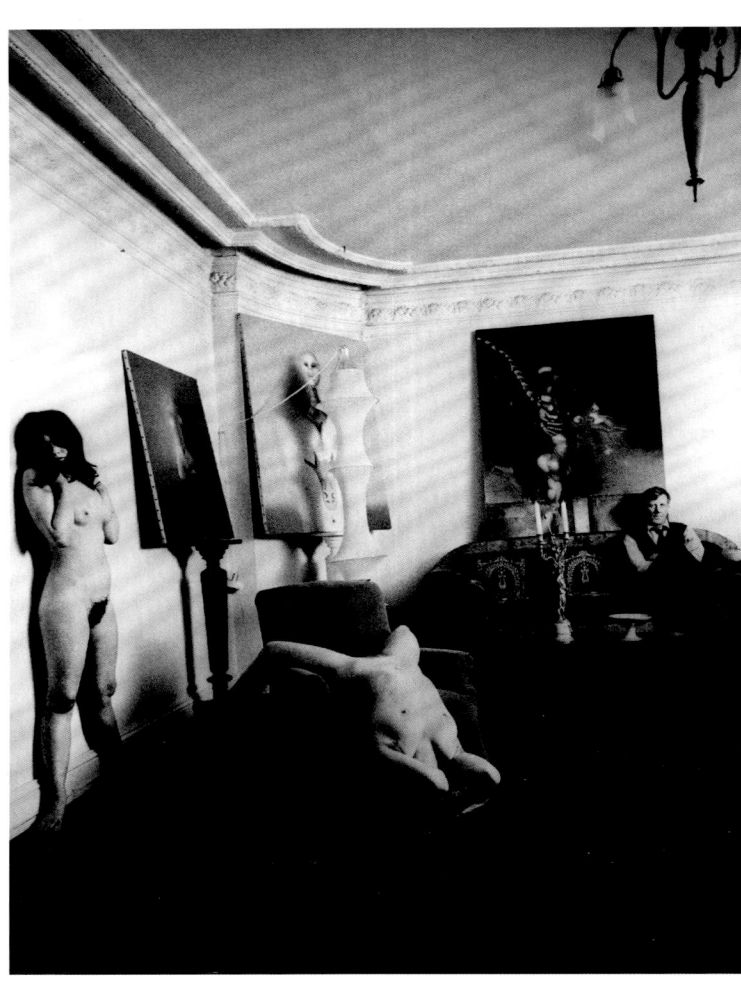

Top left:
Karin Székessy,
Poured out, 1968

Bottom left:
Karin Székessy,
Daniela posing, 1971

Bottom right:
Karin Székessy,
Daniela on a chair III, 1971

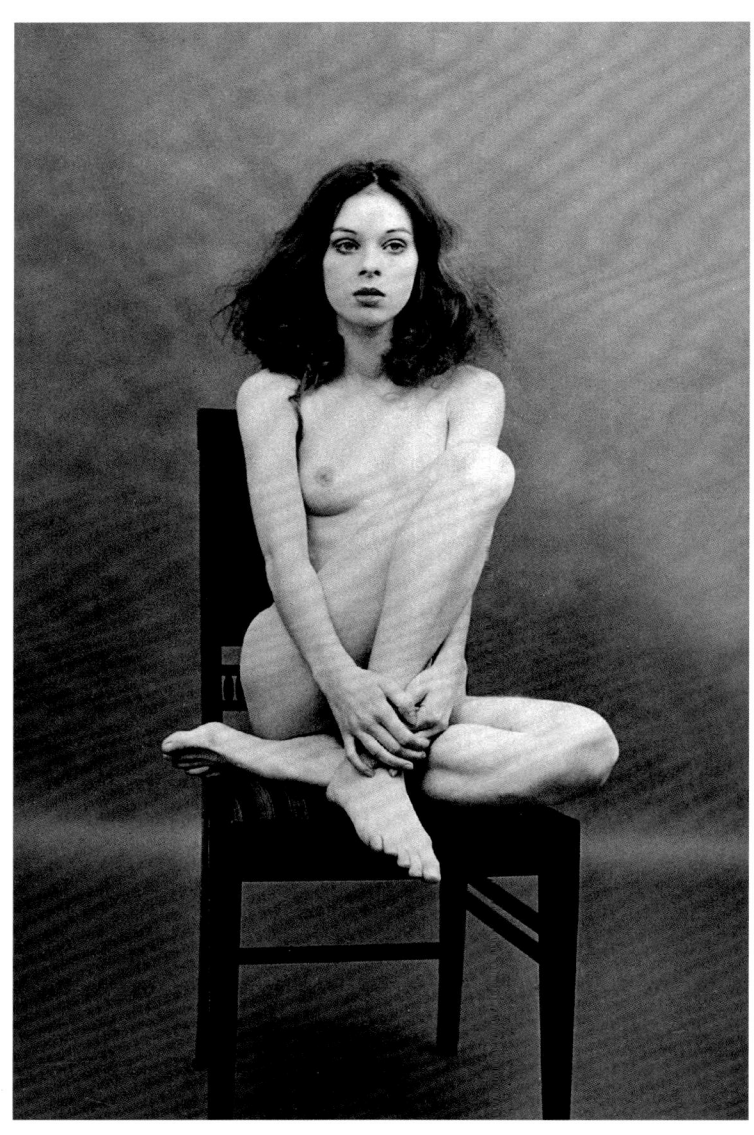

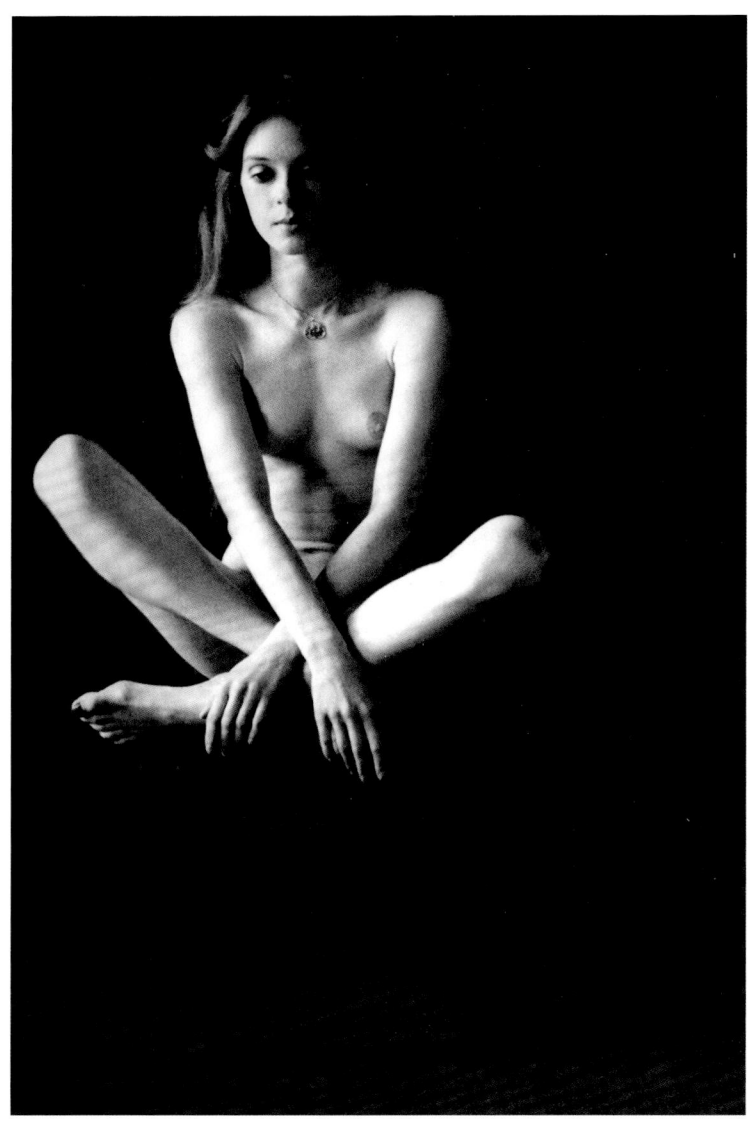

Right:
Paul Wunderlich,
*With feathered hat
and black coat*, 1973

Bottom:
Karin Székessy,
Daniela, for Lodenkämpfer,
1973
All works © Karin Székessy,
and © Paul Wunderlich,
respectively

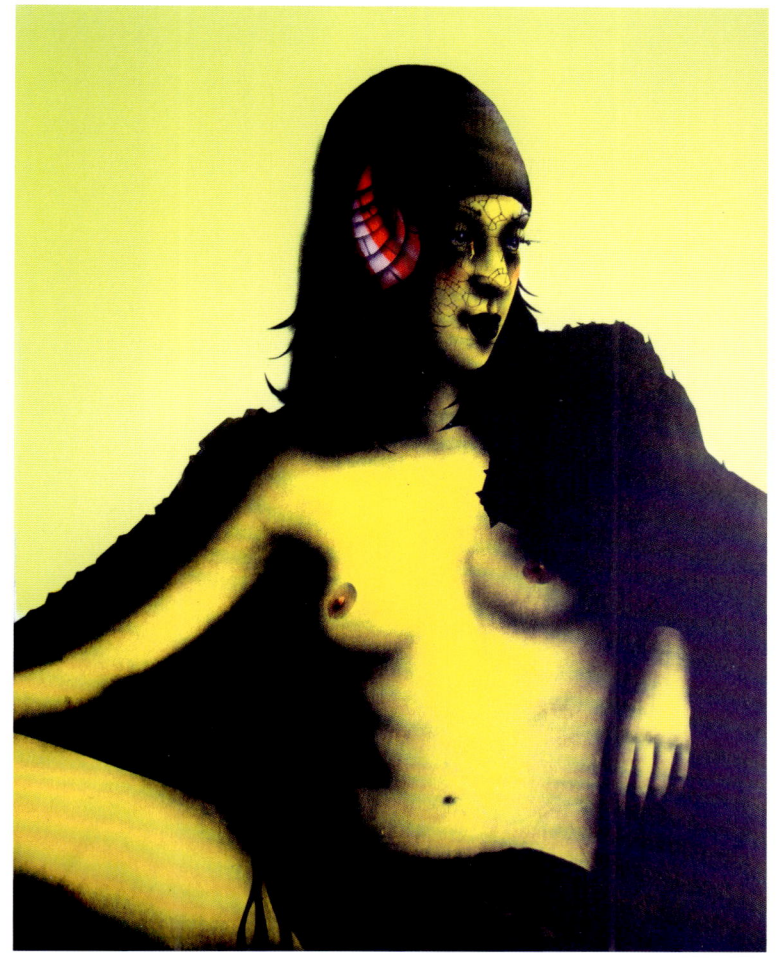

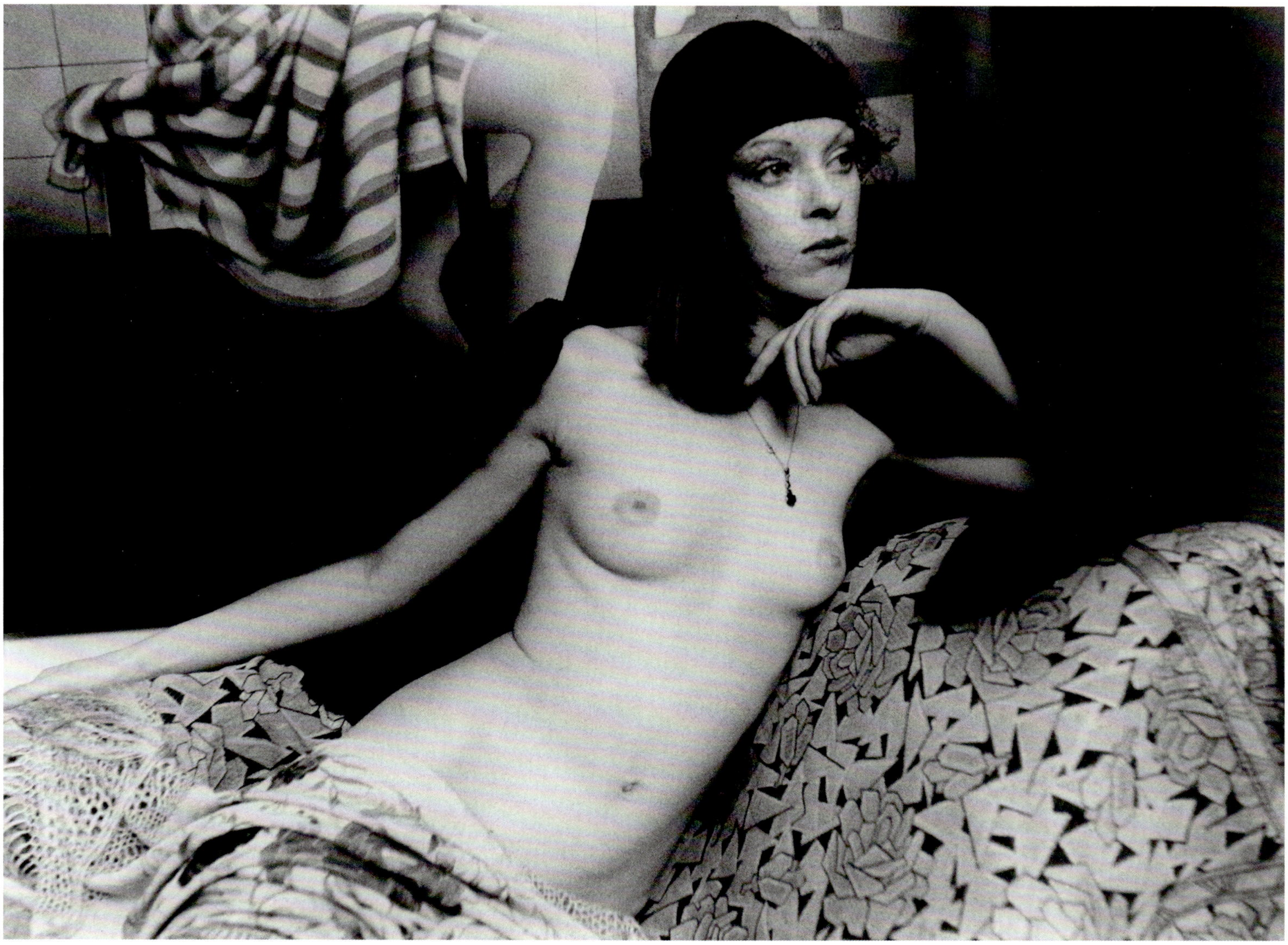

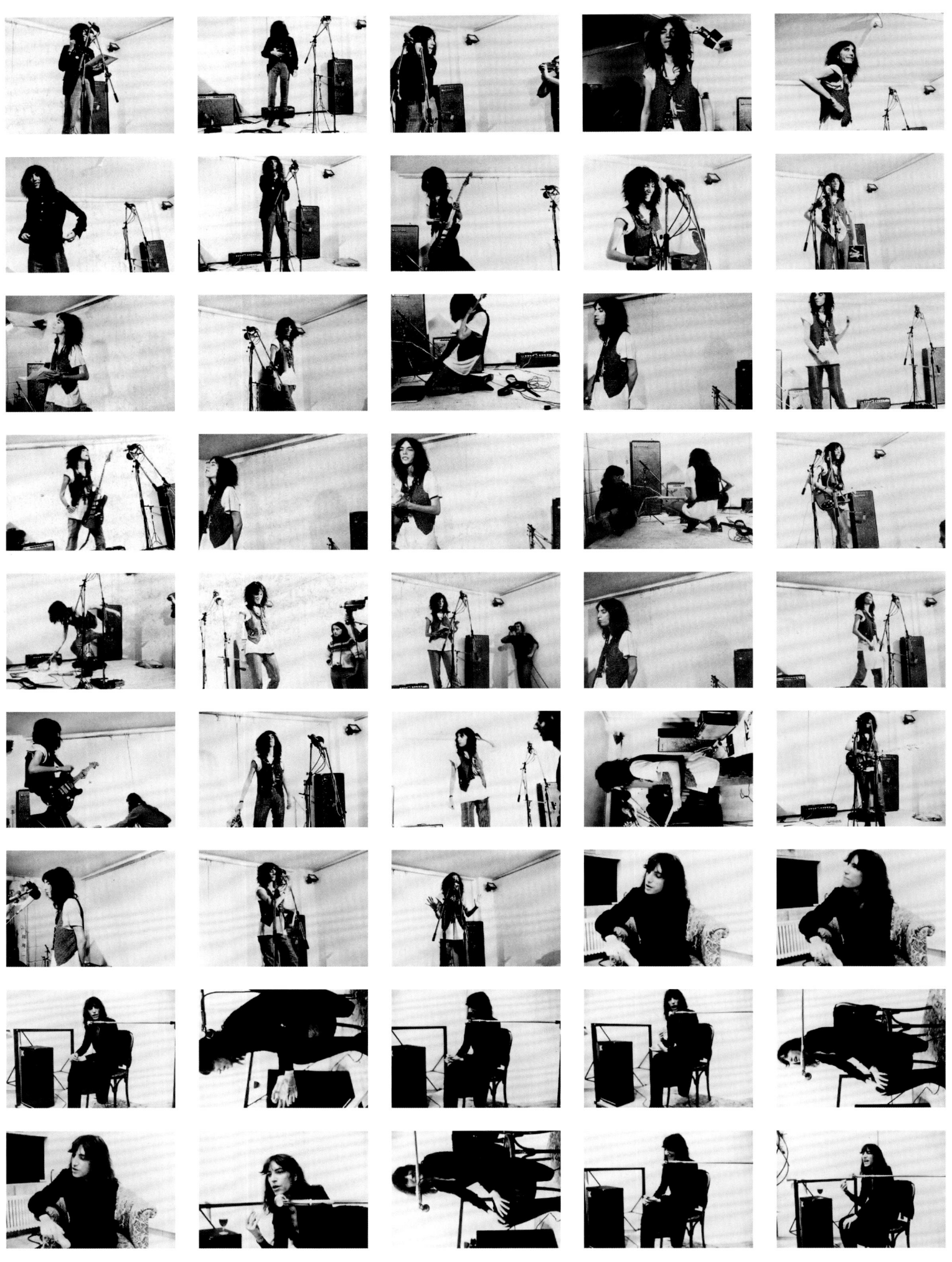

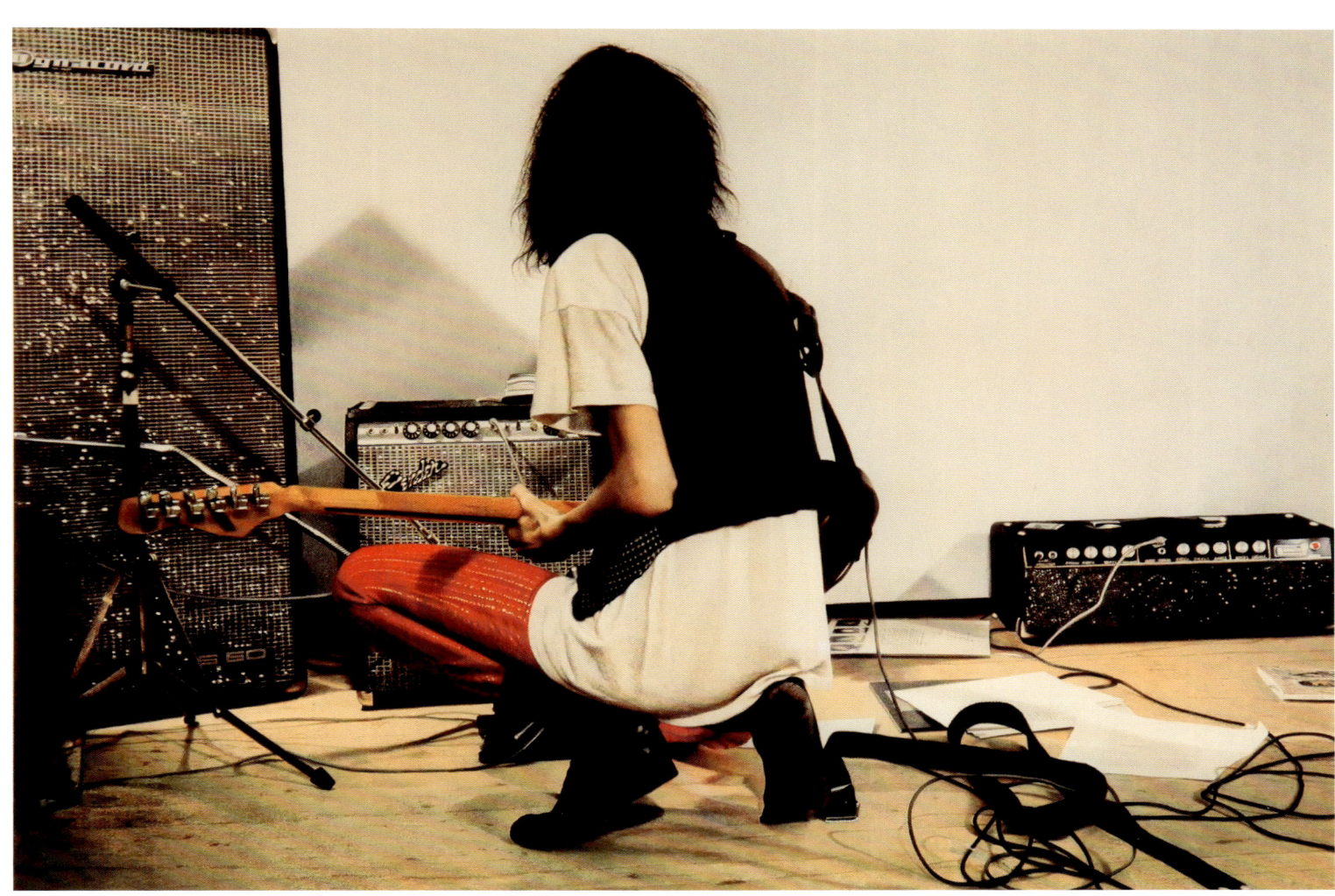

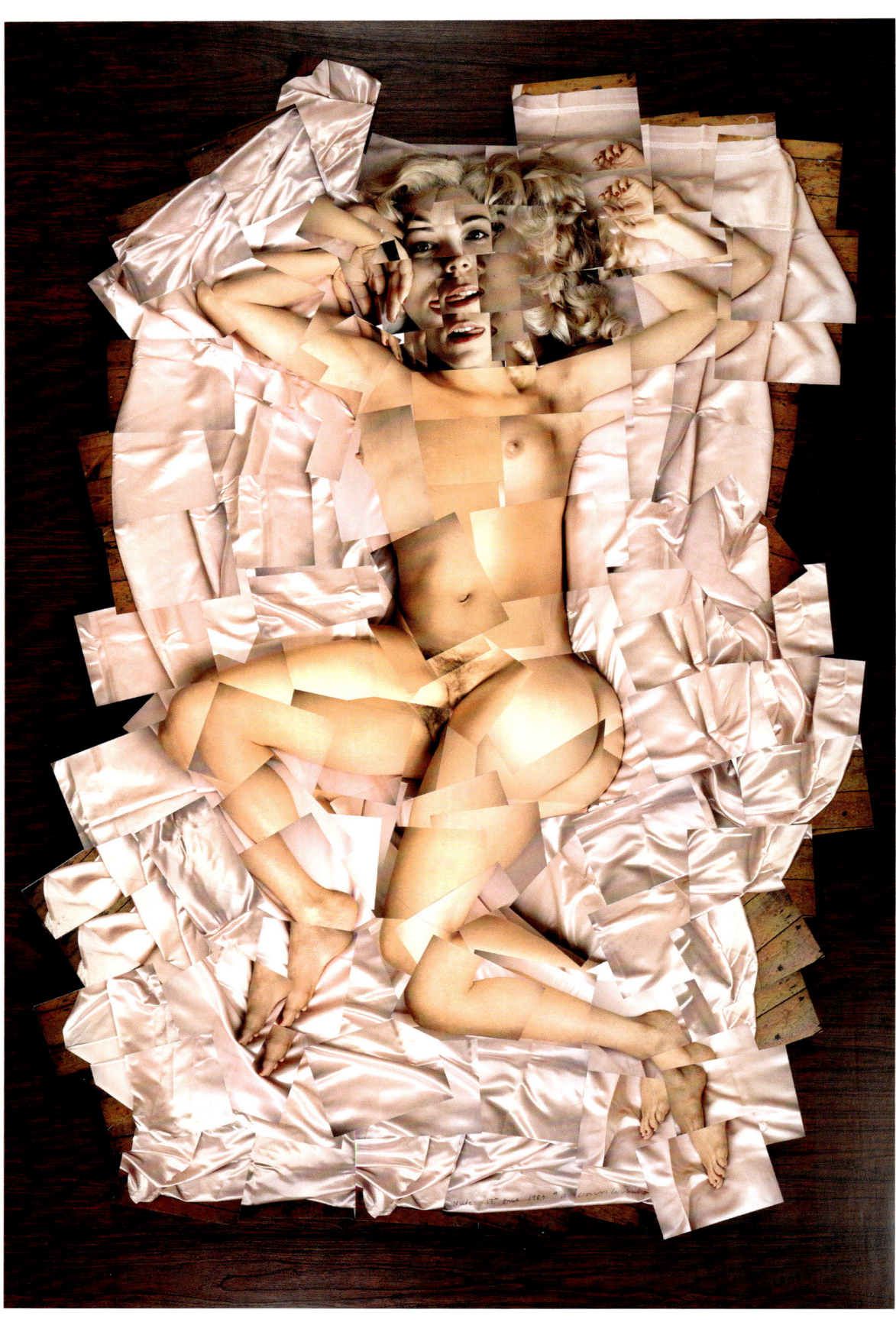

David Hockney,
Nude 17th June 1984, 1984
© David Hockney

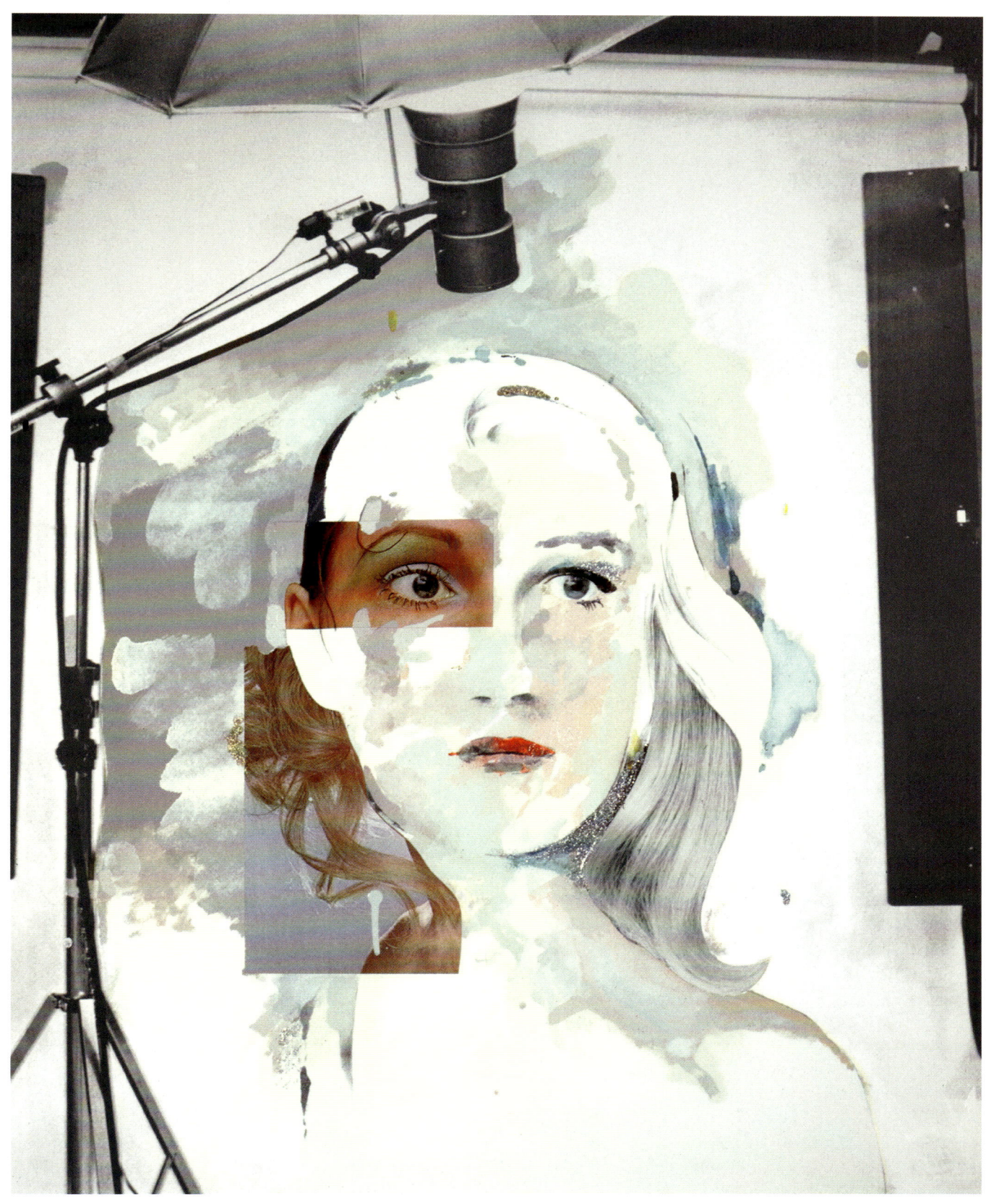

Every fashion designer is consistently delving into the past, basing a collection on a string of memories, like shoulder pads worn by clubbers in the '80s or the platform shoes David Bowie put on when he performed as Ziggy Stardust. Our photography stems from a similar nostalgia. Fashion is a language made up of a visual code of status symbols. We play with this code, and sometimes subvert it; without this play on references the images become too abstract. Building a character based on myriad elements—paintings, movies, music videos, pictures of your mother—is what keeps the process exciting. You might feel the references but you can't determine their source. What follows is a selection of images by some of fashion photography's giants, whose work has influenced four decades of fashion, photography, and advertising and has been important to the development and motivation behind our own work. One might say that in today's professional climate, in which clients want to see their campaign images before they are even shot, you're only as good as your references.

The Icons

Notes and selection by Inez & Vinoodh

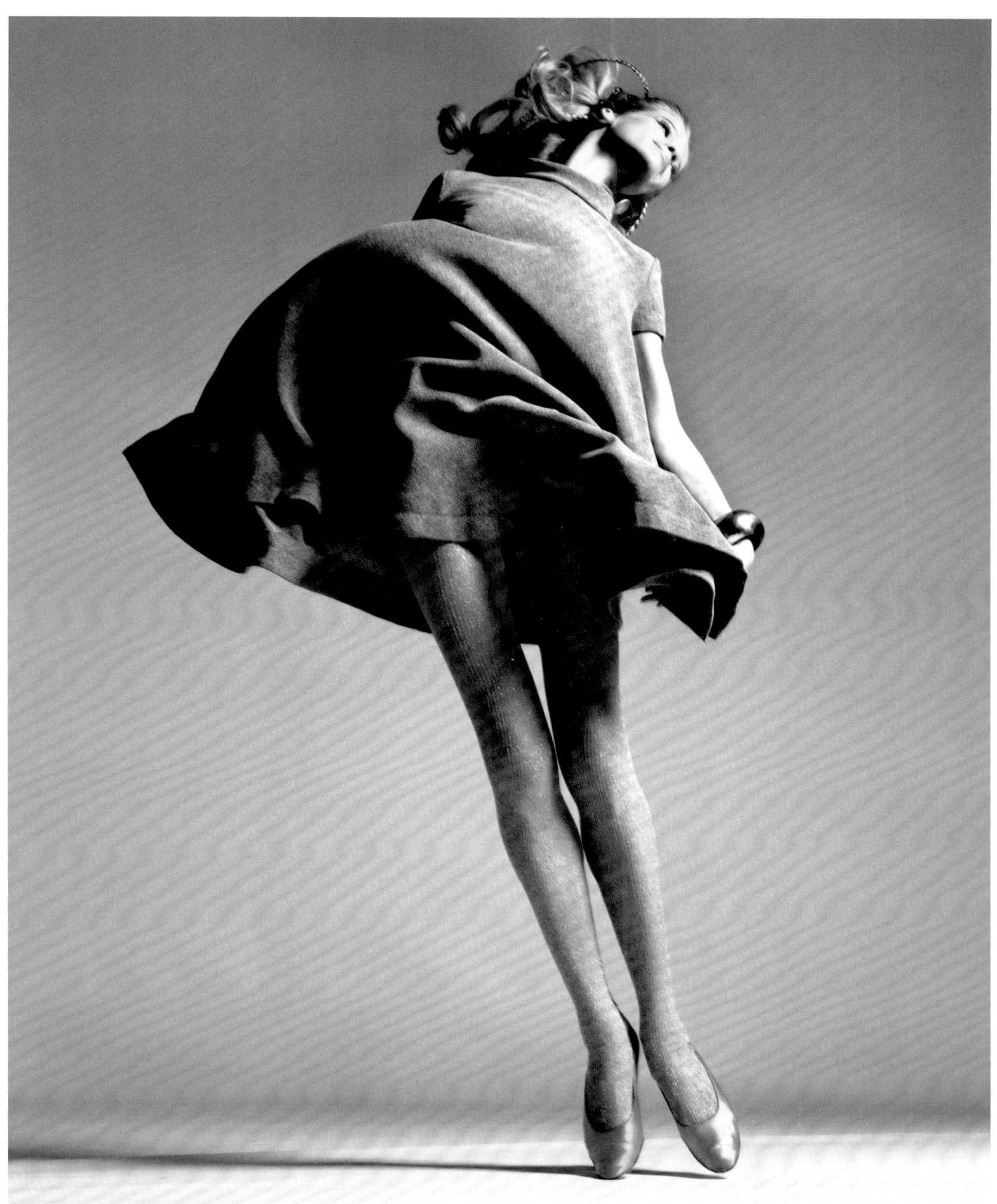

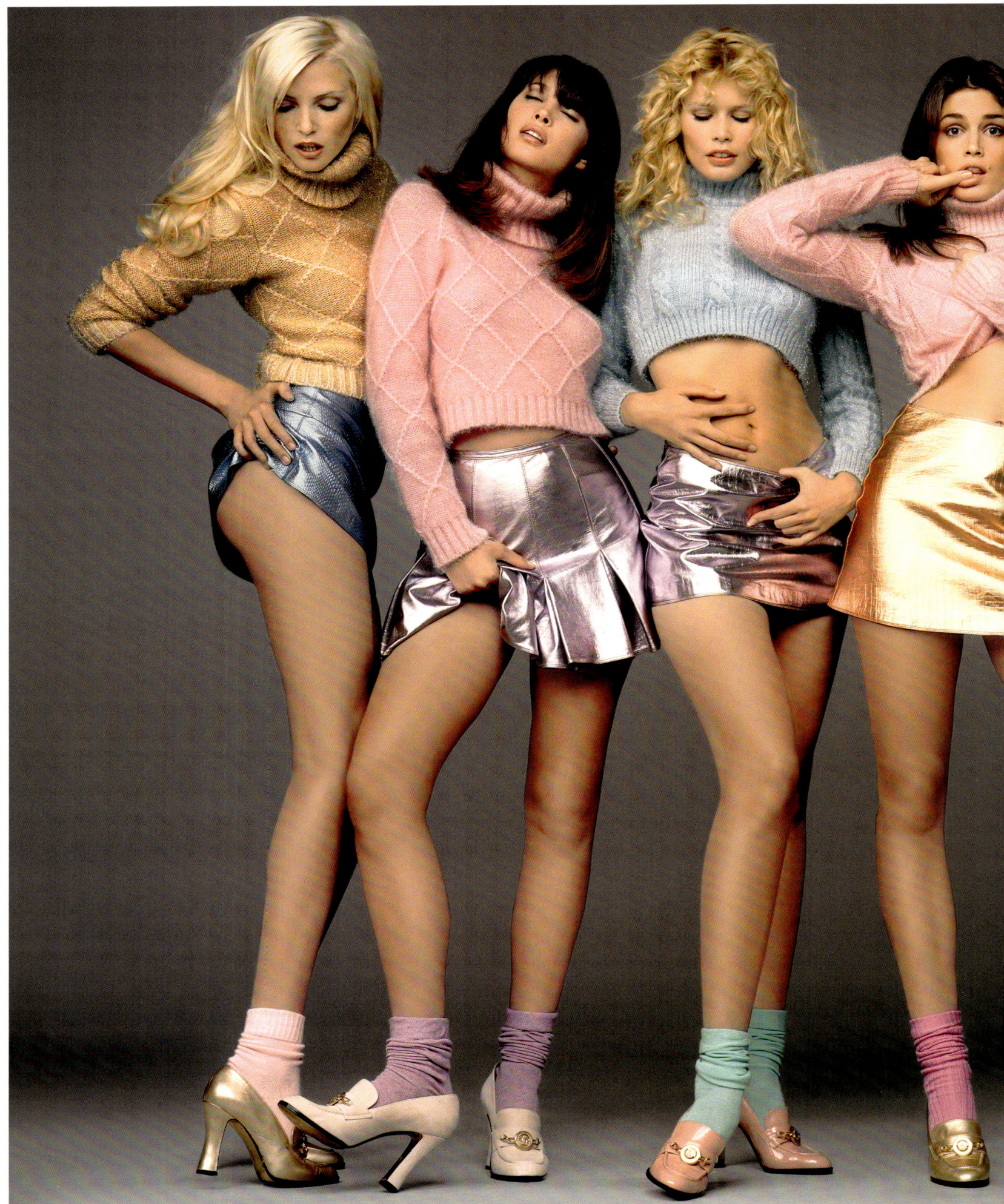

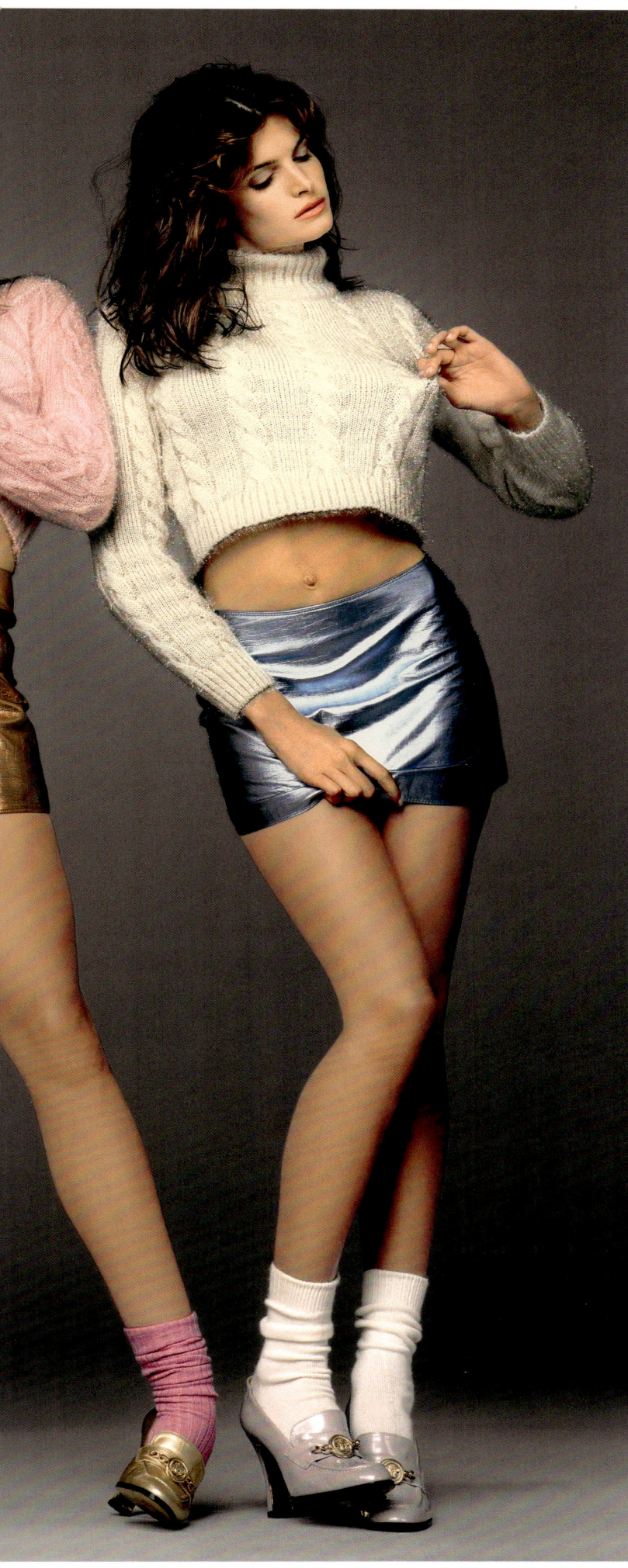

Richard Avedon,
Nadja Auermann,
Christy Turlington,
Claudia Schiffer,
Cindy Crawford,
and Stephanie Seymour,
Versace Fall/Winter
1994–95 Campaign,
New York, April 14, 1994
© The Richard Avedon
Foundation

Richard Avedon

Avedon had a brilliant way of turning everyone he photographed into a hero. It was not necessarily about beautifying people, but about making them into iconic versions of themselves. He was attentive to proportion and body positioning, and able to find that one quality of someone's physiognomy that is remarkable, whether grotesque or elegant, and bring it to the foreground. No photographer controlled body language better. Everyone is inspired by this series with Verushka (previous page), which is the epitome of movement in the studio. Almost every studio shoot today is orchestrated this way.

Avedon could translate the mood of a period but never lost his own voice. His collaboration with Versace over many years, similar to that of Yves Saint Laurent and Helmut Newton, was one of the most incredible between a designer and a photographer in which both the people and the clothing look larger than life. This photograph of five of the most beautiful women in the world is so stylized and glamorous (down to their ankle socks), yet he manages to keep their exaggerated gestures feeling candid and humorous. Apart from, of course, having the best lighting in the world, you immediately know that it's an Avedon because the people appear magnificent. He must have been truly interested in everyone he photographed.

Guy Bourdin,
*Charles Jourdan,
Spring,* 1979
© Estate of Guy Bourdin;
courtesy Michael Hoppen
Gallery, London; and
Art + Commerce, New York

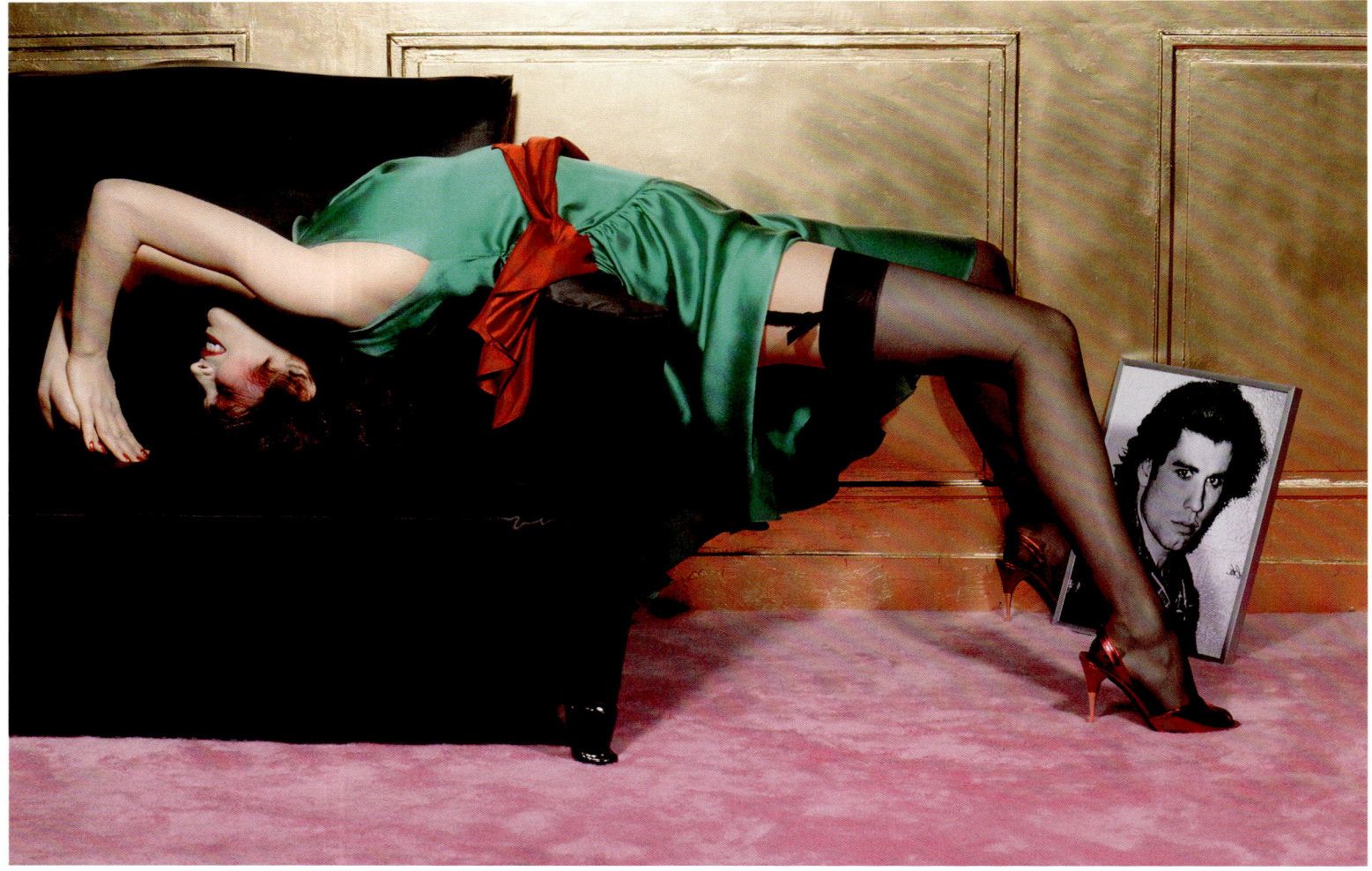

Guy Bourdin

Growing up with a mother who went to Paris twice a year
to see the runway shows and who brought back issues
of *Vogue Paris,* I (Inez) flipped through the magazine at
an early age and thought that the way Helmut Newton and
Guy Bourdin portrayed women was the way women were
meant to be: bold, strong, wild, erotic, and independent.
Bourdin definitely informed pretty much all of my early
photography.

We've all heard the stories of how precise and demanding
he was. You can tell that everything was preconceived,
that it must have started with a sketch somewhere.
This in-camera collage, in the picture opposite, shows how
he merged abstraction with content like no one else. His
consistent use of strong pink and red makeup, pale skin,
and super curly hair (ideally red) has influenced many hair
and makeup artists and is basically an industry standard.

Bourdin pushed his models to assume really wild
expressions; sometimes he actually scared them. He must
have been reacting to the '50s, when everything had to be
very perfect, proper, and clean, and then the '60s, when
everything was "peace and love." In his work from the '70s
you feel something dubious is happening outside the frame.
That dark side is inspiring, and his use of bodies, color
(his painterly approach), lighting, and humor has been a
big influence, especially this image, one of Bourdin's most
genius, in which a photograph of John Travolta is propped
between the model's legs. We love the use of color along
with her body position. And, as in all his pictures,
your eye immediately goes to the shoes.

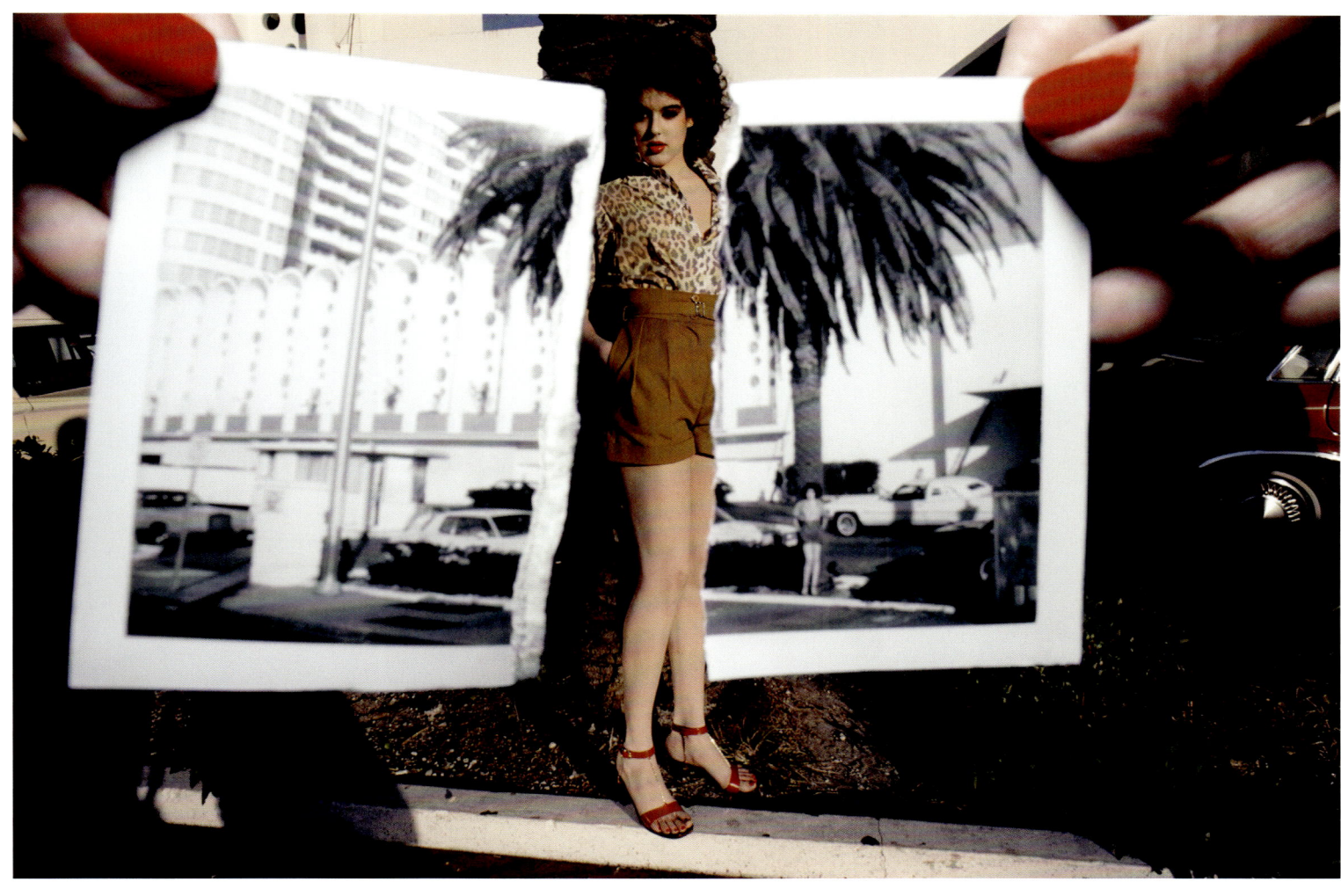

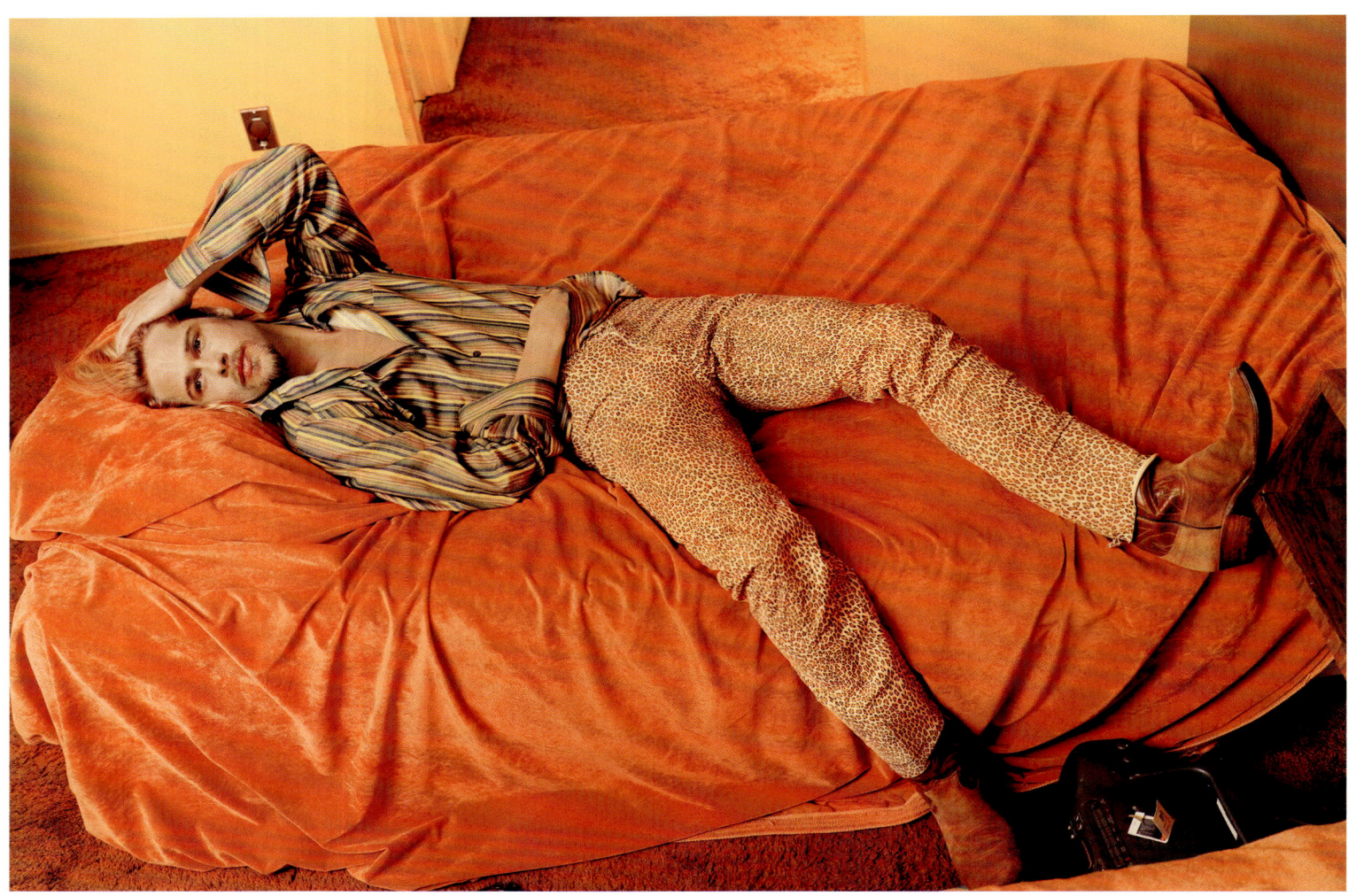

Annie Leibovitz

We saw this image of Brad Pitt for the first time at Annie's exhibition in Stockholm, and were struck by the audacity of the leopard-print pants, the boots, the pajama shirt, the red blanket on the bed, and the nasty carpet—the sharp contrast between him and his surroundings. Annie pushes her subjects to become part of a scene or plot. Others might photograph Pitt, a male superstar, as heroic and strong, whereas here he's passive but dressed so flamboyantly. On the other hand, Anjelica Huston wears a riding costume, looking very masculine, especially with her almost crotch-grabbing hand gesture. Anjelica has been hugely inspiring in our world, in fashion and fashion photography, for her work with Guy Bourdin, Helmut Newton, and Bob Richardson. These pictures are both portraits and fashion images. There is a simplicity to the images and their production, but the people are absolutely magnificent.

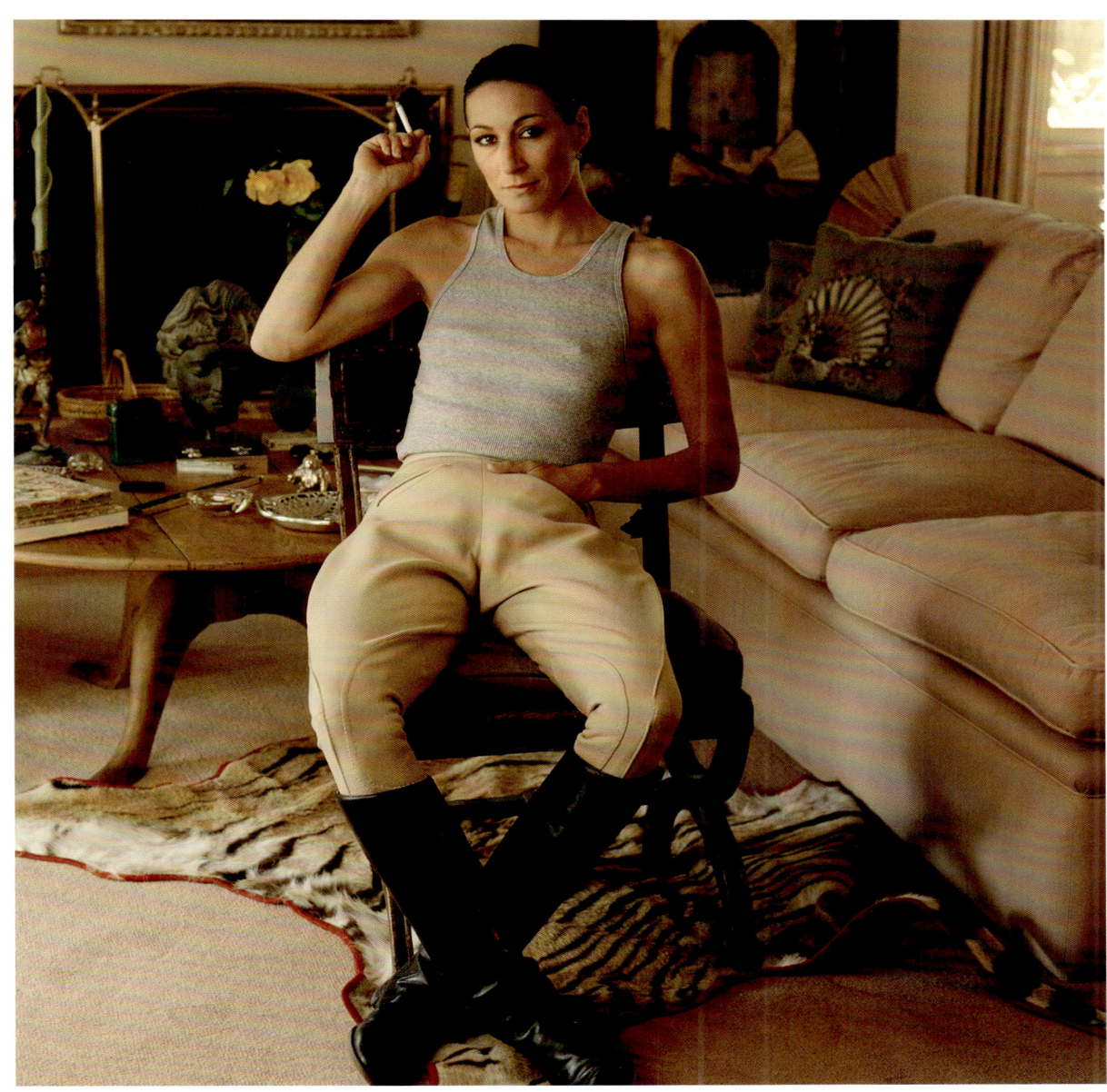

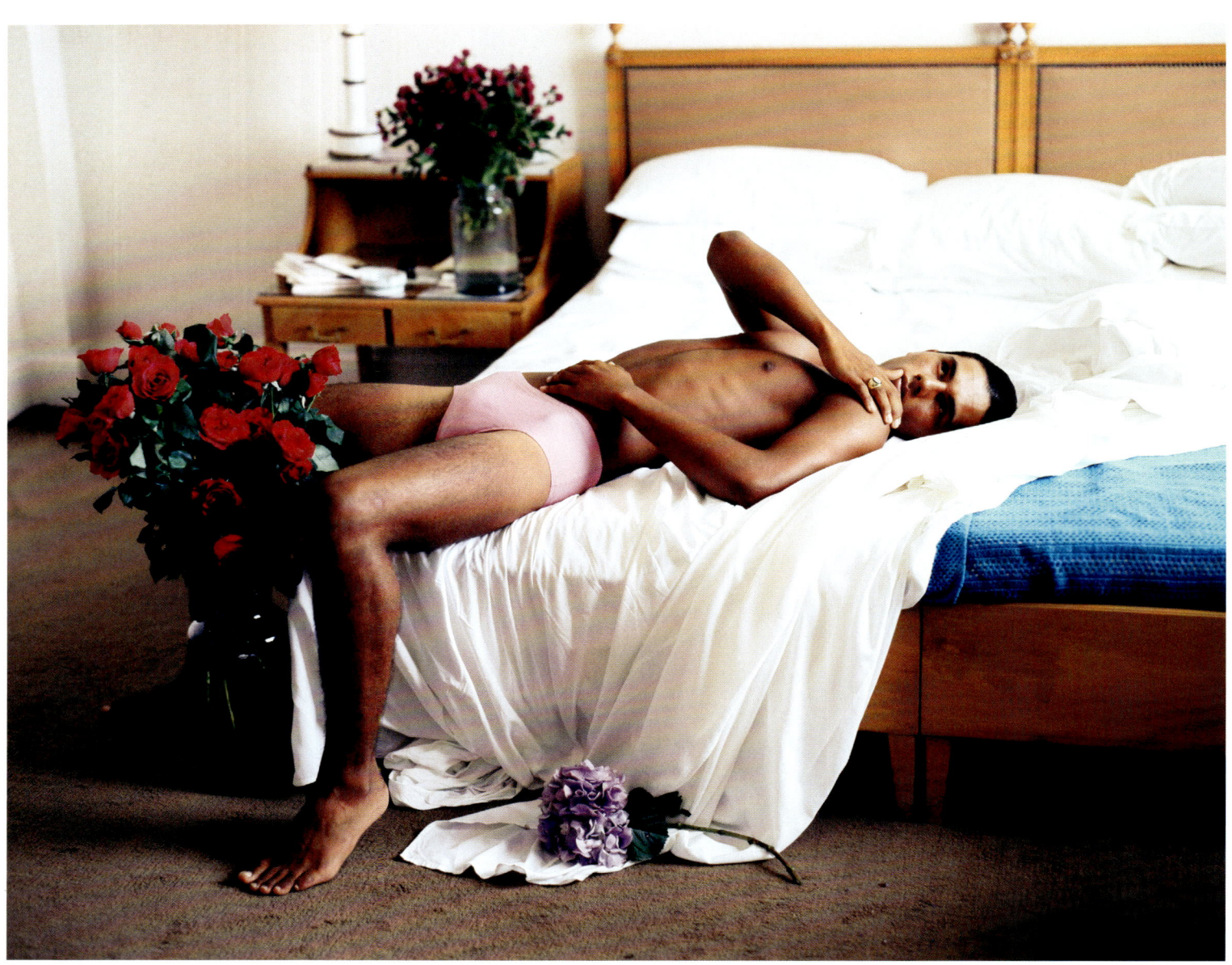

Bruce Weber

Bruce makes the most masculine men on earth look as elegant and beautiful as the most beautiful women, and he makes the most feminine women look like the strongest boys. It's androgynous without being obviously androgynous. This image at right of Talisa, in her boxing stance, is the ultimate version of that. There is a generation that is absolutely inspired by Bruce and Herb Ritts for their interpretation of this sort of androgyny. You could say Bruce comes from the line of thought that Helmut Newton started with Yves Saint Laurent, when he set women free by using masculine codes, dressing them in tuxedos and pantsuits. We're always trying to find a duality in a person: half-male, half-female, a blurring of identity.

Bruce's 1986 book *O Rio de Janeiro* has been a huge influence. His documentary approach is liberating and even stimulating. You're in a place, you have an incredible subject, the light is the light that's there. Now make that person incredible. That's what we admire in Bruce's work, that there's no artifice. But we think that's the bottom line for every photographer: when you're really interested in the people you're photographing, you get more than just the registration of someone.

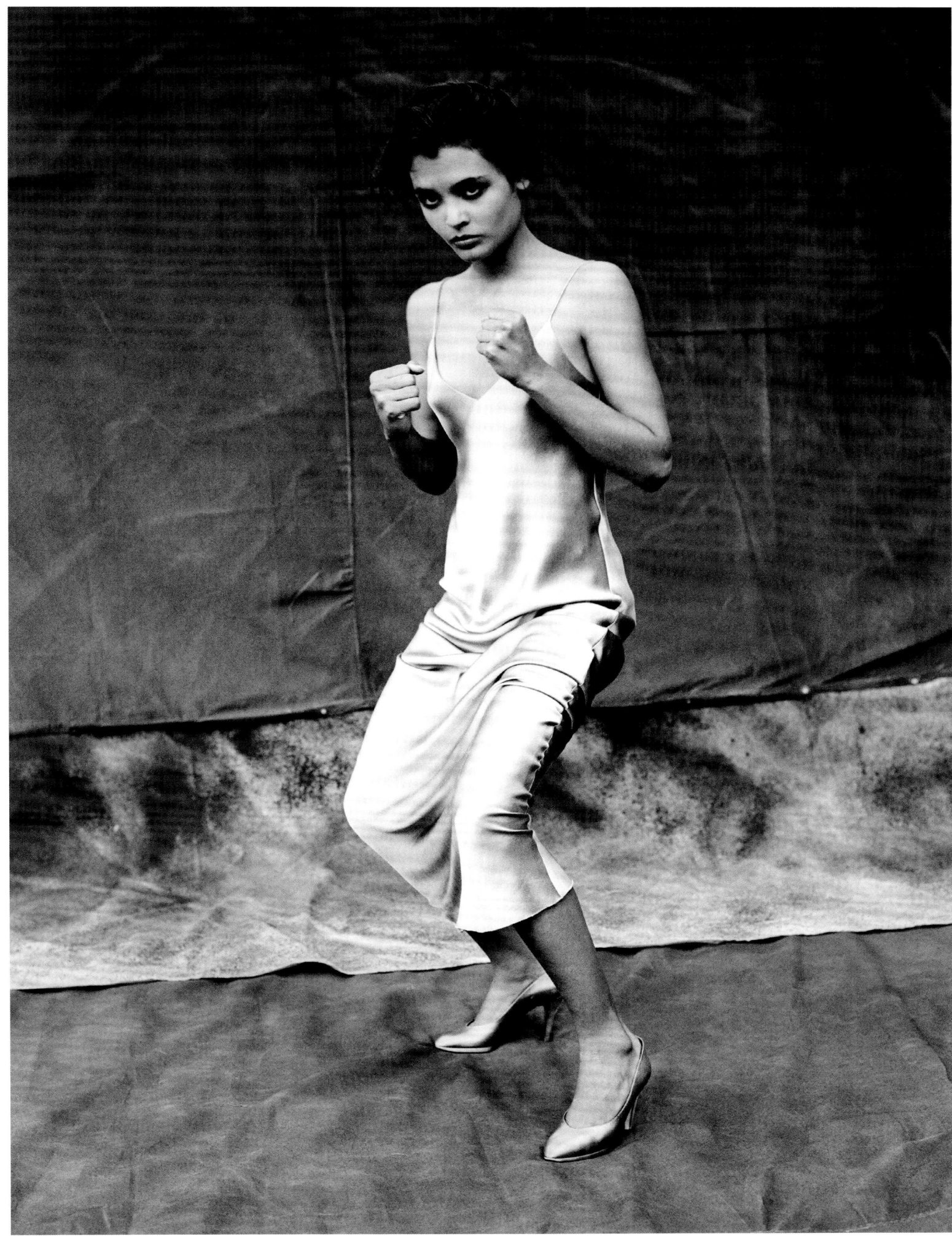

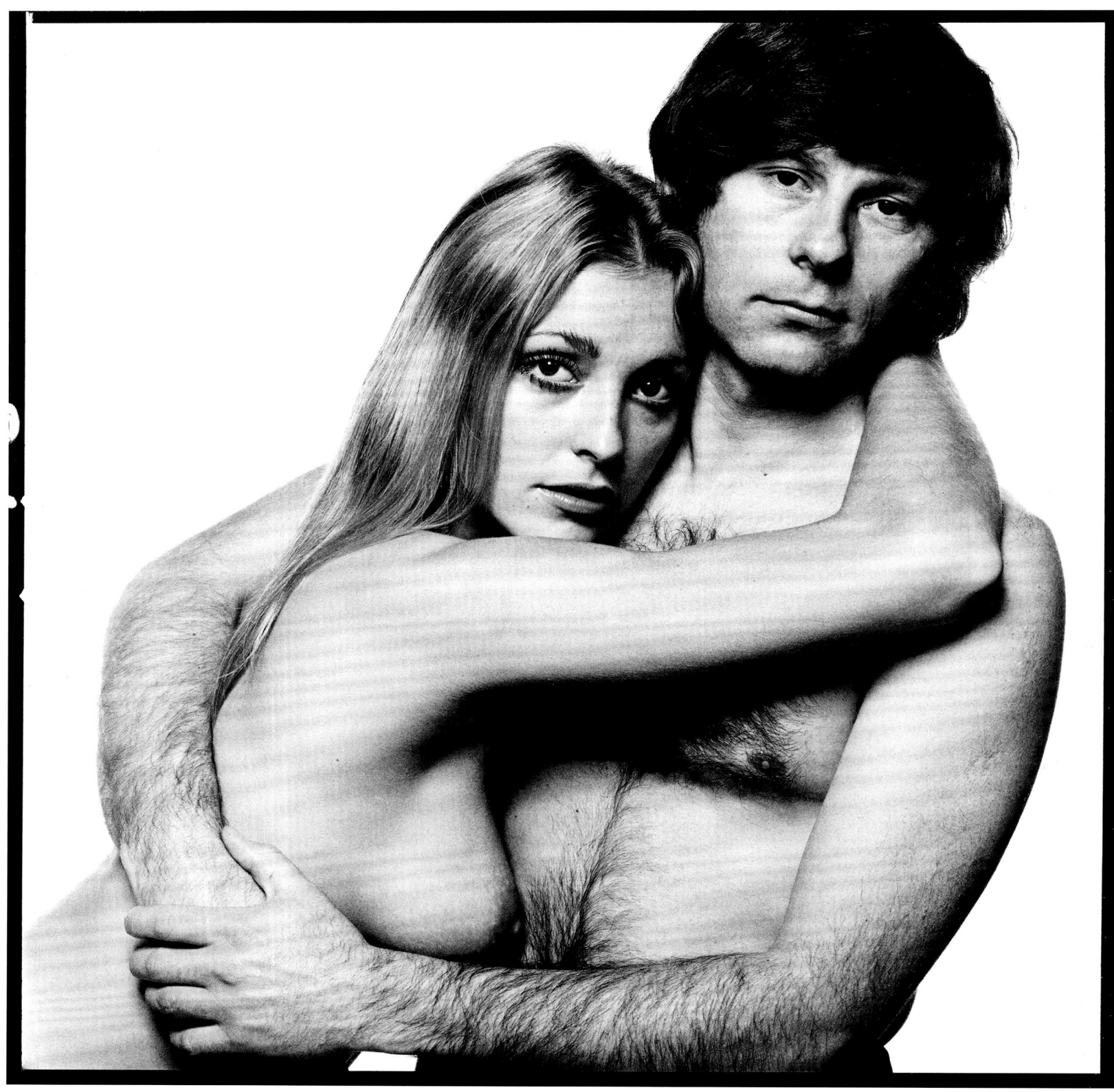

David Bailey, *Sharon Tate*
and Roman Polanski, 1969
© David Bailey

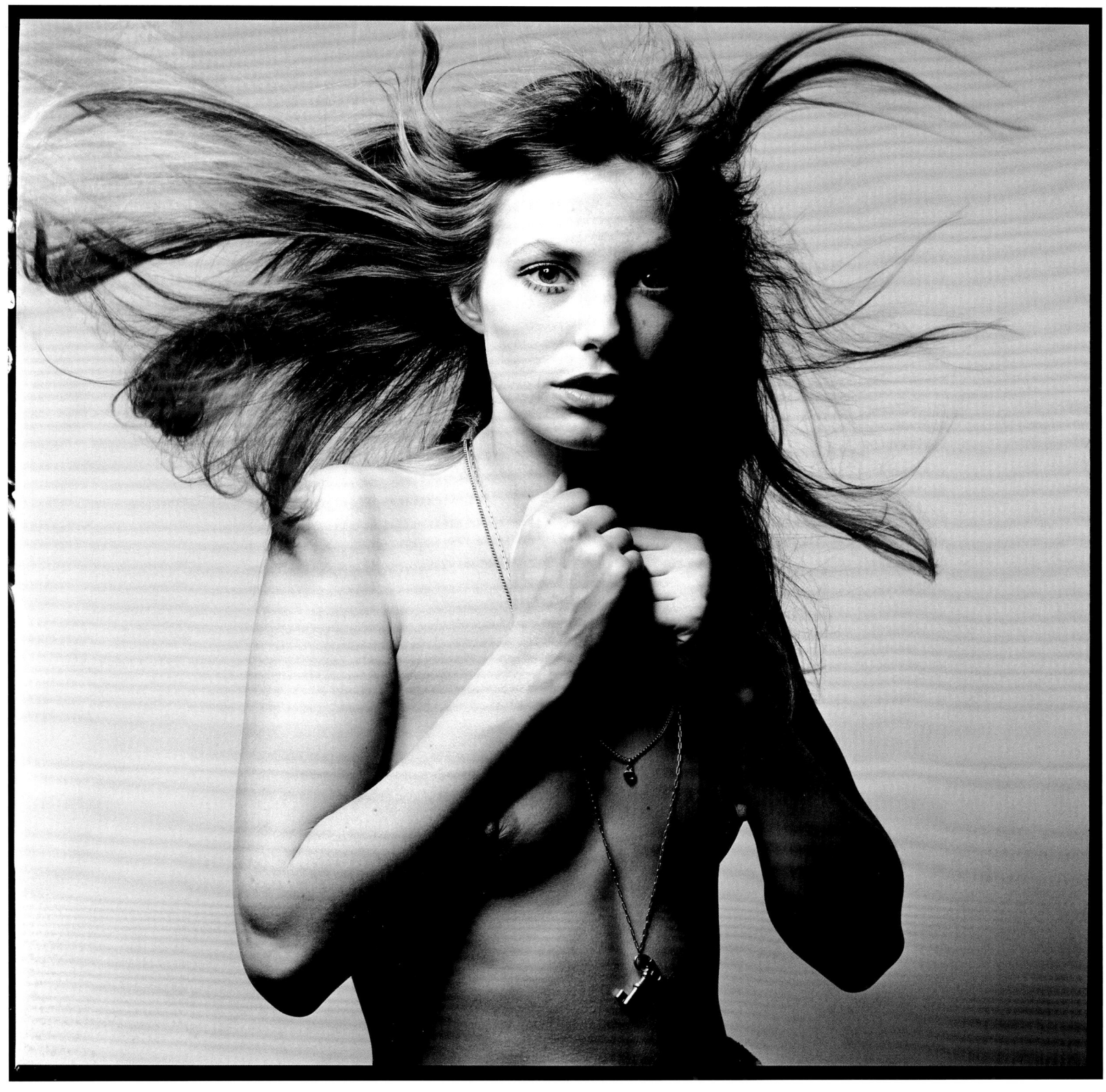

David Bailey

Bailey was a master of freezing a moment and registering
energy. In this image of Jane Birkin, the lighting is harsh
and unsubtle. Bailey went after people he really wanted
to meet, or he found models on the street if he couldn't
find the right one at an agency. Humor, bravado, and
flamboyance all come through in his raw, unapologetic
portraiture—you sense that his models made themselves
vulnerable to him. This directness is the most honest way
of working with a subject. For example, if we want to shoot
someone naked, we will tell them immediately. You feel
that kind of directness in his work. It's like: "This is what
it is. Are you going for it? Are you submitting yourself to it?
Here we go."

Deborah Turbeville,
Parco, Paris, 1986

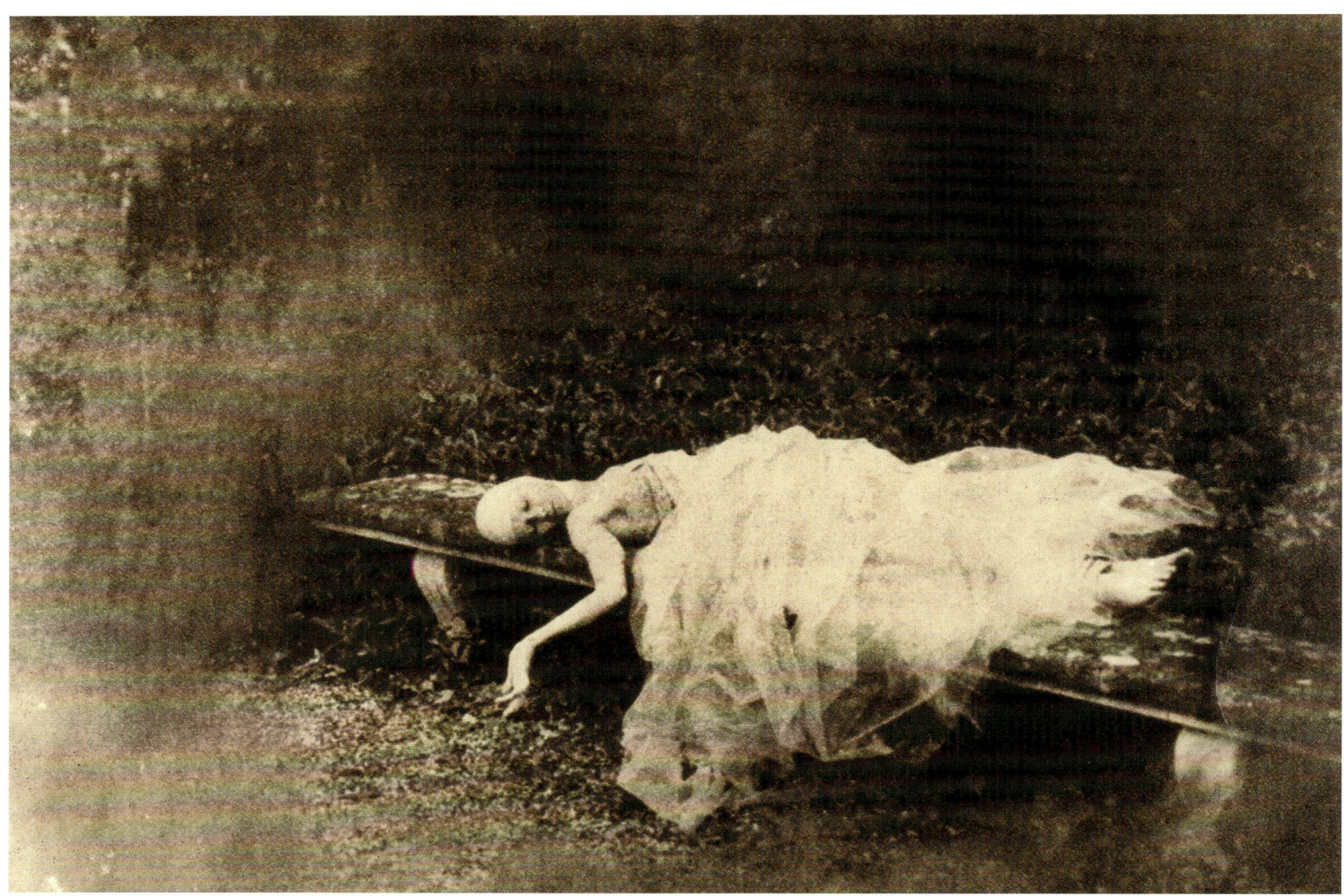

Deborah Turbeville

This image above has been in my scrapbooks ever since I (Inez) can remember looking at photography. The way the model's head is wrapped. This decaying environment. The broken-doll position; the faded, uncanny romantic atmosphere that seems based on an old painting; the way Turbeville would lay out her books with pieces of tape stuck to her photographs—all of that influenced me. There's a series that we did for *The Face*, with the model Maggie Rizer, based on this image; she had a headwrap like this girl's.

Group shots, like the one opposite, are so difficult to do, at least successfully. Turbeville was a master at using negative space and catching everyone at the right moment. She must have been amazing at directing people in such a way that they would let go. Her models are often a little bit neurotic, a little on the verge of falling apart. They are unsure and unavailable, which we find attractive, but there is an incredible delicateness. We're always amazed at how she manages to construct these group shots so beautifully, which is again a hard thing to do because you're setting up a fashion photograph. You're dealing with shoes and clothes. It's incredible how she directed her subjects, and found a way to make things feel personal, as though there is complicity among the women.

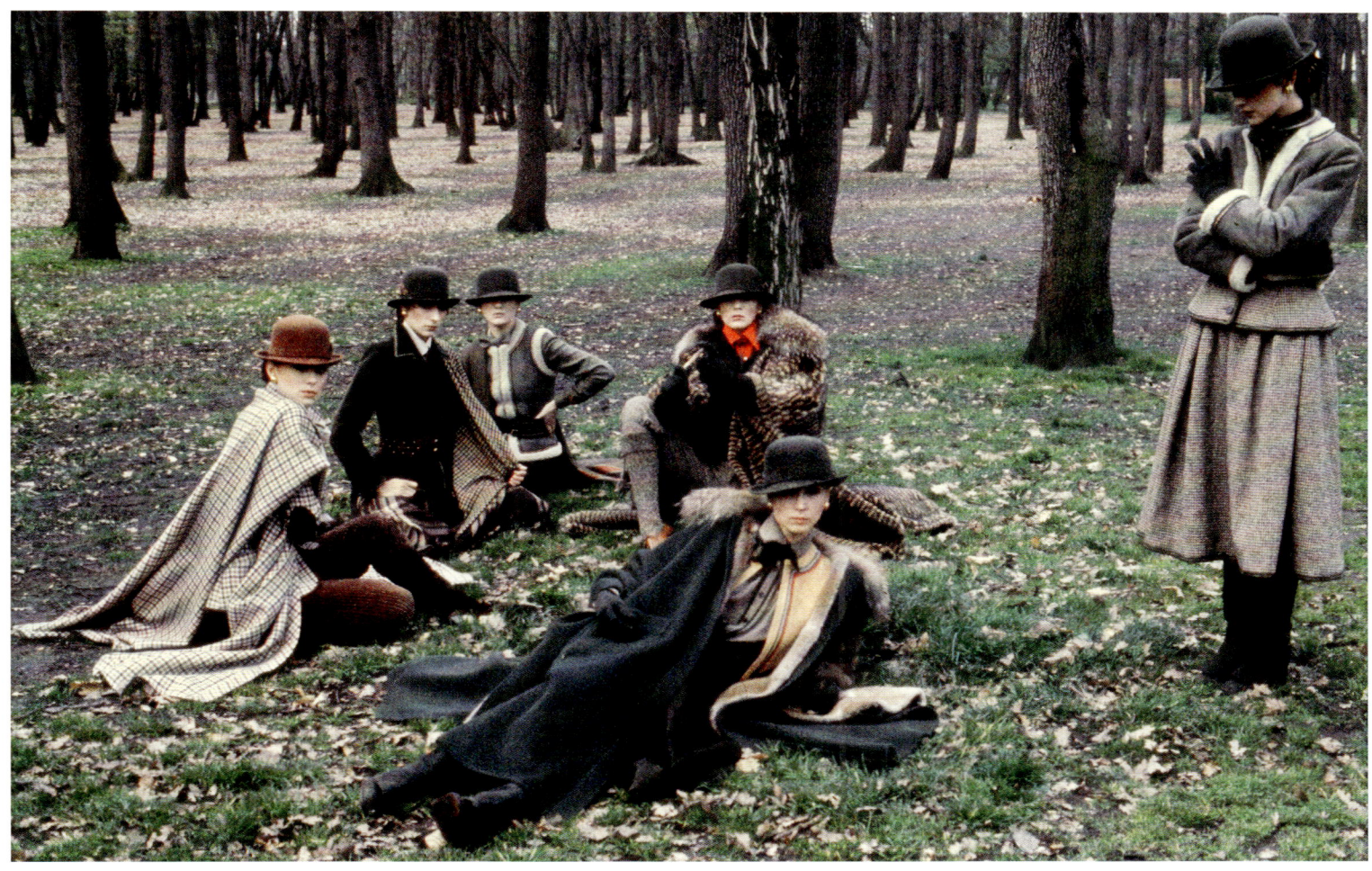

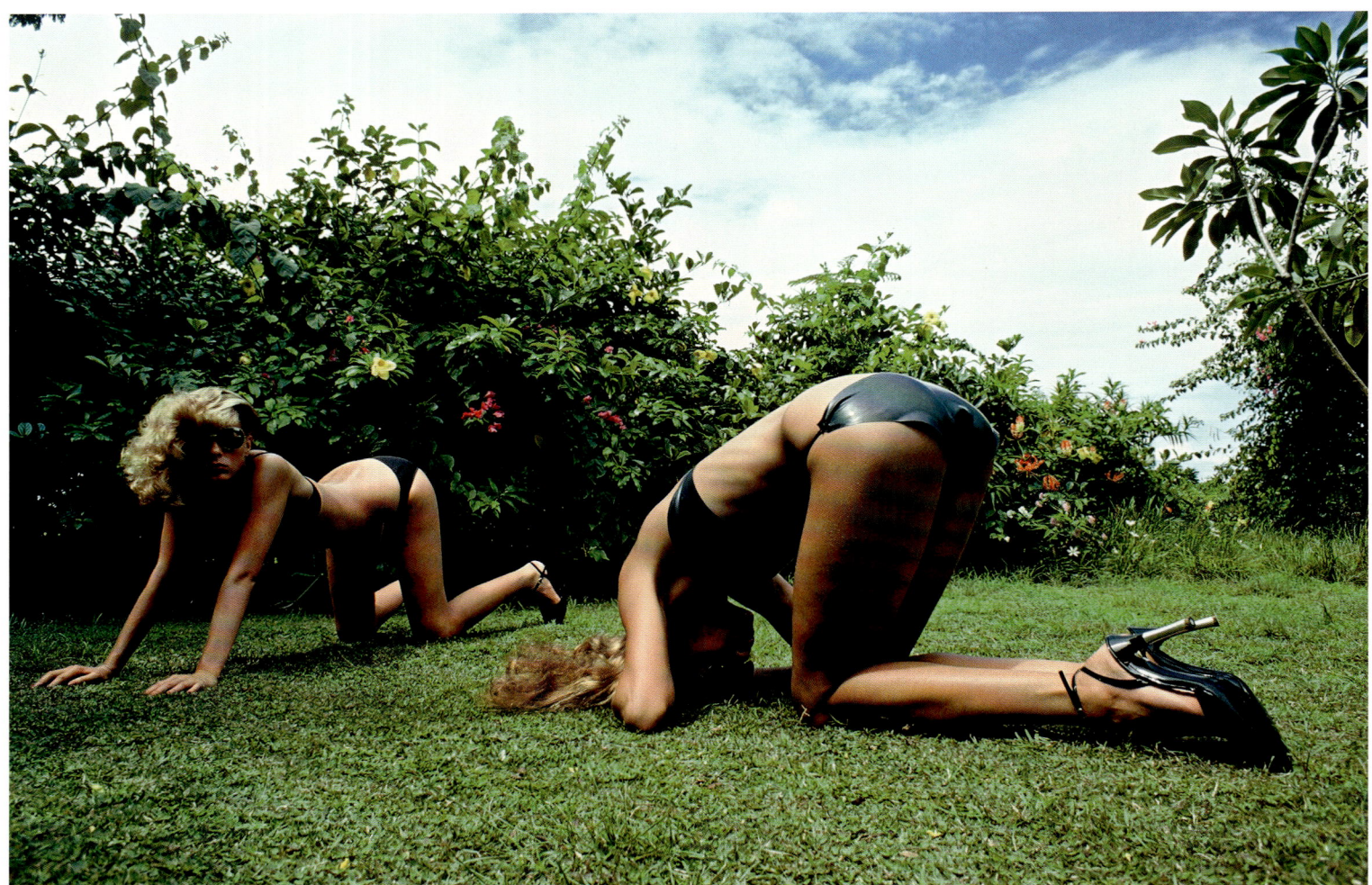

Hans Feurer

In the 1970s, Feurer opened up a studied, controlled idea of the fashion photograph while shooting for Kenzo. He worked with a long lens, at a distance, directing models with a megaphone in the early morning and at the end of the day when the light was the right temperature. Maybe using the long lens had to do with him not really wanting to engage with the women in the photographs but rather capturing them voyeuristically. The energy and the movement of the women in his photographs is sexy and creates a very unexpected body language. Women float in space in such an incredible way, showing the clothes so beautifully. When he worked with Kenzo it was a time in fashion that mixed utilitarian clothes and elegance. In this photograph at right, you're not sure what's going on: she's wearing a very folkloric outfit with a military hood and gloves and mountain-climbing shoes. There are all these different messages.

This image above we honestly thought was by Guy Bourdin. But then we found out, along the way, that this was a Feurer. Let's say there is his work with Kenzo, and then there is his work that has a sporty, fitness side to it. With this image, because of the contorted bodies and the strangeness of the composition, there is eroticism, but in his work it's never obvious nor cheap.

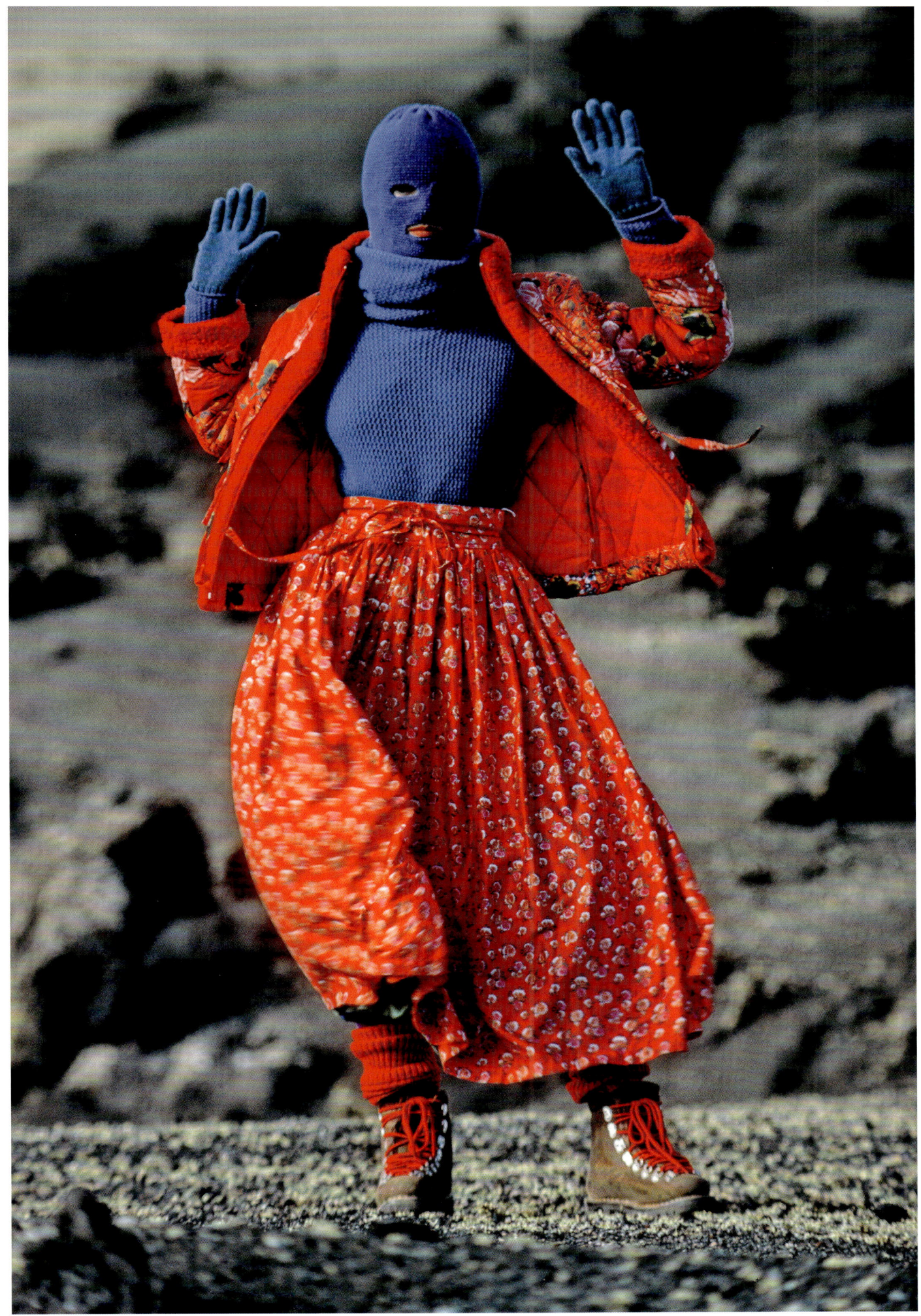

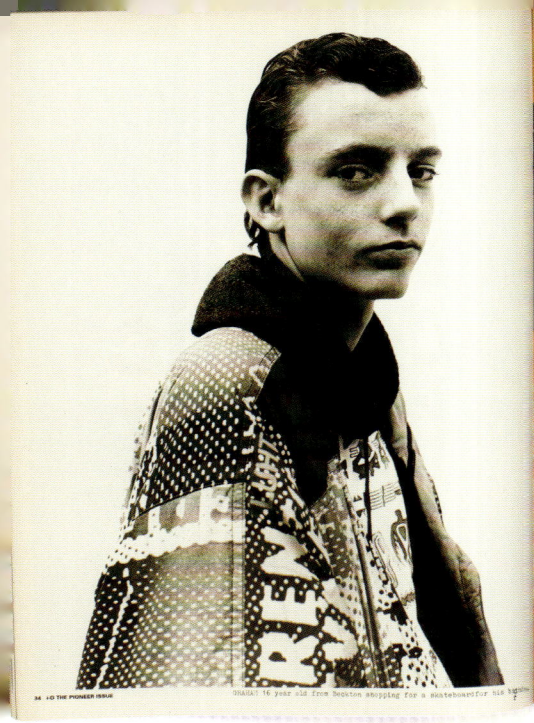

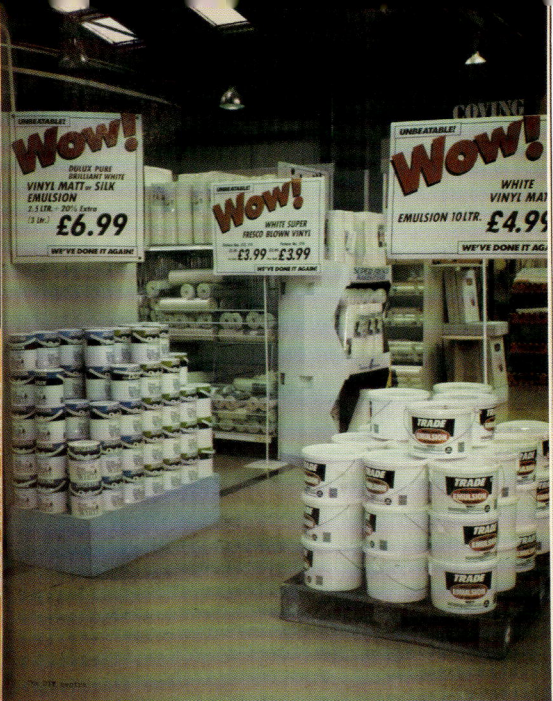

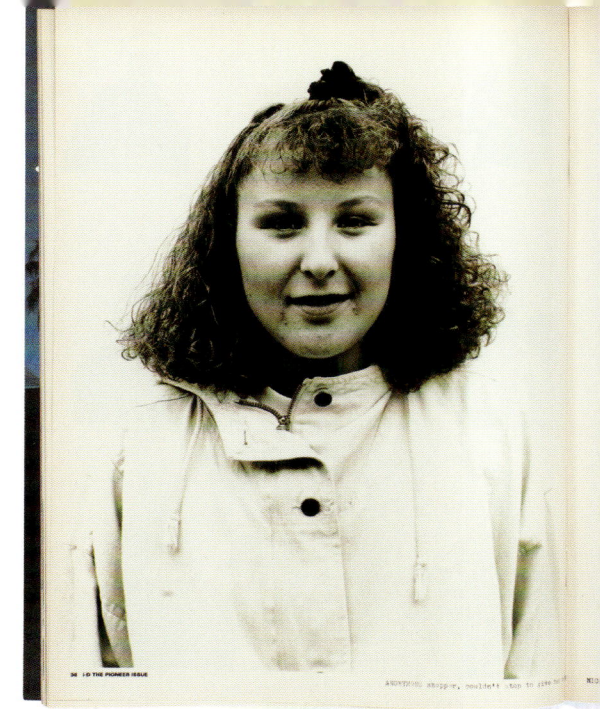

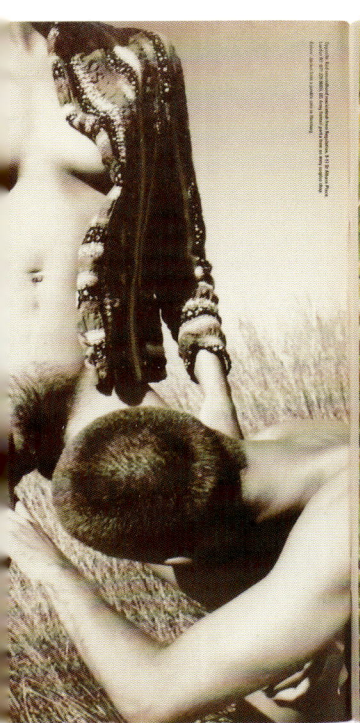

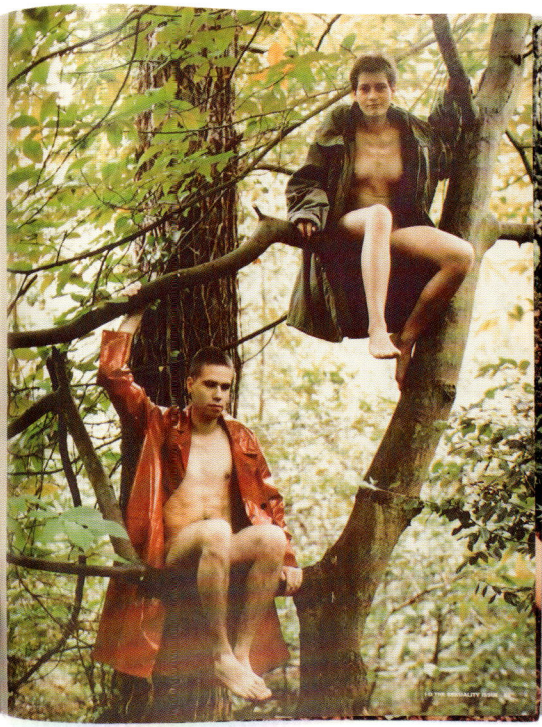

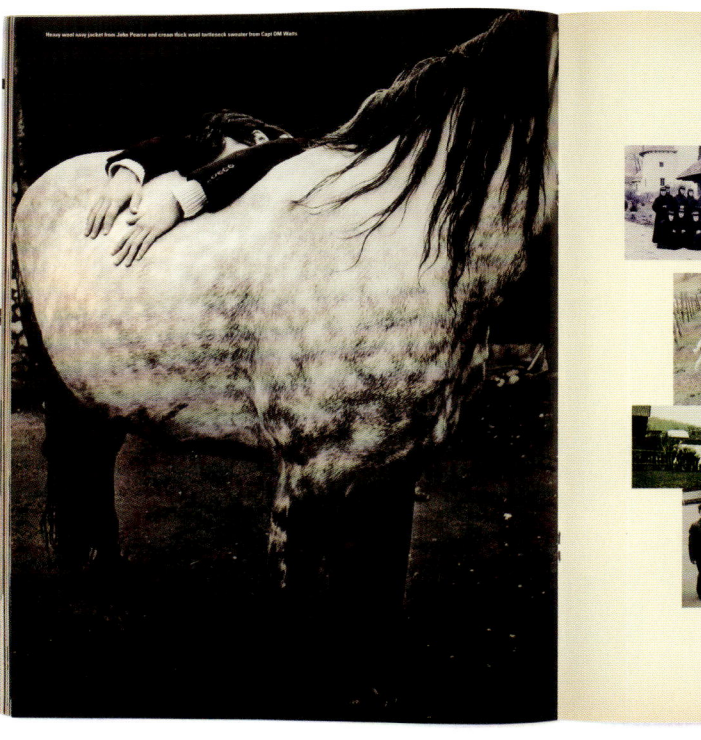

Heavy wool navy jacket from John Pearce and cream thick wool turtleneck sweater from Capt SM Watts

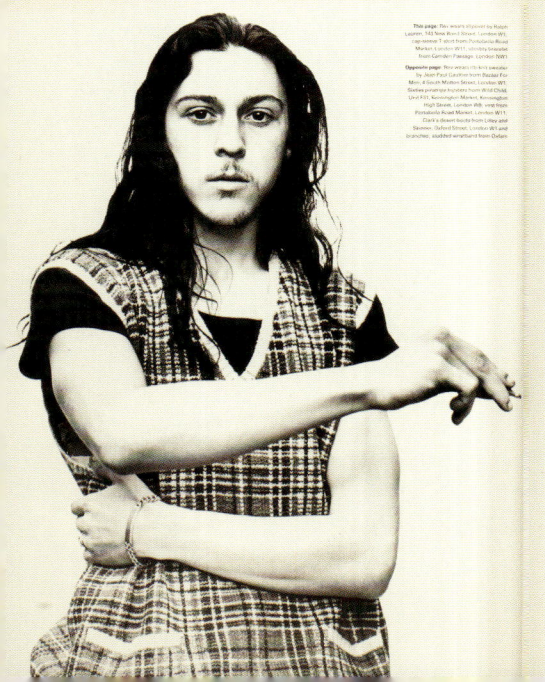

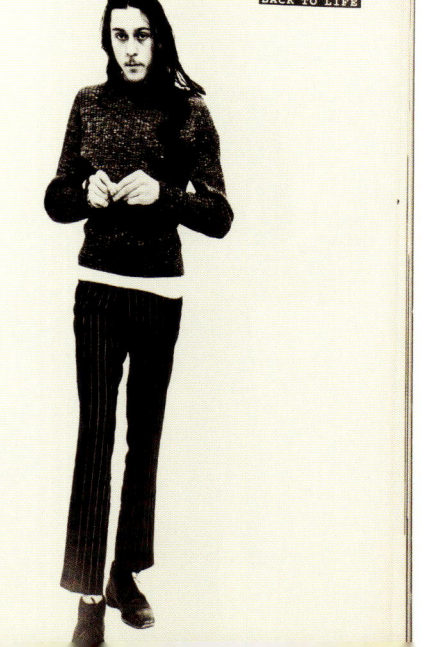

BACK TO LIFE

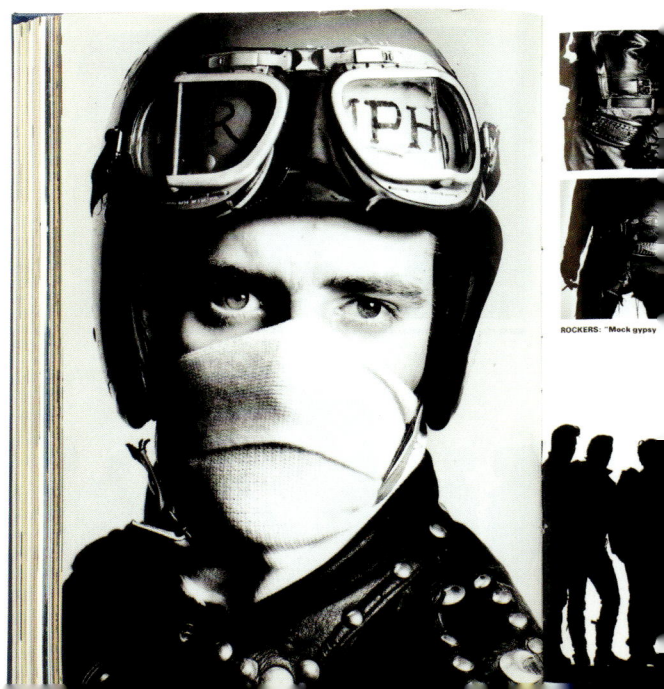

ROCKERS: "Mock gypsy

The year 1980 saw the birth in London of *The Face* and *i-D*, two independently published and quintessentially British magazines. *i-D* was the invention of former British *Vogue* art director Terry Jones, and *The Face* was created by former *NME* (*New Musical Express*) editor Nick Logan. These new publications signaled a bold, catalytic moment in magazine publishing, offering an escape from the constraints of mainstream media for their founders and a platform for instinctive self-expression for their contributors. As the last vestiges of punk waned and transitioned to New Wave and then New Romantic, the first issue of *The Face* was produced and launched by Logan using his personal savings, and *i-D*'s early landscape-format issues (with silk-screened graphic covers) were designed and distributed in small runs in keeping with punk's DIY mantra and post-punk aesthetic. Both magazines covered similar facets of youth culture; however, given the respective backgrounds of their founders, it was unsurprising that from the outset *The Face* was music-focused, while *i-D* was more interested in fashion. The first issues of *i-D* introduced the "Straight-Up"—formal full-length street portraits photographed against blank urban walls—that documented the personal and individual style of British youth. While many of the photographers responsible for those early images remain as little known as the majority of the passing strangers they documented, the names of other early contributors would become more familiar. As *i-D*'s format rotated from landscape to portrait, Nick Knight made its first "photographic" cover, featuring Sade, and Marc Lebon made the second, featuring Madonna.

i-D, Jill, and *The Face*

Fashion's Maverick Magazines

Phil Bicker

Both photographers would become *i-D* regulars, integral to the magazine's evolution. Lebon's work was raw and visceral, an experimental mash-up, fashion photography without boundaries. Knight's tireless creative contribution—one of his stories, art-directed by Marc Ascoli, was aptly titled "In Pursuit of Excellence"— was as inspiring as it was pivotal. For the magazine's fifth anniversary issue, Knight created a series of one hundred portraits, a styled topology of Britain's rich history of tribal youth culture, signaling the photographer's constant inventive hunger; he continued to produce dozens of fashion stories, more often than not made with his trusted collaborator, stylist Simon Foxton. Along with the contributions of stylists Judy Blame, Caroline Baker, and Ray Petri, these and other stories over the next half-decade augmented and magnified street style, taking the magazine to another level.

The early issues of *The Face* inherently touched on style in their portrayals of musicians, but the magazine's fashion coverage was, at least in its formative issues, less overt. While the irreverent *i-D* embodied the spirit of its logo— a wink and a smile—*The Face* took a more classical approach to cool. As the publication found its audience and confidence, the experimental graphics and custom typography of designer Neville Brody defined the magazine's identity, framed its content, and spread its influence. As the publication moved beyond its music roots, it took more risks. *The Face* chose "style" over "fashion," and stylist Helen Roberts initiated the magazine's evolution with photographer Jamie Morgan. Other stylists followed— Joe McKenna, Michael Roberts, Caroline Baker, and Debbie Mason among them— but none would have the impact or lasting influence of Ray Petri, or "Sting Ray," as he first chose to be credited. Petri was the godfather and unquestionably the leader of the creative West London "Buffalo" collective, a group of photographers (including Jamie Morgan and Marc Lebon), stylists (including Mitzi Lorenz), musicians (Neneh Cherry, Nick Kamen), artists (Barry Kamen), and models (including a fourteen-year-old Naomi Campbell), who brashly defined the look of '80s youth culture.

Petri made the MA-1 bomber jacket ubiquitous and mixed secondhand clothes and Army surplus, skiwear, sportswear, and accessories to create a brave new world of street style, urban cowboys, rude boys and ragamuffins, men in boxer shorts, collaged gangsters, and even men in skirts. He made the radical desirable

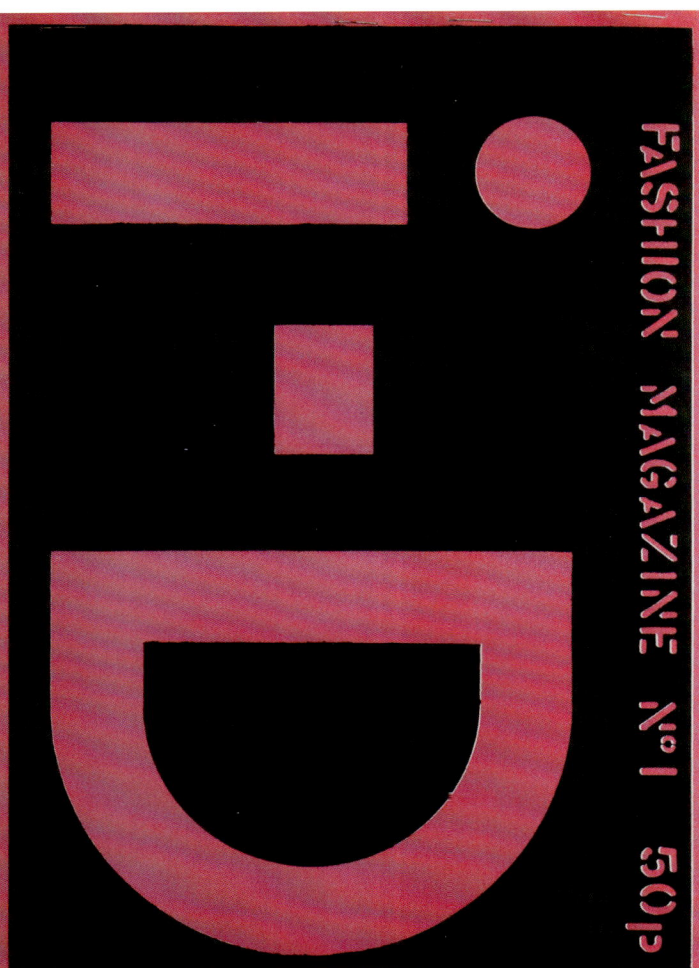

i-D no. 1, August 1980.
Cover design by Terry Jones

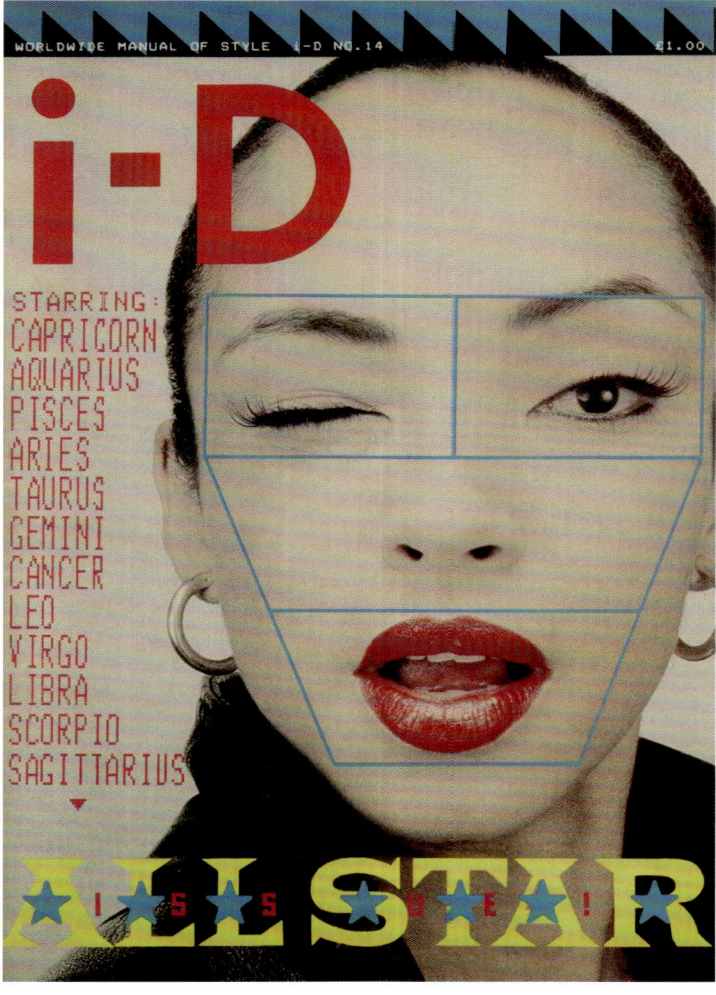

i-D no. 14, April 1983.
Cover photograph
by Nick Knight

and the outrageous believable, until his career was cut short when he died in August 1989 of AIDS. His legacy would include his later work with photographer Norman Watson for *Arena*, but it was his original vision and idiosyncratic styling, photographed by Jamie Morgan, that provided *The Face* with its first "style" cover—a photograph that publisher Nick Logan would later describe as a "fuck-off image from another planet"— and some of the magazine's most memorable stories, iconic covers, and "Killer" images. "New," "Hard," "Bold," the cover lines rang out; "Buffalo: The Harder They Come the Better," one portfolio's introductory text announced.

While Petri reimagined British style, the short-lived *Jill* magazine in Paris, under the direction of stylist Elisabeth "Babeth" Dijan, also embraced liberty, and the spirit of the new. As French as *i-D* and *The Face* were British, the independently published *Jill* was more fashion-centric but no less influential. The magazine was alternately at times a little softer and romantic, and at times a little darker and fantastic than its English counterparts. In its short run of eleven issues, published between 1983 and 1985, Dijan's inspired vision and styling and the photography of her contributors, including Peter Lindbergh, Jean-Baptiste Mondino, Jean-François Lepage, and a young Ellen von Unwerth, embraced the work of Jean Paul Gaultier and his generation of young French designers who turned the fashion world's attention once more firmly back to Paris.

A year after *Jill* folded, Dijan's distinctive styling was featured in a special Paris issue of *The Face*. By the end of the '80s Dijan had contributed a series of highly stylized fashion stories to the magazine, including the twenty-six-page comic-book-inspired opus, "Fashion Heroes," with photographer Stephane Sednaoui. The story featured designers Jean Paul Gaultier, Thierry Mugler, Martine Sitbon, Vivienne Westwood, Azzedine Alaïa, and a fantastical, intricately collaged series of images that preempted the digital era.

As the decade turned, a new generation of photographers, including David Sims and Corinne Day, and stylists, including Melanie Ward, emerged. Both Knight as photo editor at *i-D* and I as art director at *The Face*, nurtured and published their work. Inspired by rave music and, later, "grunge," the pared-down photographs related more to personal style and self-expression than to manufactured fantasy for commercial ends.

The images that appeared in *The Face* and *i-D* at the time were an antidote to fashion's high glamour and excess. In the summer of 1990, *The Face* ran an eight-page black-and-white story featuring a sixteen-year-old, then-unknown model, Kate Moss, and put her on the cover. The antithesis of the supermodel, the thin and refreshingly natural Moss stood just five-foot-seven. Photographed by Corinne Day and styled by Melanie Ward at England's Camber Sands beach, in feather headdress, Birkenstocks, cheesecloth, and daisy chains, Moss challenged the prevalent concept of beauty and, in doing so, embodied a new attitude and spirit for the age.

Simultaneously, David Sims further challenged mainstream ideals and archetypes, photographing a story for *The Face* in 1990 that featured a lank-haired, unlikely "model" named Rev against a stark white studio background. Styled by Ward and choreographed by Sims, Rev looked like a gypsy, clad in his own ill-fitting secondhand pinstripes and knitwear, as he alternately floated, posed, and cut a graphic figure. In another key 1990 story that ran in *i-D*, stylist Venetia Scott and photographer Juergen Teller traveled across Romania, dressing and photographing real people of various ages they encountered to produce a wonderfully nuanced, understated, and ultimately unfashionable fashion story. And, recalling and refining the simple approach of *i-D*'s early "Straight-Ups," Nigel Shafran in 1991 photographed the personal style of "Teenage Precinct Shoppers" unadorned.

These photographs, especially those by Day and Sims, made waves. A startled fashion world—unable to comprehend the casting, styling, or aesthetic—was at first caustic and dismissive. But the work could not be ignored. It was exciting, new, and challenging. Eventually the contagious individual visions of nonconformity made an impact on the mainstream and became a fashionable way of photographing fashion.

Both *i-D* and *The Face* continued their creative celebration of intuition, instinct, and individuality; Wolfgang Tillmans emerged through the pages of *i-D* in 1992 to blur and break down the boundaries between art and fashion photography, and *The Face* published pioneering stories by Inez & Vinoodh in 1994 and Elaine Constantine in 1997, before eventually folding in 2004. But despite both magazines' years of commercial and cultural success, the spirit of originality and global influence that defined their work in the late '80s and early '90s would never be surpassed.

Top: Pages from *i-D* no. 1, August 1980, "Straight-Up." Photographs by Steven Johnston

Bottom: Pages from The Face no. 32, May 1991, "Slapheads." Photographs by Corinne Day; styling by Melanie Ward

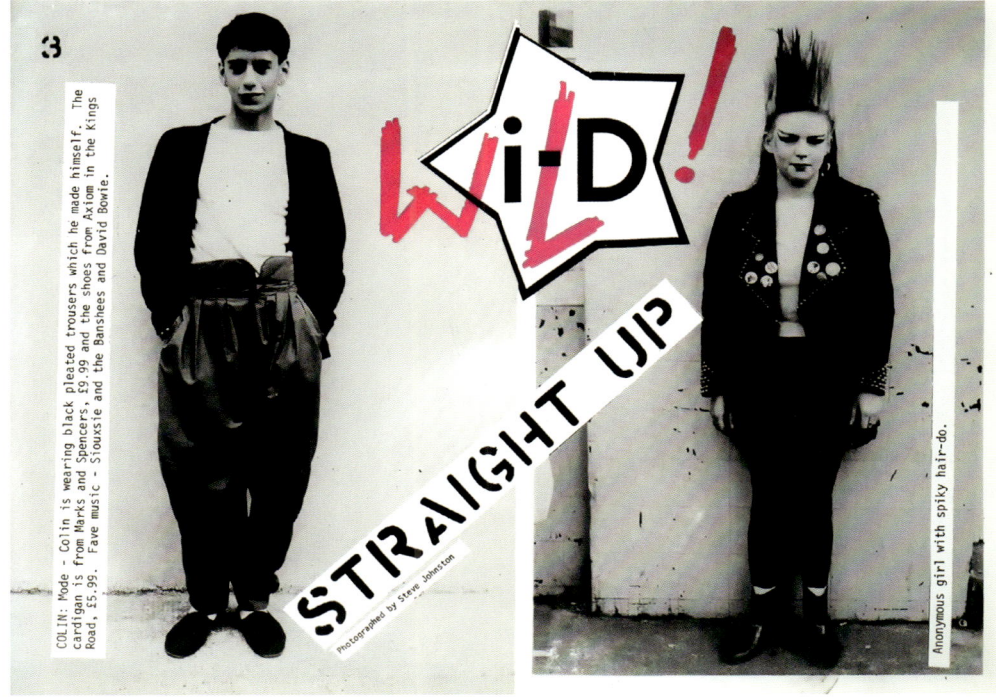

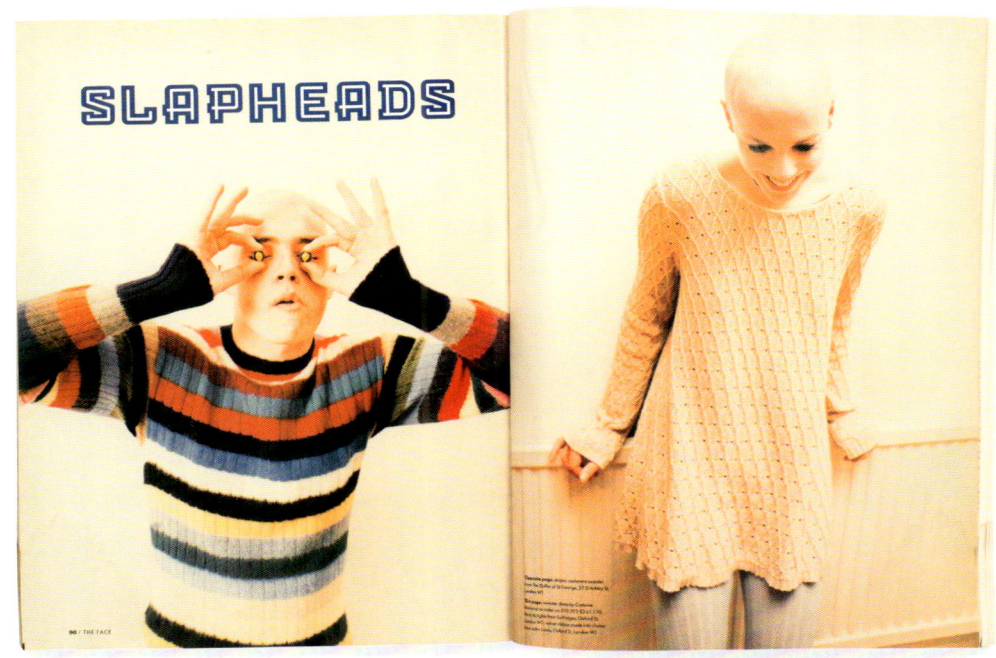

Phil Bicker, a creative director, designer, and photography editor, was the art director of *The Face* from 1987 to 1991.

IDENTITY PARADE

FIVE YEARS

Here, for the first time are a selection of portraits by Nick Knight from a forthcoming book of People Of The 80s. Specially commissioned by i-D Magazine, these are just a few of the stars that Nick has photographed for inclusion in this book. This is both a celebration of the success of five years of i-D's catalogue of protagonists, and a starting point for what will become the definitive tome of the 80s.

The Scam: During May and June of this year, Dylan Jones and Nick Knight studiously contacted over 100 people who had at some time or another appeared in i-D Magazine. All the faces. From the fashion designers who weren't fashion designers then, to the pop stars who weren't, from the already famous to the ones who still aren't. The aim? A retrospective photo portrait gallery to appear in the 5th Anniversary edition of i-D. Day in, day out they sweated over hot-to-the-touch telephones, tracking down their subjects in all parts of the world. In they came, traipsing through the i-D offices, sipping coffee and chewing the fat – waiting to be immortalised on film. And the result . . .? Here for your eyes only . . . Read on . . .

". . . all the fat skinny people, and all the all short people, and all the nobody people and all the somebody people . . ."

YOW! The Worldwide Manual Of Style!! Let fashion live!!! Live fashion!!!

In the Eighties the revolts into style and the plunders of fashion have been rife, ripe and cheeky – turning Britain into a living, breathing catwalk of style where every living person is a dress code, a law unto themselves. And in these eclectic Eighties, i-D Magazine has undertaken to line the gallery of all these sartorial snapshots – a rogues' gallery, a beauty gallery – The Gallery Of Style.

The Eighties produced not only thousands of people with thousands of dress modes, but it also produced legions of duplicates – multiplying, cross-dressing and cross-fertilising like crazy; insatiable and inscrutable.

The Bowie generation did come to life – not just the 'soul-boy' ethic, but the configuration of all manner of as-yet-unseen yute cults from the early Seventies: the baggied, the skinned, the long-haired the overcoated, the cropped, the goth-ckeed, the wonder-whicked . . . the whatevered. Style is now consumers market, and once you let the genie out of the bottle it's impossible to put back the cork – everybody wants a piece of the action. Buy, wear and be merry!

The fashion-zealots narcissistically confronted themselves with a multitude of public climactic moments – and the media ate with Pacman-like intensity, chewing over things they'd normally have the scantest opinion on: real life street showbusiness.

If the fantasy cycle started in 1975 with the advent of punk, then lo and behold we are at the end of an era –

ten years of unmitigated brazen showoffishness. The late Seventies were the mulling period – the puberty stage for harbingers and stylists, garnished with colloquial hokum – an inspiration and invitation to protagonists and plunder-mongers.

But the Eighties is where the fun began, and also when i-D took the lens cap off. From 'To Cut A Long Story Short' to the end of DoDos – five years stuck on your eyes, five years what a surprise – we had to cram so many things to store everything in these. In between the fashion phantasmagoria, the die-hard decals, the festered fashions, the victims and the victimised there obviously came a backlash – along with cossetted surrogate pop came casualty of chrome-plated and streamlined times: people who started to dress like the people who once beat them up for looking different. Pah! Humbug!! But the force remains, and exclusivity still holds its own, even if it is being pocketed by twice as many people (we are filling up with even more surefooted and versatile young things.

Loonine clashing threads, ambiguity, iconoclastic fads and cest-petite dress are coming at us faster than ever – and at the third stroke the time will be 1996 precisely – so here's to it. Let's sink the big boats! Vive le rock!!

Dylan Jones

The book will be released during the next 18 months, written by Dylan Jones and designed by Terry Jones.

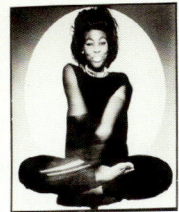
SHERRON – Singer.

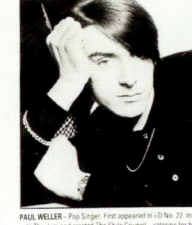
PAUL WELLER – Pop Singer.

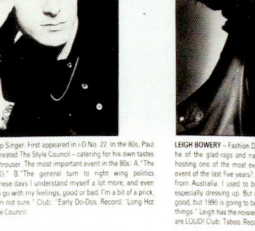
LEIGH BOWERY – Fashion Designer.

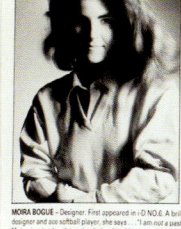
MOIRA BOGUE – Designer.

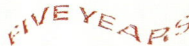

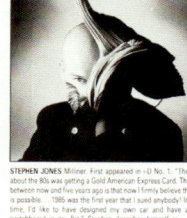
PAM HOGG – Fashion Designer.

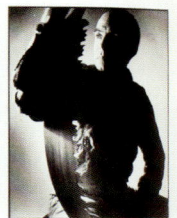
STEPHEN JONES – Milliner.

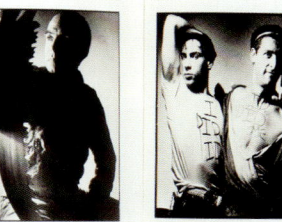
KEITH FROM SMILE – Hairdresser.

JAMES & MARC LEBON – Hairdresser & Photographer.

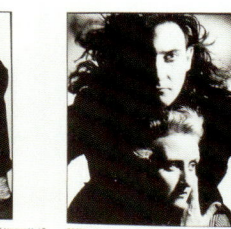
DYLAN JONES – Journalist.

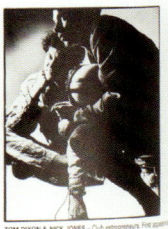
SCOTT CROLLA & GEORGINA GODLEY – Fashion Designers.

TOM DIXON & NICK JONES – Club entrepreneurs.

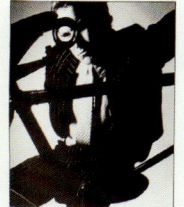
STEPHEN BAYLEY – Museum Commando.

Gatefold pages from *i-D*
no. 30, October 1985,
Fifth anniversary issue,
"*i-D* Identity Parade."
Photographs by Nick Knight

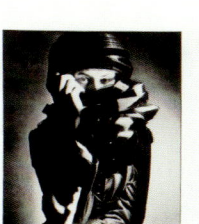
CERITH WYN EVANS – Film-maker.

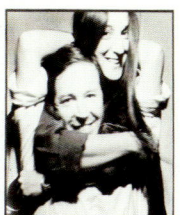
TERRY & TRICIA JONES – Editor Art Director/Dog Handler and Extra Pair of Hands/Teacher/Mum.

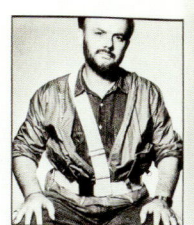
JOHN PEEL – DJ.

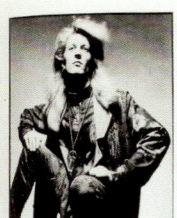
KEANAN – Fashion Designer.

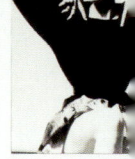
KATE – Model.

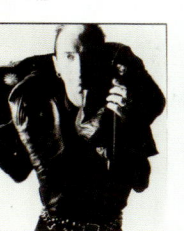
MARC ALMOND – Pop Singer.

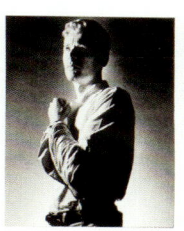
JAY STRONGMAN – DJ & Journalist.

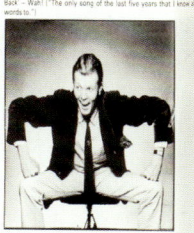
RUSTY EGAN – Club Entrepreneur & Record Producer.

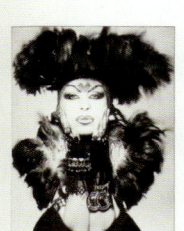
JANE KHAN – Fashion Designer.

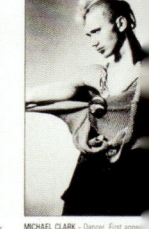
MICHAEL CLARK – Dancer.

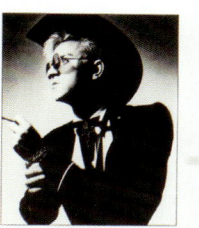
STEVE STRANGE – Nightclub Entrepreneur, Singer.

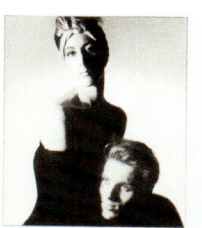
CARYN FRANKLIN & NICK TRULOCKE – Fashion Editor & Club Entrepreneur.

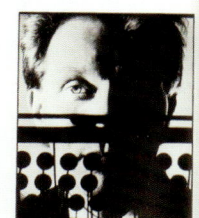
DAVID JOHNSON – Journalist with The London Standard.

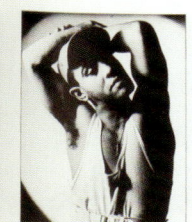
CHRISTOS TOLERA – Singer & Interior Decorator.

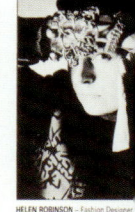
HELEN ROBINSON – Fashion Designer.

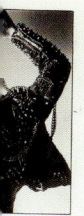
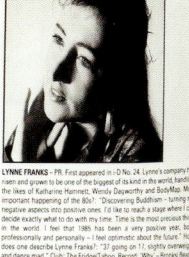
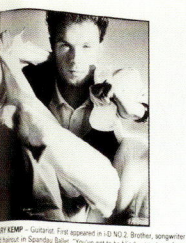
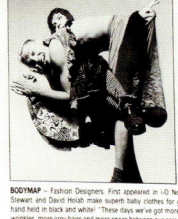
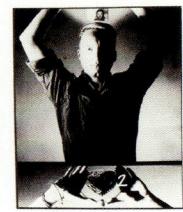

LYNNE FRANKS – PR. First appeared in i-D No. 24.

GARY KEMP – Guitarist. First appeared in i-D No. 2.

BODYMAP – Fashion Designers. First appeared in i-D No. 11. Steve Stewart and David Holah make superb baby clothes for grown-ups.

JEFFREY HINTON – Video-maker. First appeared in i-D No. 17. A former self-confessed nightclub hedonist, Jeffrey is now the country's leading video-scratcher.

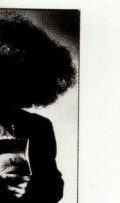
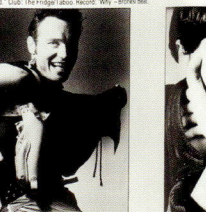
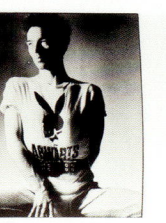
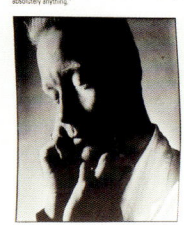

ADAM ANT – Pop singer. First appeared in i-D No. 5. Prince Charming's alter ego, a regular rock 'n' roller.

MITZI LORENZ – Stylist. First appeared in i-D No. 19. Little Mitzi has tried successfully to appear in every other issue of i-D.

ALIX SHARKEY – Singer, Journalist, Star. First appeared in i-D No. 7. Stimulin, Out, i-D, Essential.

RICHARD OSTELL – Fashion Designer. First appeared in i-D No. 3. A 1981 St Martin's graduate and a former member of Notre Dame X.

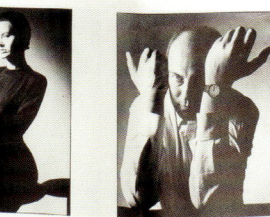
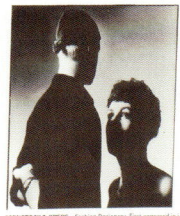
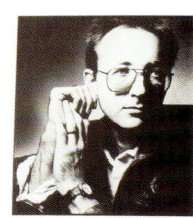

KATE GARNER – Singer. First appeared in i-D No. 10. Once a model and photographer, then the better half of Haysi Fantayzee – now forging ahead with a solo career.

STEPHEN KING – Fashion Designer. First appeared in i-D No. 24.

BERNSTOCK & SPIERS – Fashion Designers. First appeared in i-D No. 22.

NICK LOGAN – Editor. First appeared in i-D No. 30.

18

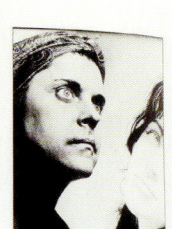
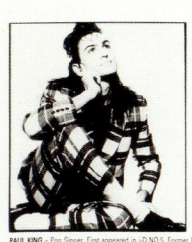
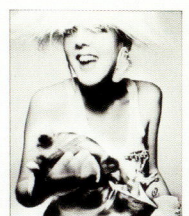
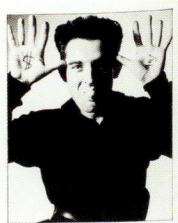
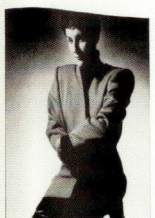
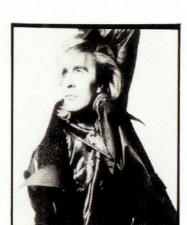
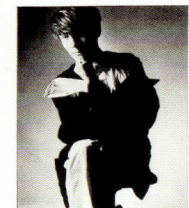

GENESIS P. ORRIDGE – Pop singer. First appeared in i-D No. 1. Throbbing Gristle, Psychic TV.

PAUL KING – Pop Singer. First appeared in i-D No. 5. Former Reluctant Stereotype – now King Big-wig.

SCARLETT – Model. First appeared in i-D No. 2. Scarlett was the face that every foreign magazine photographed when they catalogued the Blitz scene.

TOM BINNS – Jewellery Designer. First appeared in i-D No. 18.

ALICE RYCROFT – Fashion Designer. First appeared in i-D No. 20.

MARTIN FRY – Singer/Songwriter. First appeared in i-D No. 8. As the frontman to ABC, Martin has travelled the world.

SOPHIE HICKS – Fashion Journalist. First appeared in i-D No. 16.

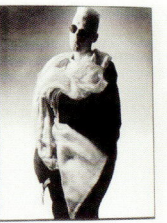
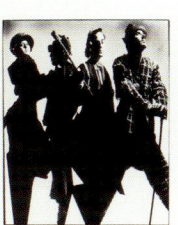
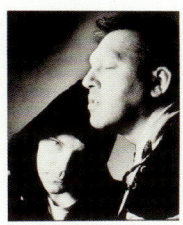
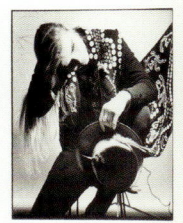
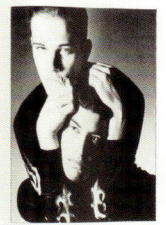
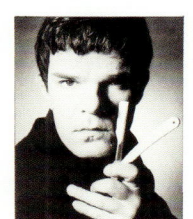
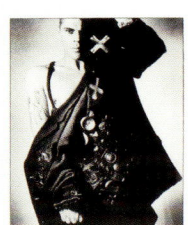

JOHN CRANCHER – Fashion Designer. First appeared in i-D No. 2.

JOHN GALLIANO – Fashion Designer. First appeared in i-D No. 21. Left St Martin's in summer 84.

ANDY CZEZOWSKI & JIMMY FOX – Club Entrepreneur & Club Performer, respectively. First appeared in i-D's No. 19 & 13.

LIZZY TIER – Singer. First appeared in i-D No. 4. Former model.

WILLIAM FALKNER – Make Up Artist. First appeared in i-D No. 25.

SIMON FORBES – Hairdresser and creator of Antenna. First appeared in i-D No. 7.

JUDY BLAME – Jewellery Designer. First appeared in i-D No. 6.

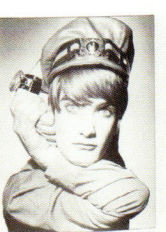
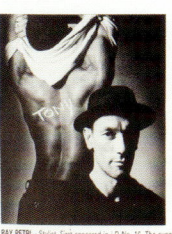
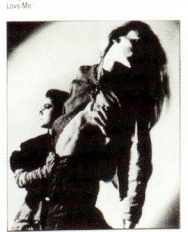
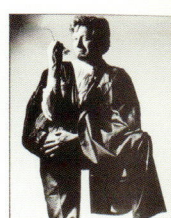
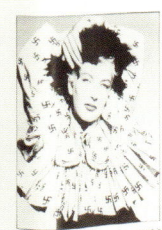
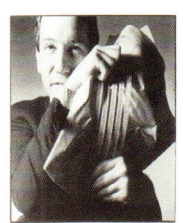
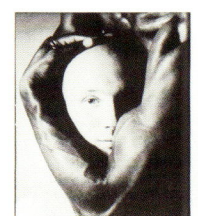

JALLE BAKKE – Make Up Artist. First appeared in i-D No. 20.

RAY PETRI – Stylist. First appeared in i-D No. 10. The supreme Buffalo Boy, whose pork-pie hats, big lapel jackets and 'Killer' cards have invaded the streets of London.

JOHN RICHMOND & MARIA CORNEJO – Fashion Designers. First appeared in i-D Nos. 18 and 13 respectively.

TONY WILSON – TV Presenter, Record Mogul and Club Owner. Every one's favourite Factory Records and Manchester's Hacienda.

RACHEL AUBURN – Fashion Designer. First appeared in i-D No. 27.

NEIL SPENCER – Journalist. First appeared in i-D No. 27. Neil was editor of the NME between Nick Logan and Ian Pye.

SIMON FOXTON – Stylist & Fashion Designer. First appeared in i-D No. 12.

22

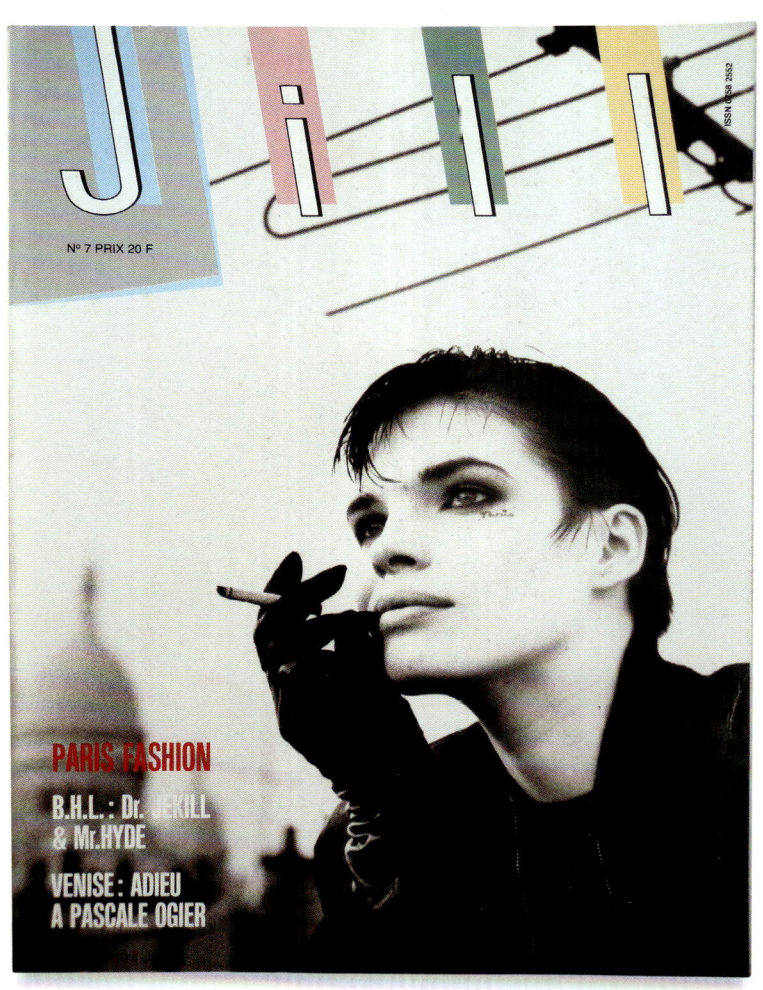

Left:
Jill no. 7, Fall 1984

Bottom:
Pages from *Jill* no. 8,
February 1985, "Vestiges."
Photographs by Jean-
François Lepage;
art direction by Frédérique
Lorca and Claudia Huidobro

Opposite, top:
Pages from *Jill* no. 8,
February 1985, "Rococo
& Co." Photographs
by José Arman Pita;
art direction by Caroline
Baker

Opposite, bottom:
Pages from *Jill* no. 8,
February 1985, "Le bal
des vamps" (The vampires'
ball). Photographs
by Ellen von Unwerth;
art direction by Anna
Lawlowski

Following pages:
Pages from *Jill* no. 8,
February 1985,
"J'suis snob" (I'm a snob).
Photographs by
J.-J. Castres; art direction
by Mitzi Lorenz

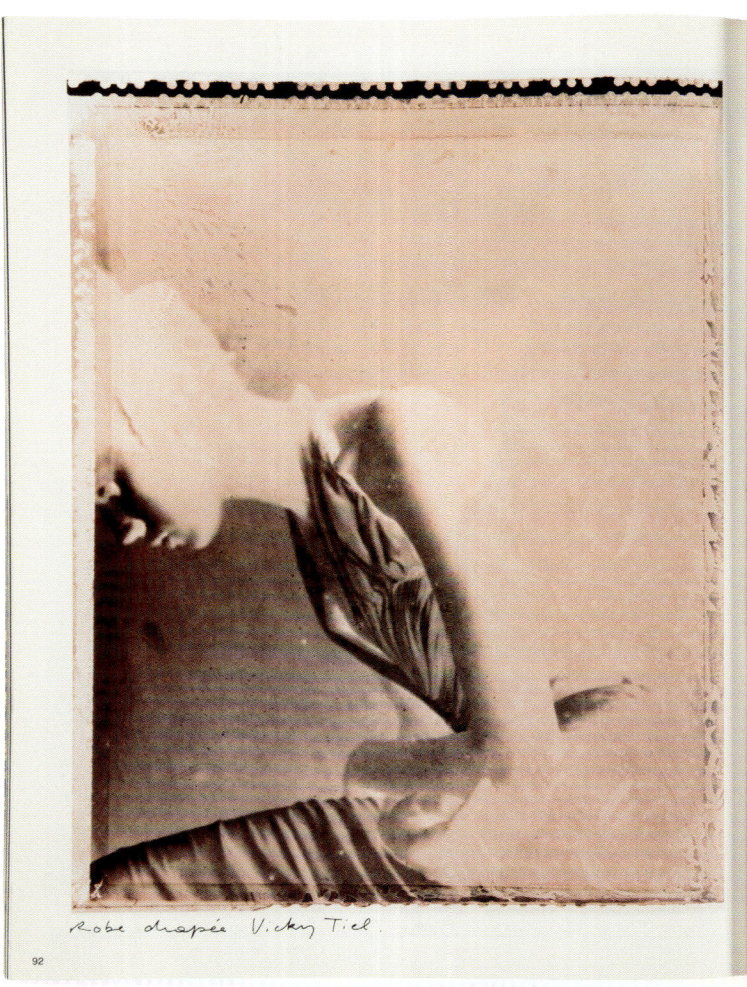

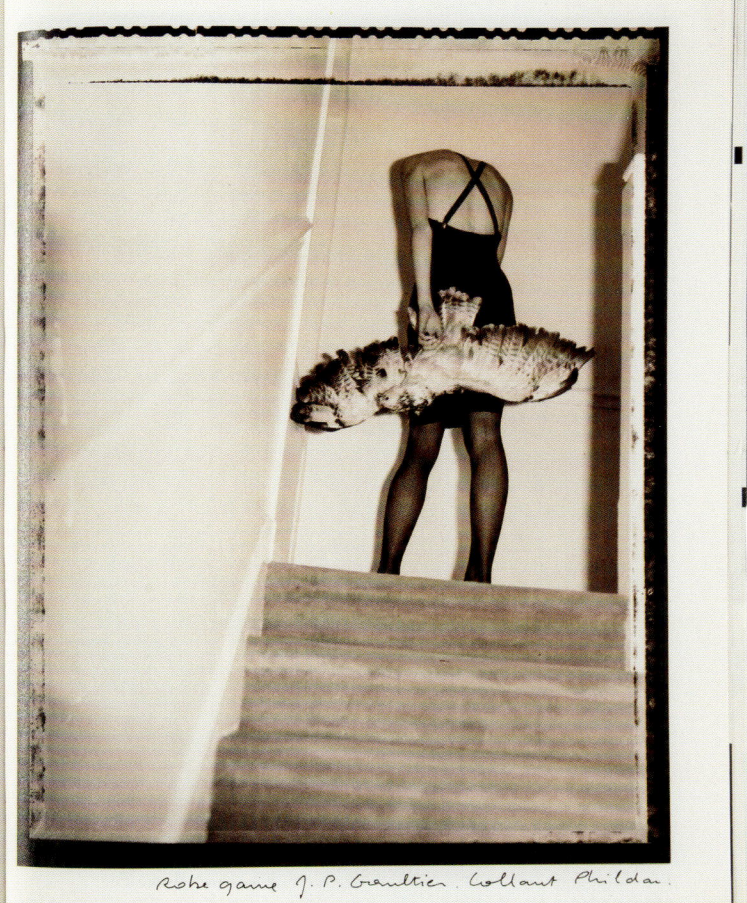

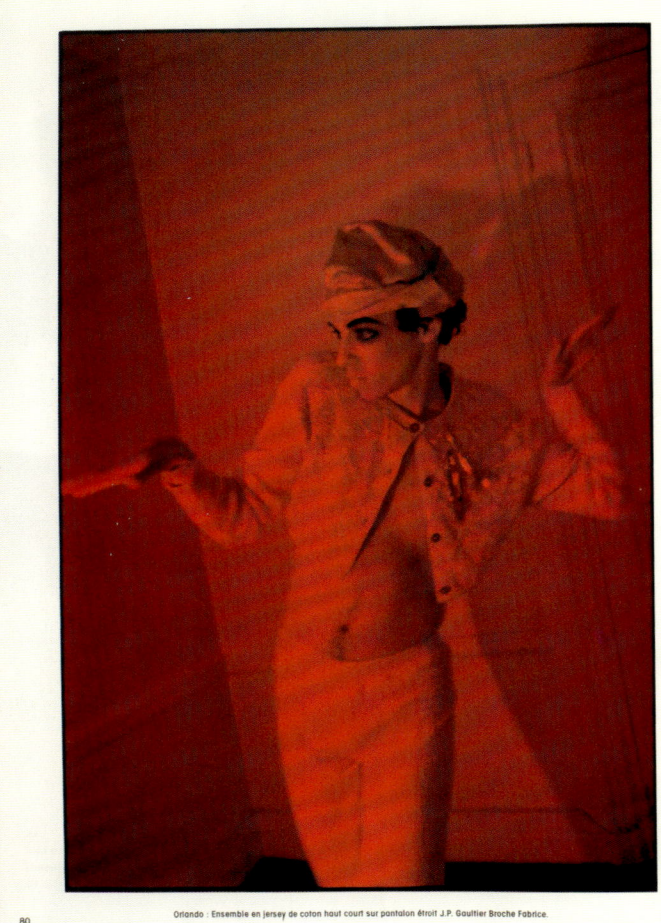

80   Orlando : Ensemble en jersey de coton haut court sur pantalon étroit J.P. Gaultier Broche Fabrice.

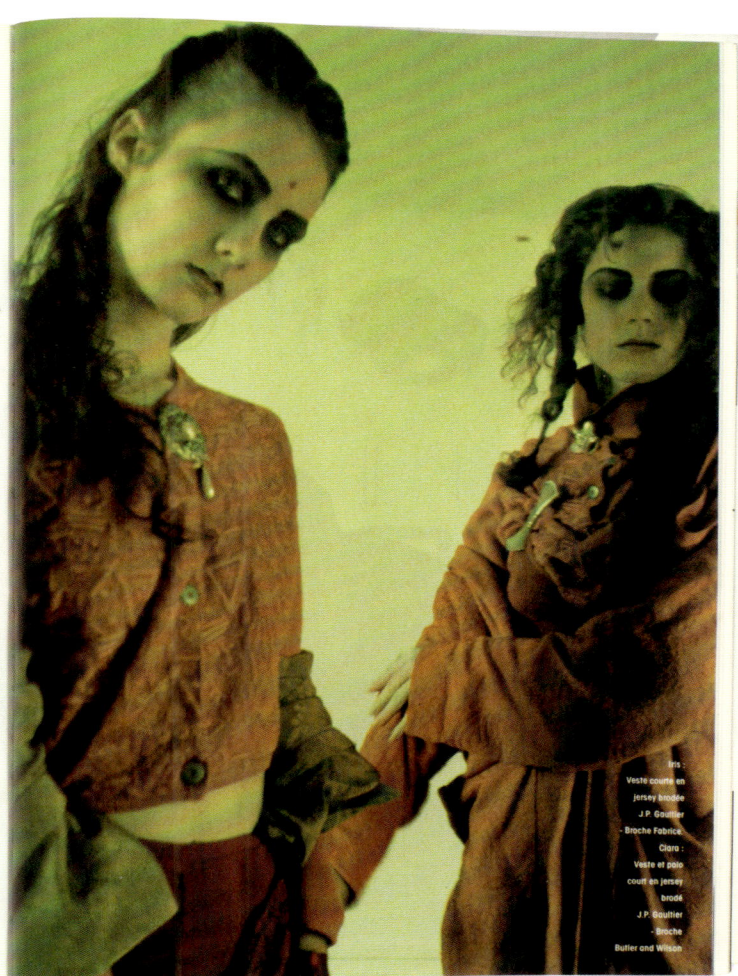

Iris :
Veste courte en
jersey brodée
J.P. Gaultier
- Broche Fabrice
Clara :
Veste et polo
court en jersey
brodé
J.P. Gaultier
- Broche
Butler and Wilson

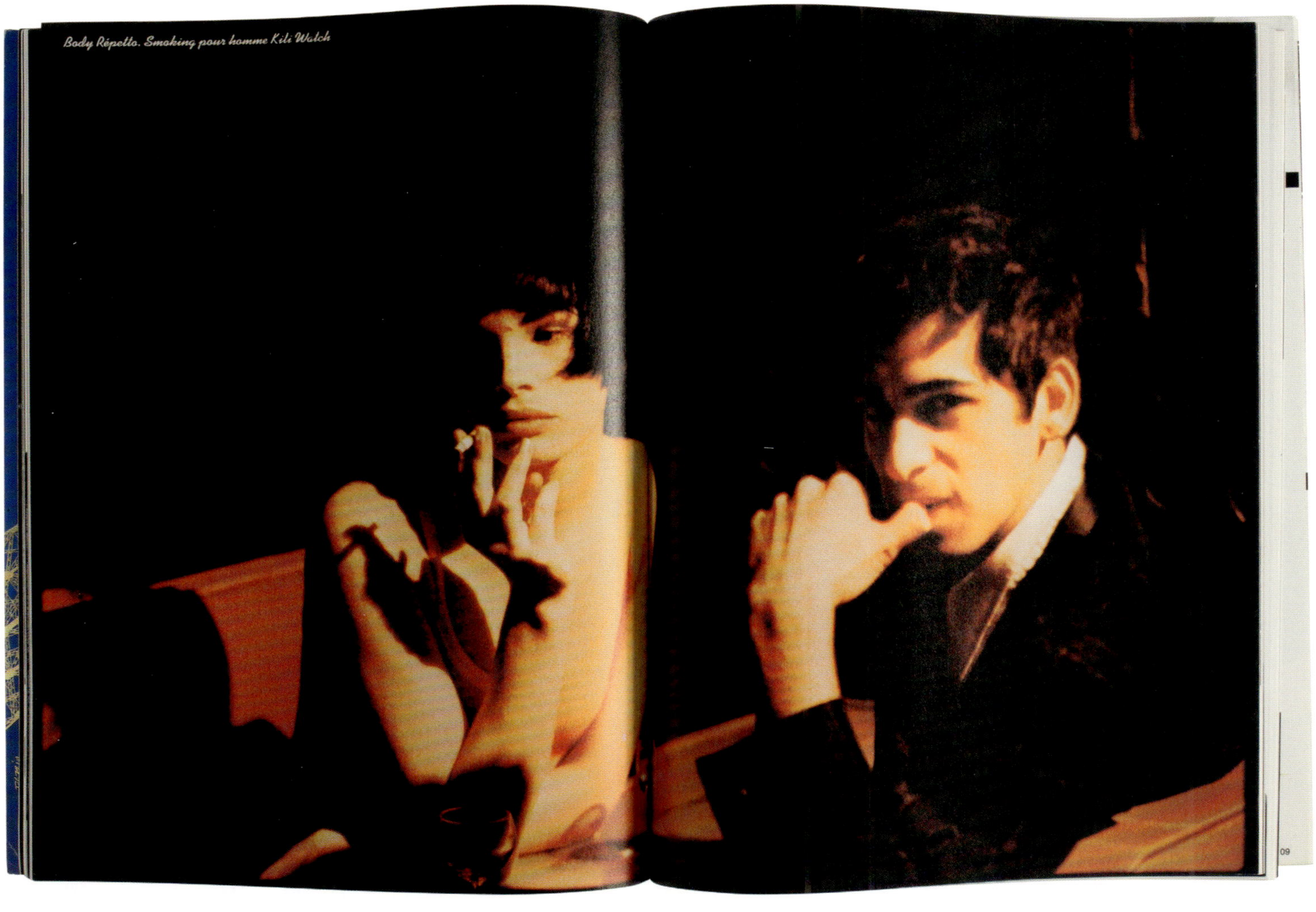

Body Répetto. Smoking pour homme Kili Watch

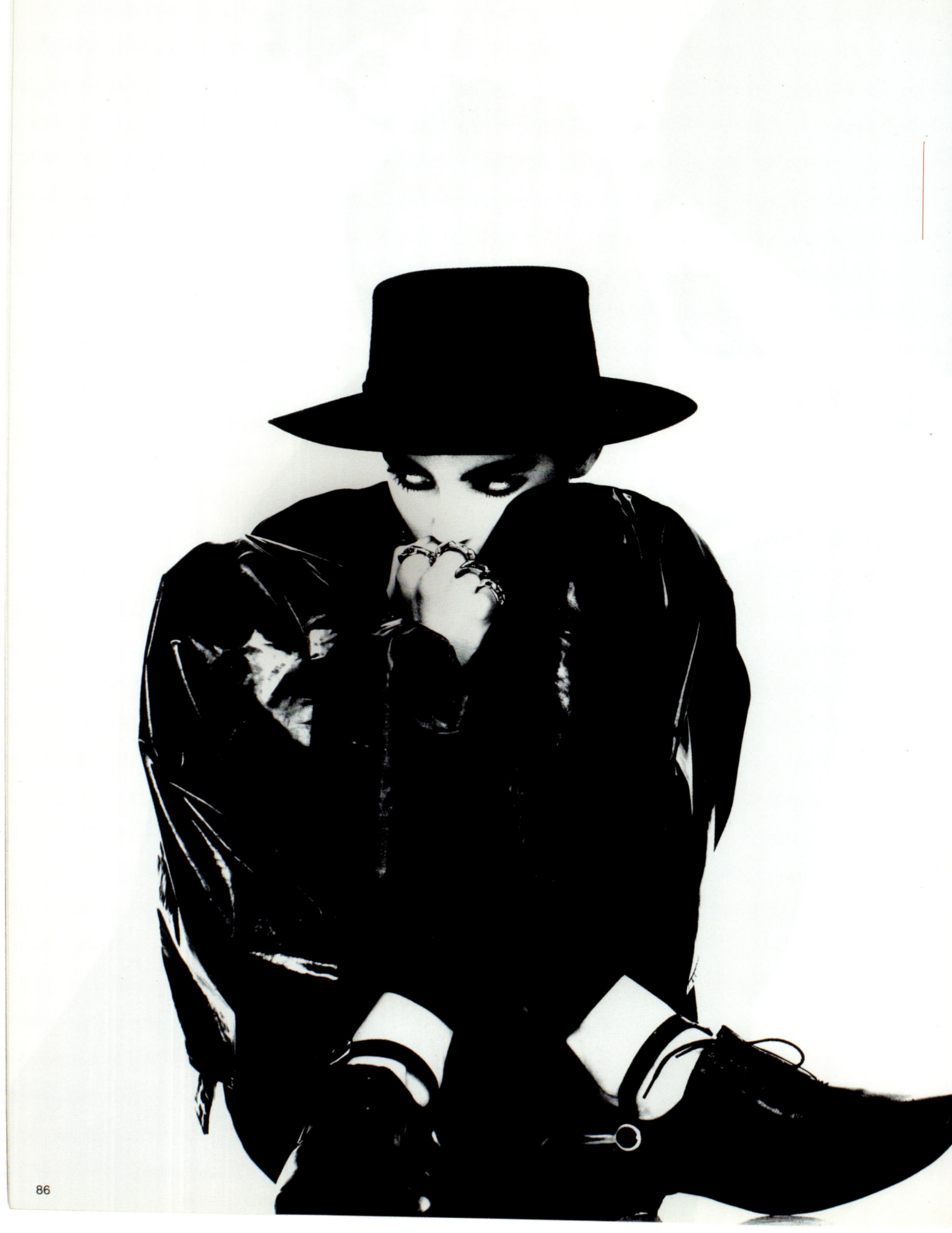

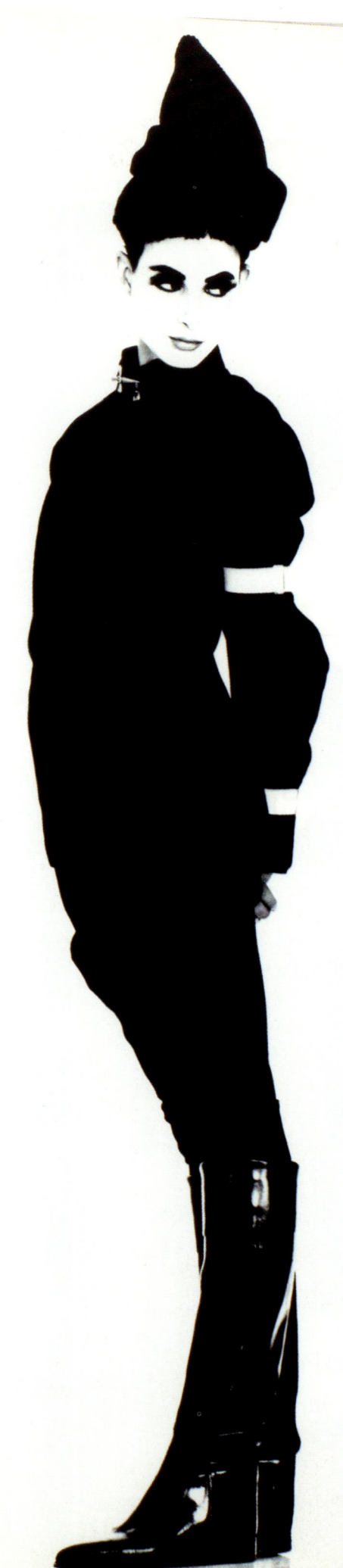

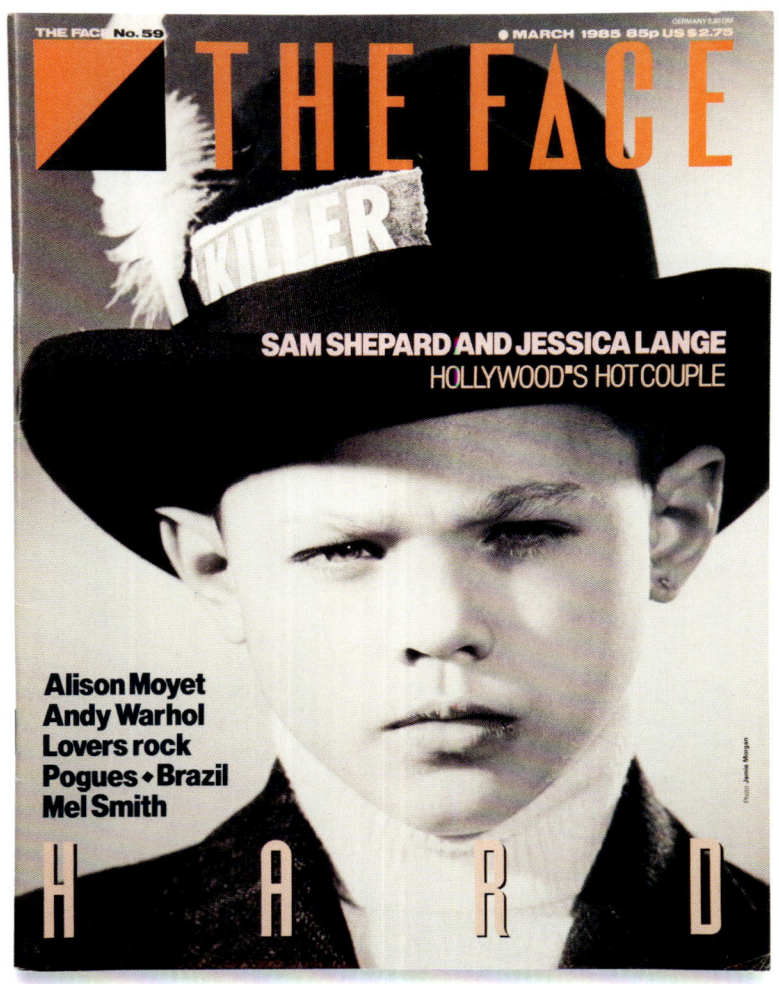

Cover and pages from
The Face no. 59, March
1985, "The Harder They
Come." Photographs
by Jamie Morgan;
styling by Ray Petri

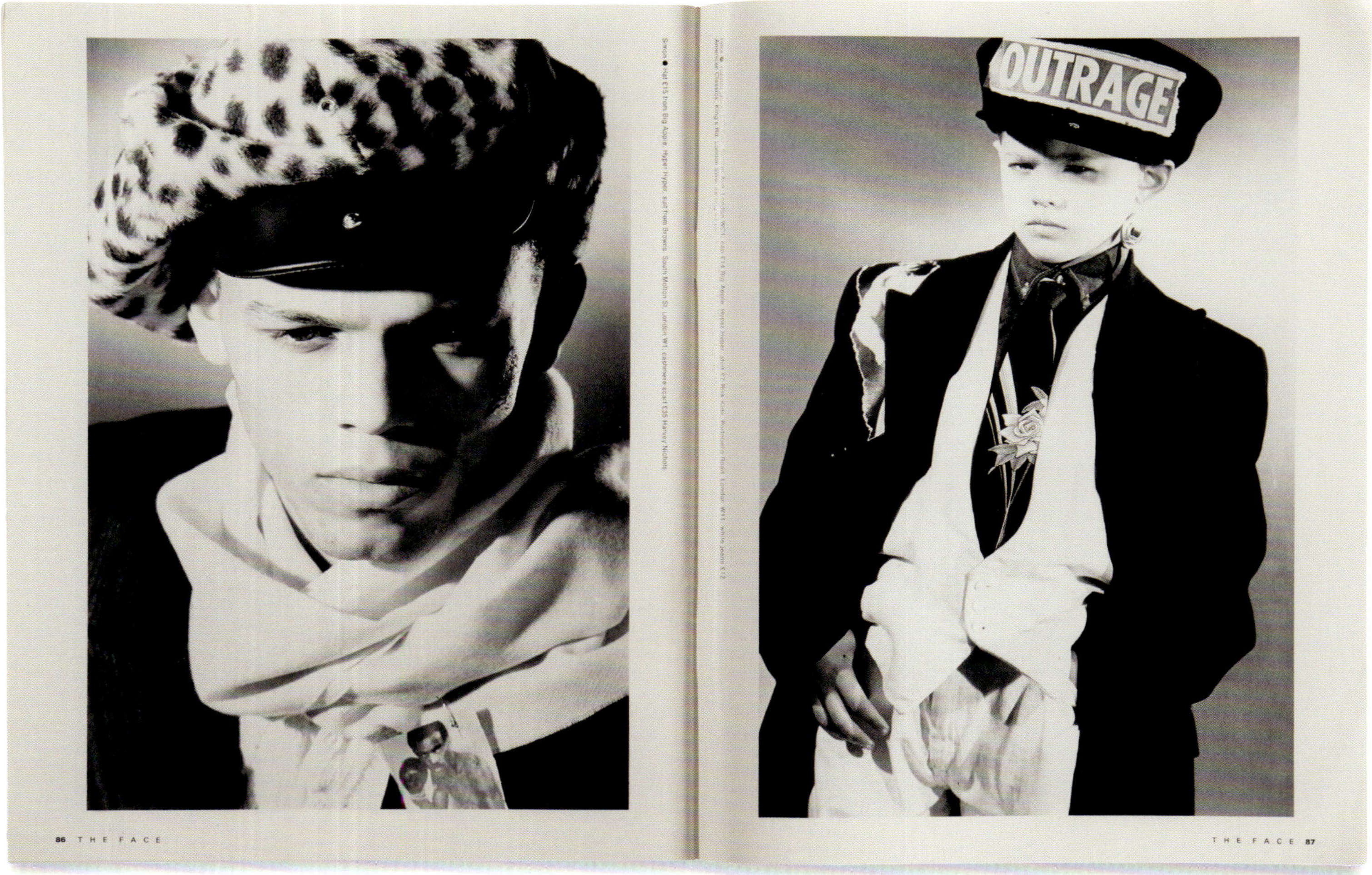

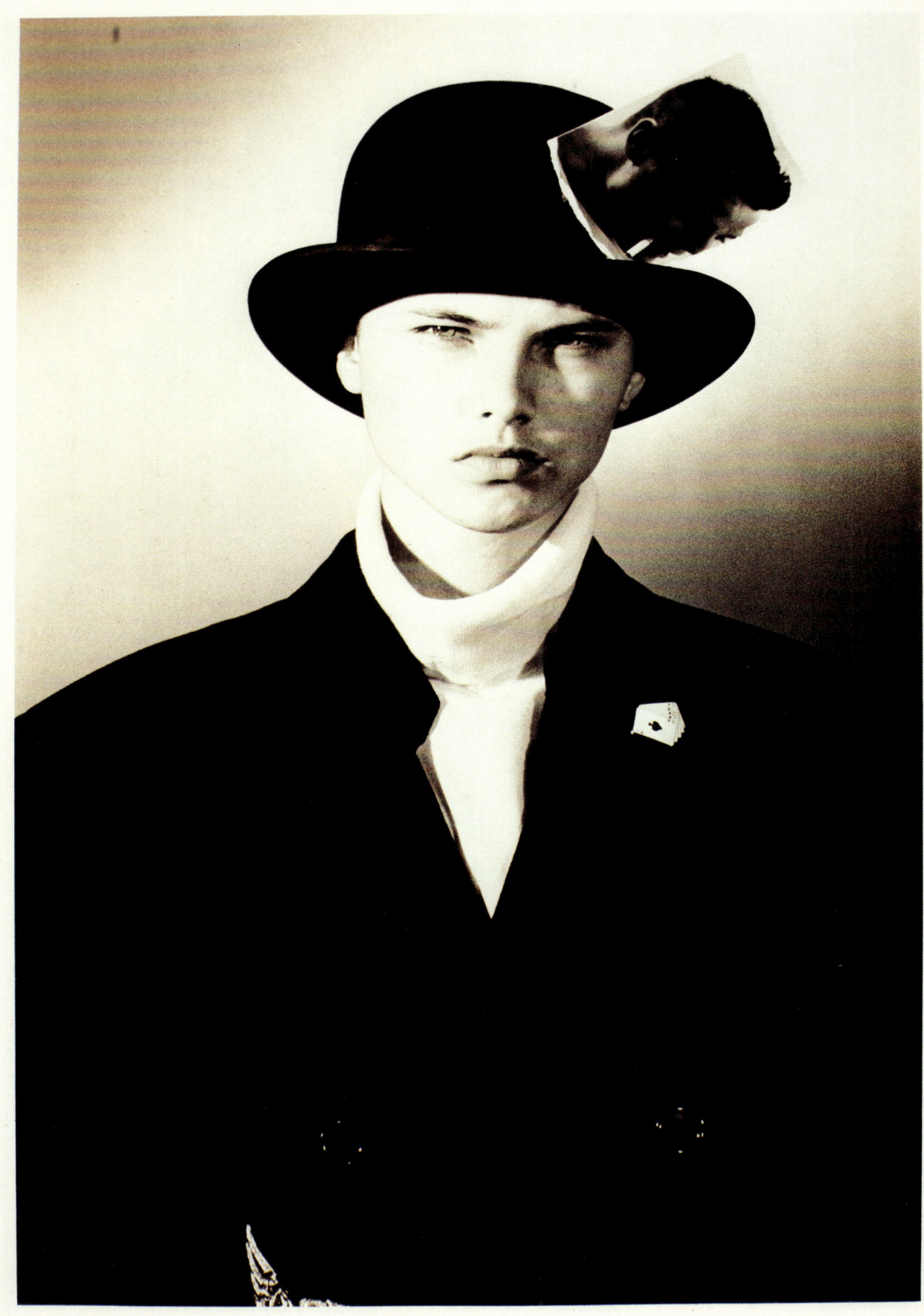

Lynsey ● Cashmere coat £195, jumper £29 from Harvey Nichols; ace of spades badge £8 Western Styling; Ken Mkt; bowler from Cligancourt, Paris

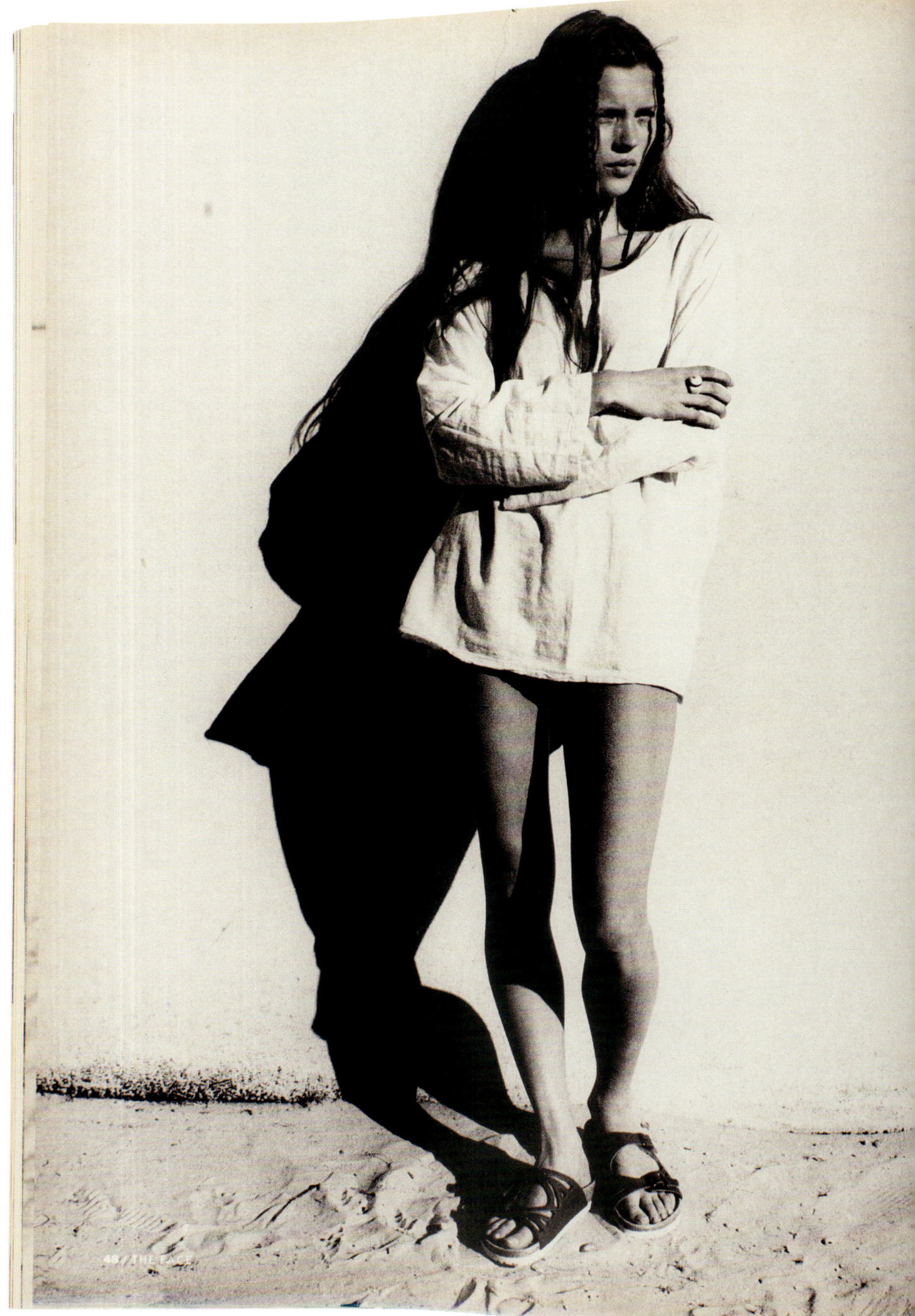

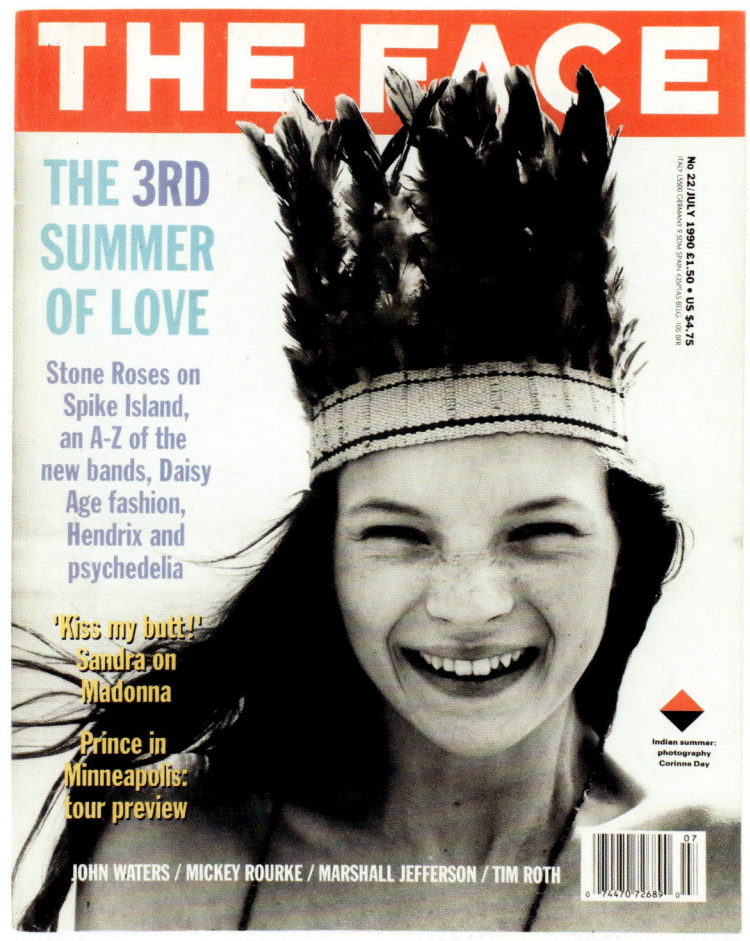

Cover and pages
from *The Face* no. 22,
July 1990, "The Daisy Age."
Photographs by
Corinne Day; styling
by Melanie Ward

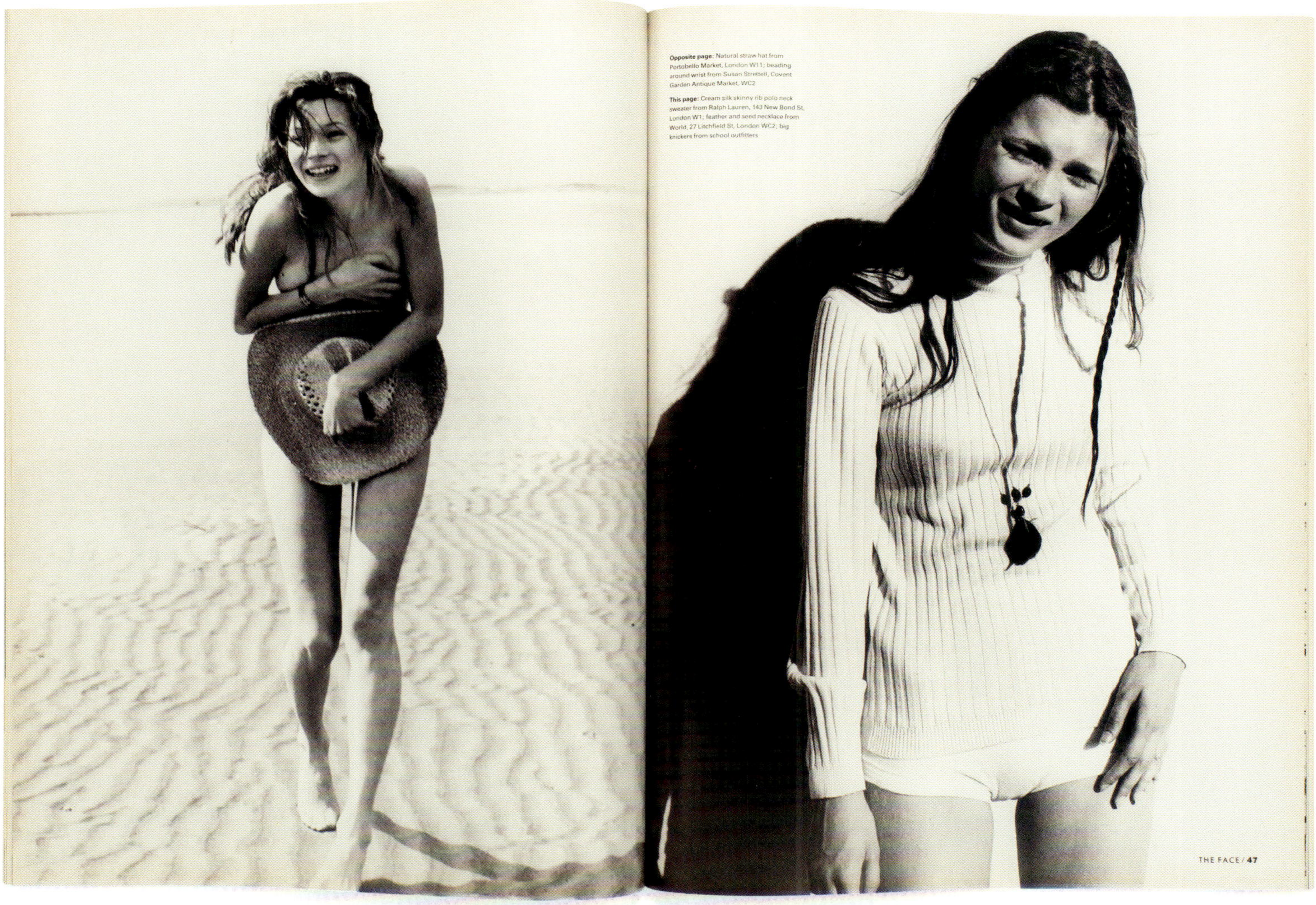

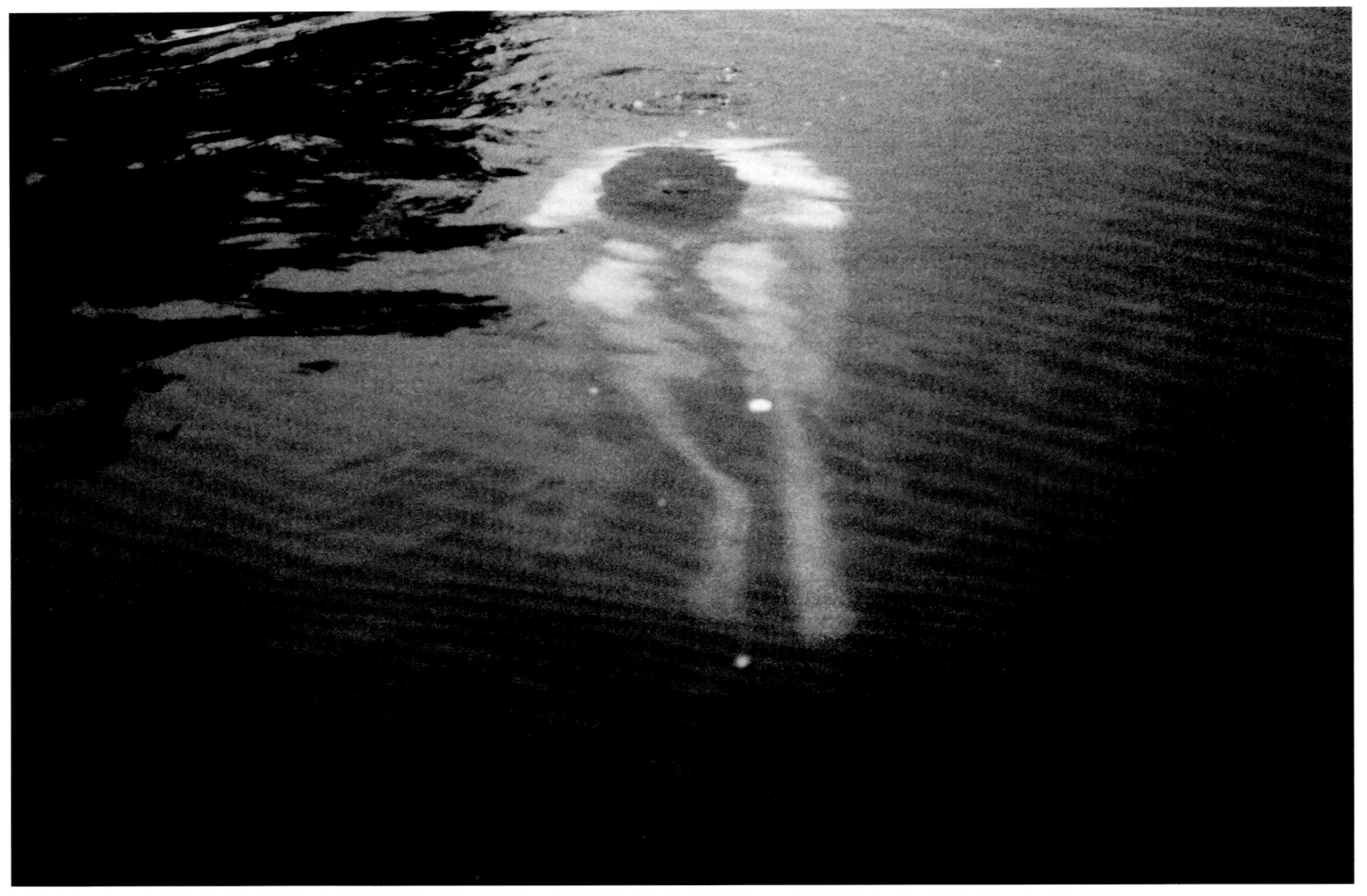

Margaret Durow

New Romantic

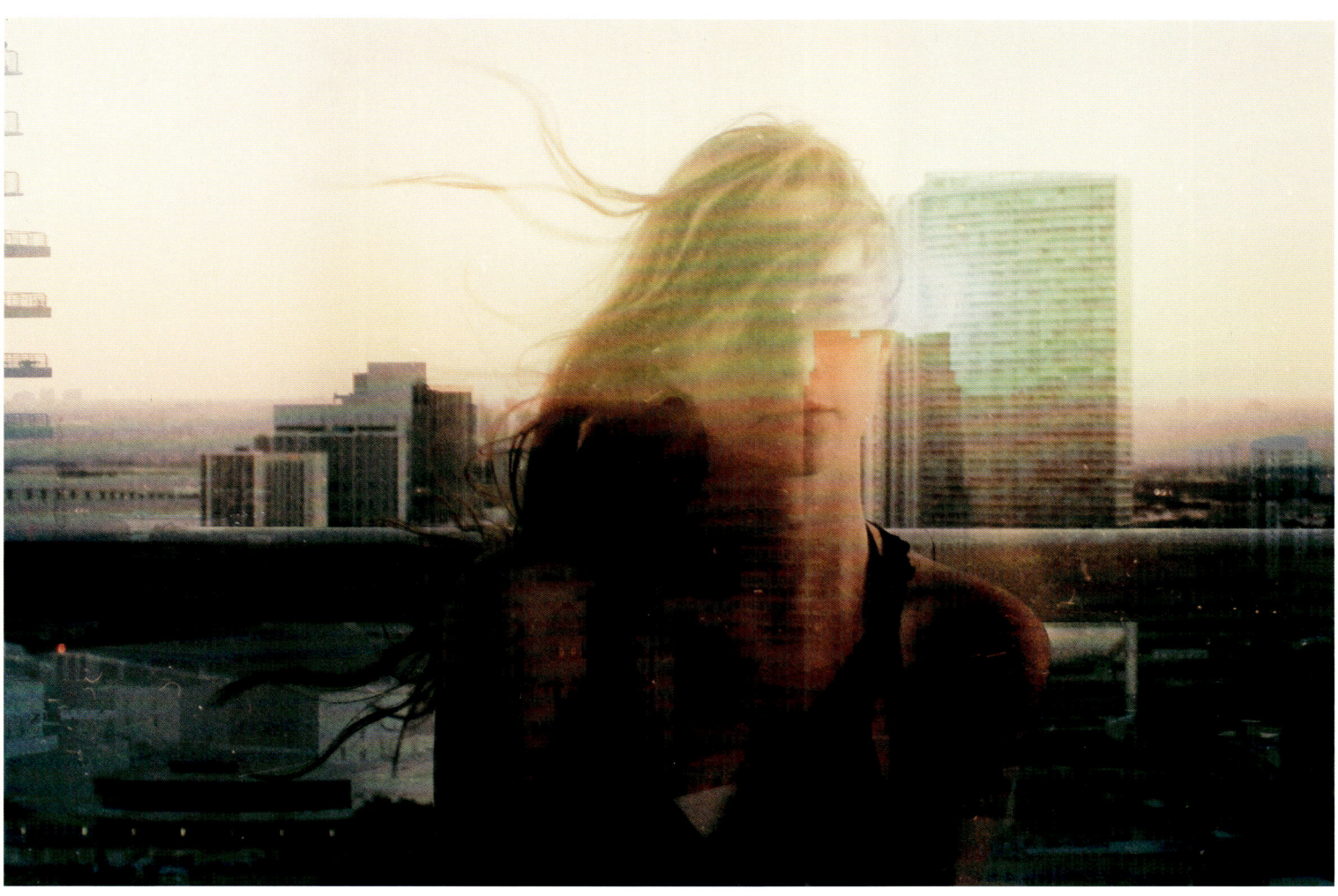

Though Margaret Durow came of age surrounded by digital sensors, the twenty-four-year-old Wisconsinite prefers the aesthetic of 35mm celluloid. Inez & Vinoodh discovered her work on Instagram and praise her lighting and the feeling of "solitude but not loneliness." Durow's pictures don't follow the "hard, flashy, and straight-on" quality of much contemporary photography; the photographer's romantic pictures focus on quiet moments to convey a feeling rather than just an image. Echoing memories from her childhood along the shores of Rock Lake in rural Wisconsin, water is often the central character in her moody landscapes and foggy vistas. Various portraits reveal her curiosity in playing with form: we see Durow through a hazy color double-exposure, reading on her bed in a black-and-white frame reminiscent of Nouvelle Vague films, or as a puzzling fragment—nothing but legs.

Last year, Durow self-published a collection of black-and-white photographs under the title *Ephemeral Springs*. Her interest in photography is directly tied to her awareness of the natural environment and life's cycles; she is a burgeoning scientist with degrees in biological conservation and environmental studies from University of Wisconsin–Madison. After a recent internship cataloging plant specimens for the Wisconsin State Herbarium, Durow is planning to combine her interests in memory, images, and biology through further studies in library science—an appropriate calling for someone who desires to record, recall, and retrieve memories.　　—The Editors

Above:
Miami, 2012

Following spread,
clockwise from top left:
George, 2009;
Sister, 2009;
Legs and Light, 2012;
Door County, 2012
All photographs courtesy
the artist

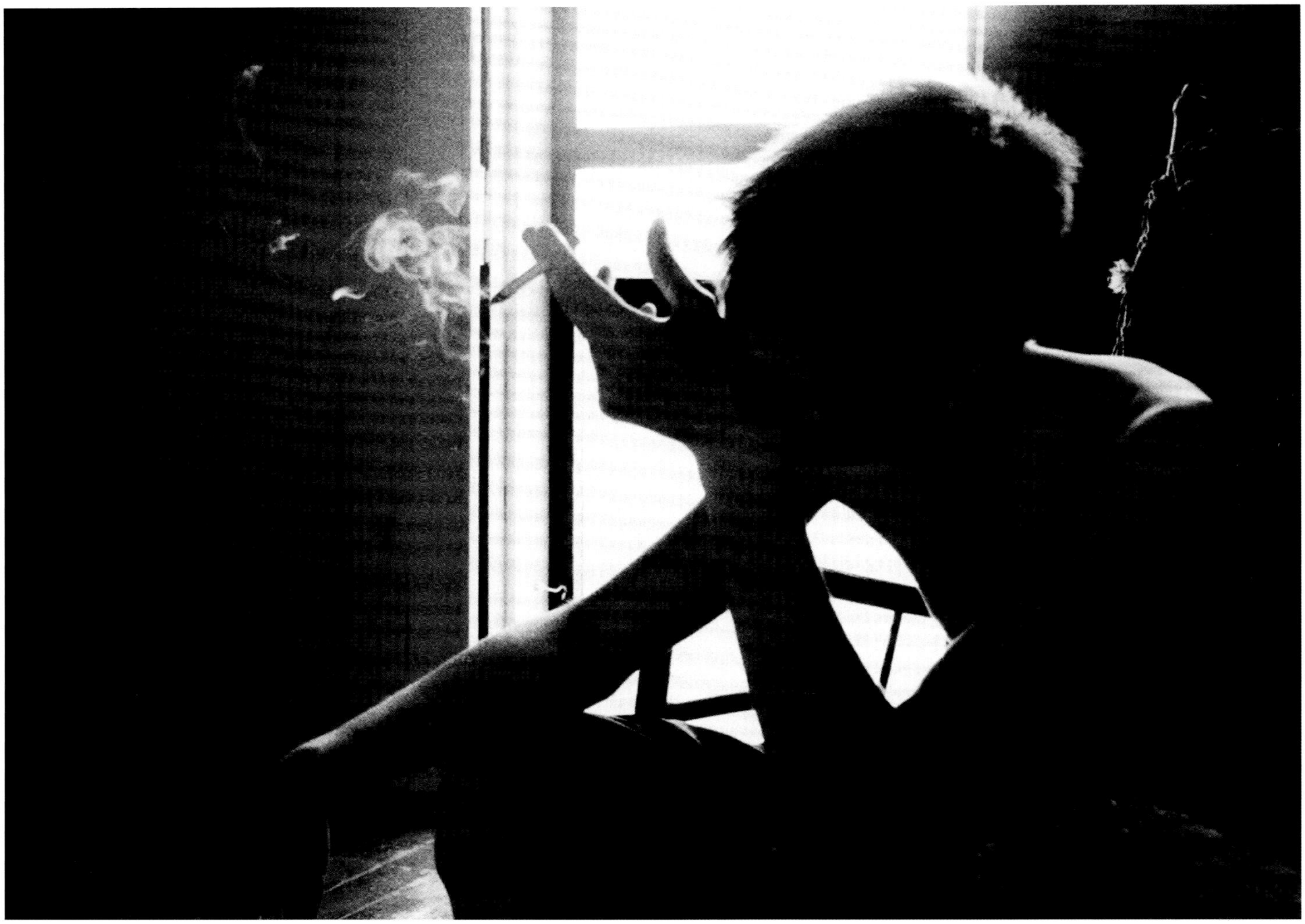

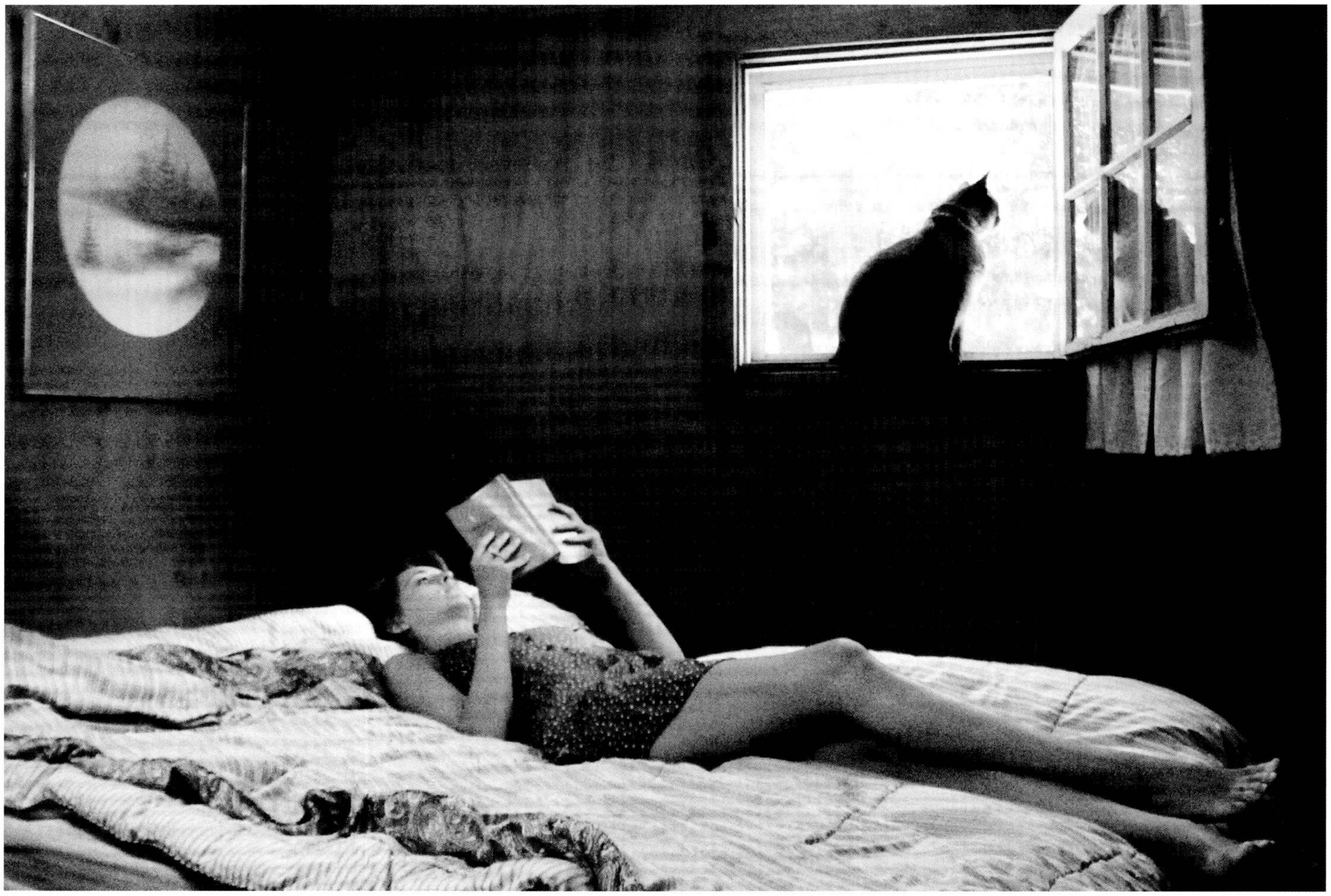

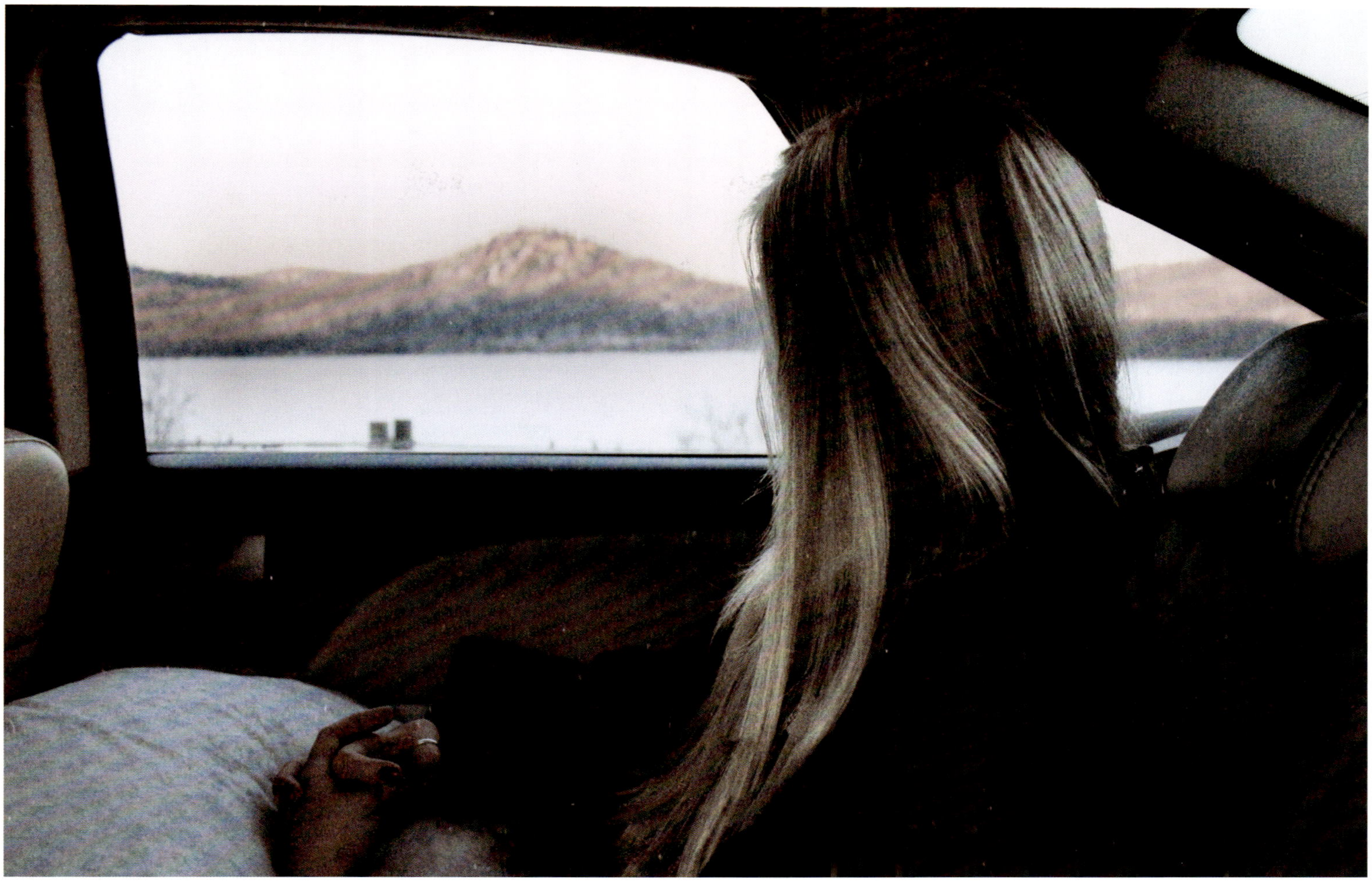

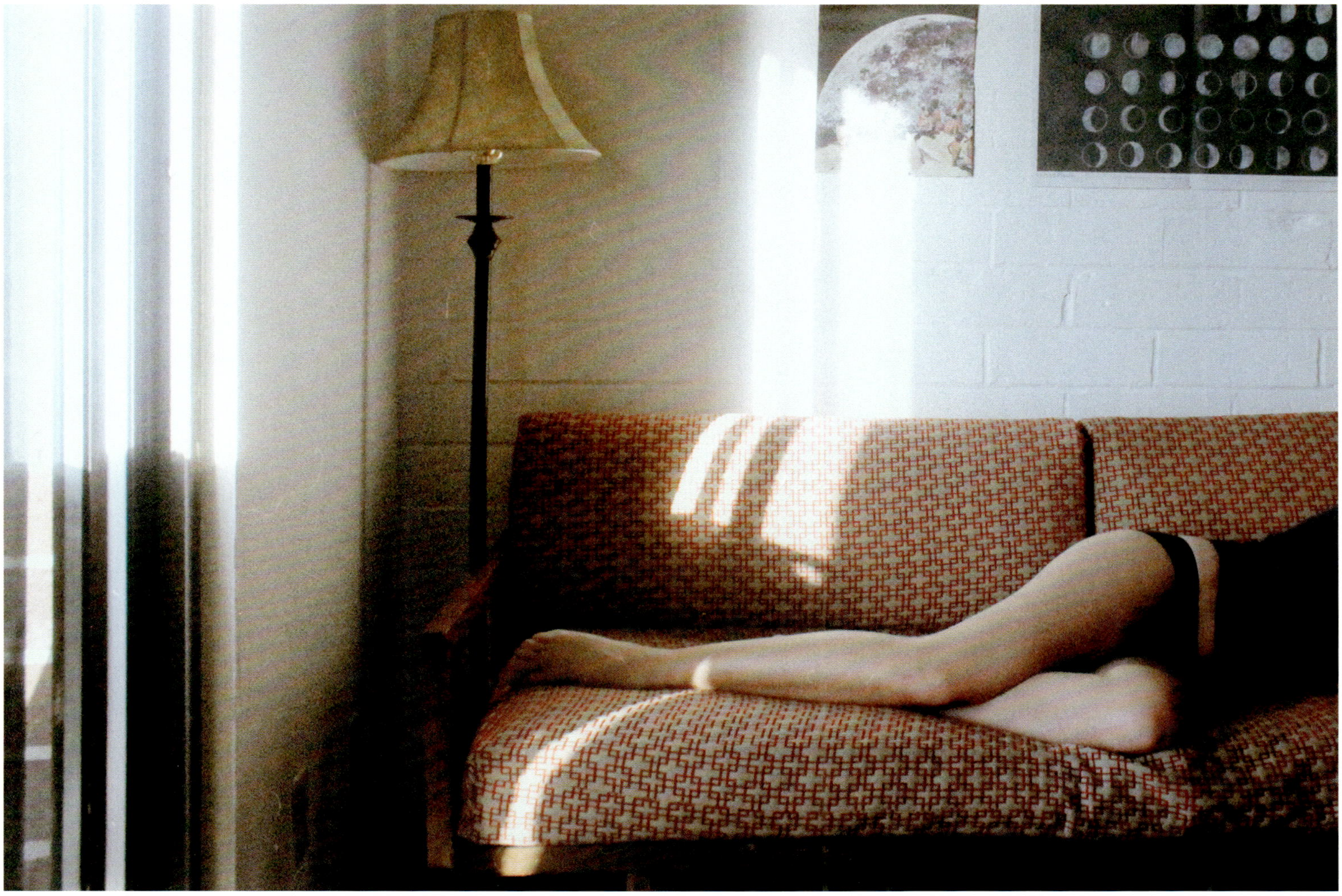

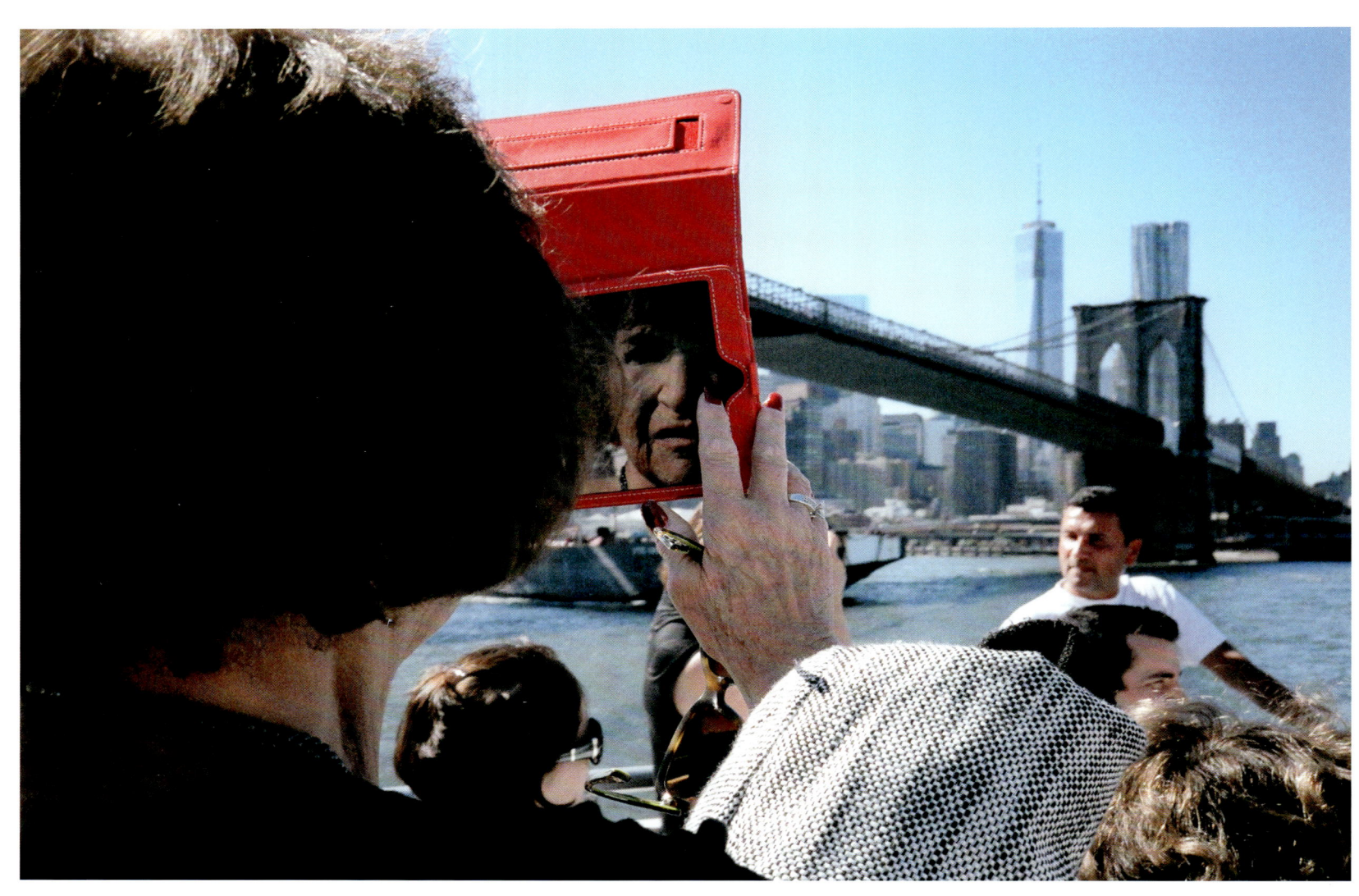

Daniel Arnold worked as a writer before switching to photography, but the mark of a storyteller is felt in his photographs, made on New York's streets and subways. Following in the tradition of street photographers of decades past who organized chaotic urban life into harmonious frames, Arnold creates images that are comedic, surreal, and sometimes a little scary. He is confrontational with his camera, not shying away from subjects who often appear to be unaware of his presence. This urban sleuthing has caught the attention of magazines and galleries. Last spring Arnold rode a different subway to the end of its line each day of the week for the *New Yorker*'s Instagram feed; a new fashion magazine titled *Lady* commissioned him to follow a model around the city and onto the subway while surreptitiously photographing her. An exhibition in San Francisco came about with characteristic spontaneity: he landed in the Bay Area ten days before the show, shot and printed all the exhibition's images in six days, and in the course of working walked one hundred miles (the pedometer he wore clocked his distances). For all the structure and hard work involved, the photographs are casual and spontaneous. As with any convincing chronicler of the street, the act of photographing, if a hustle, is instinctual. "I can't go a block without working," Arnold says. The result of that obsession is an enormous catalog of pleasurable off-the-cuff moments and street style. —The Editors

Daniel Arnold

The Itinerant

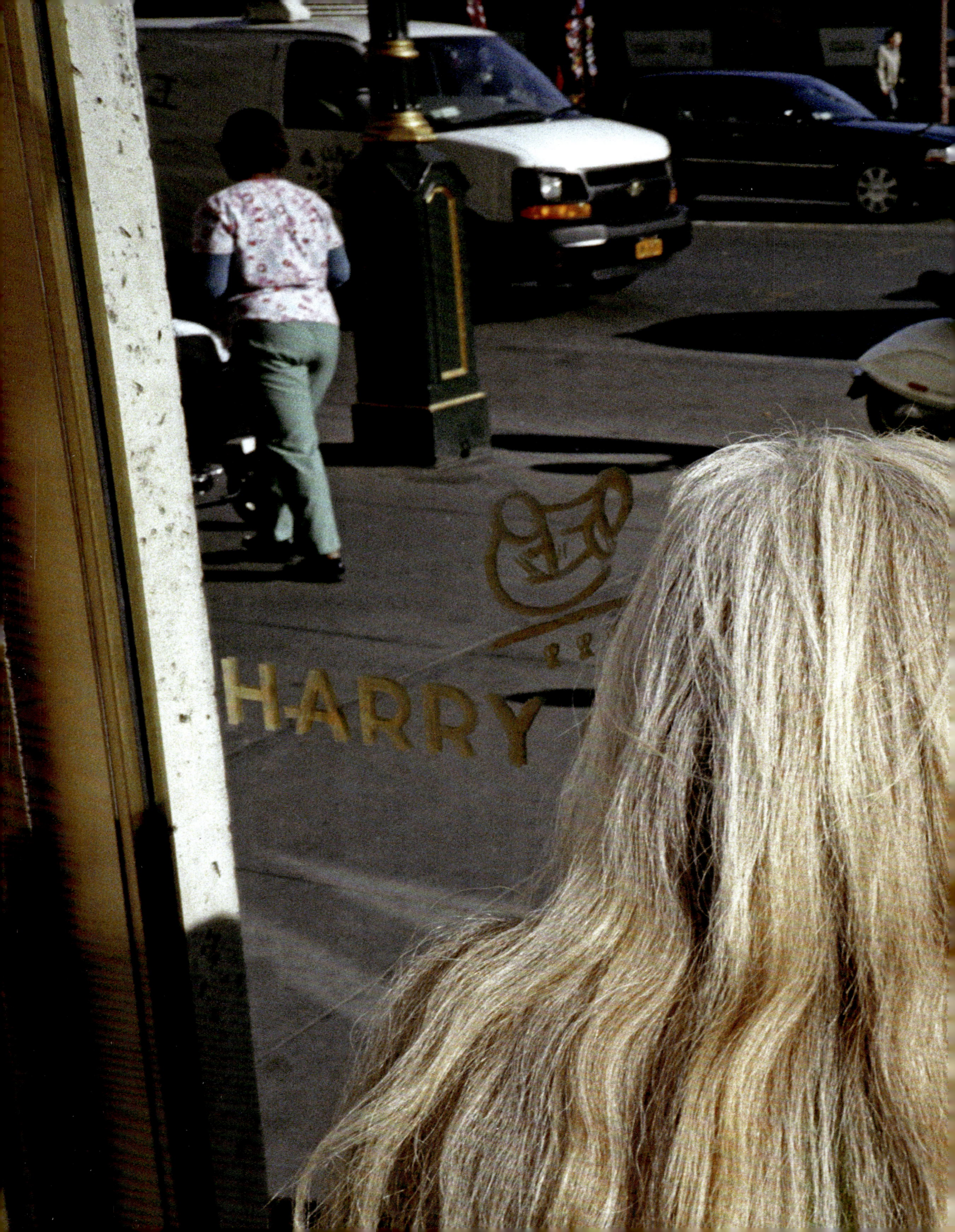

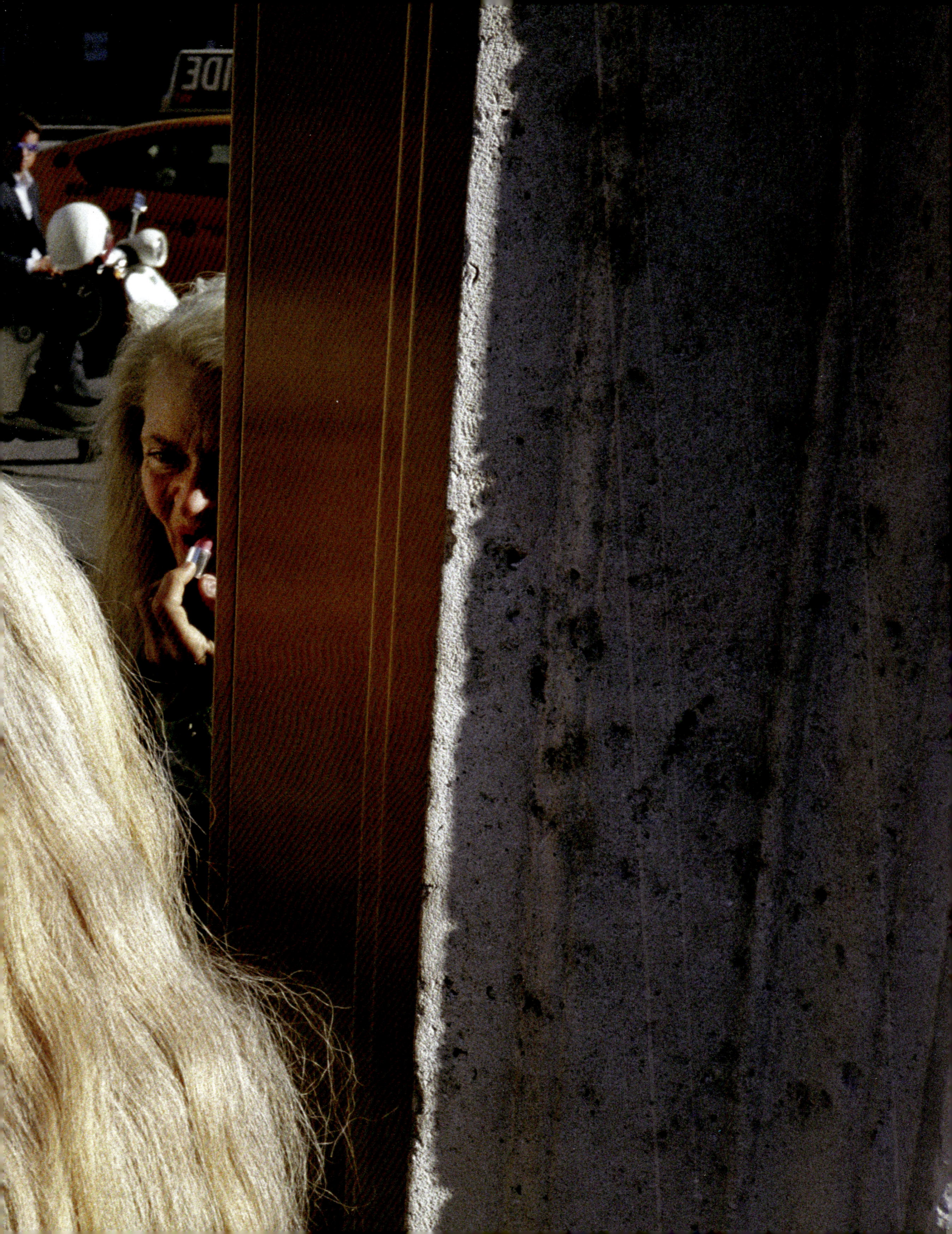

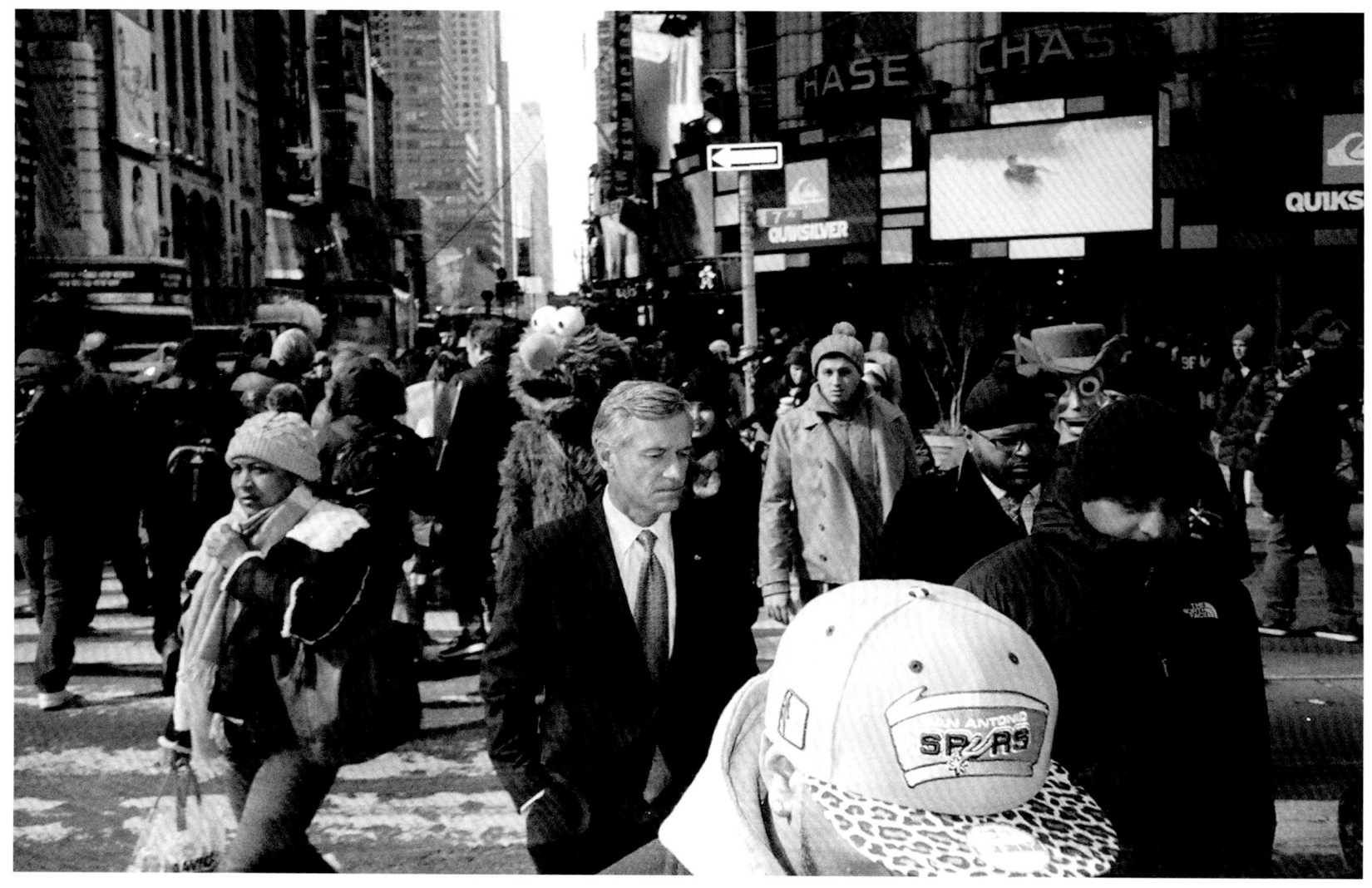

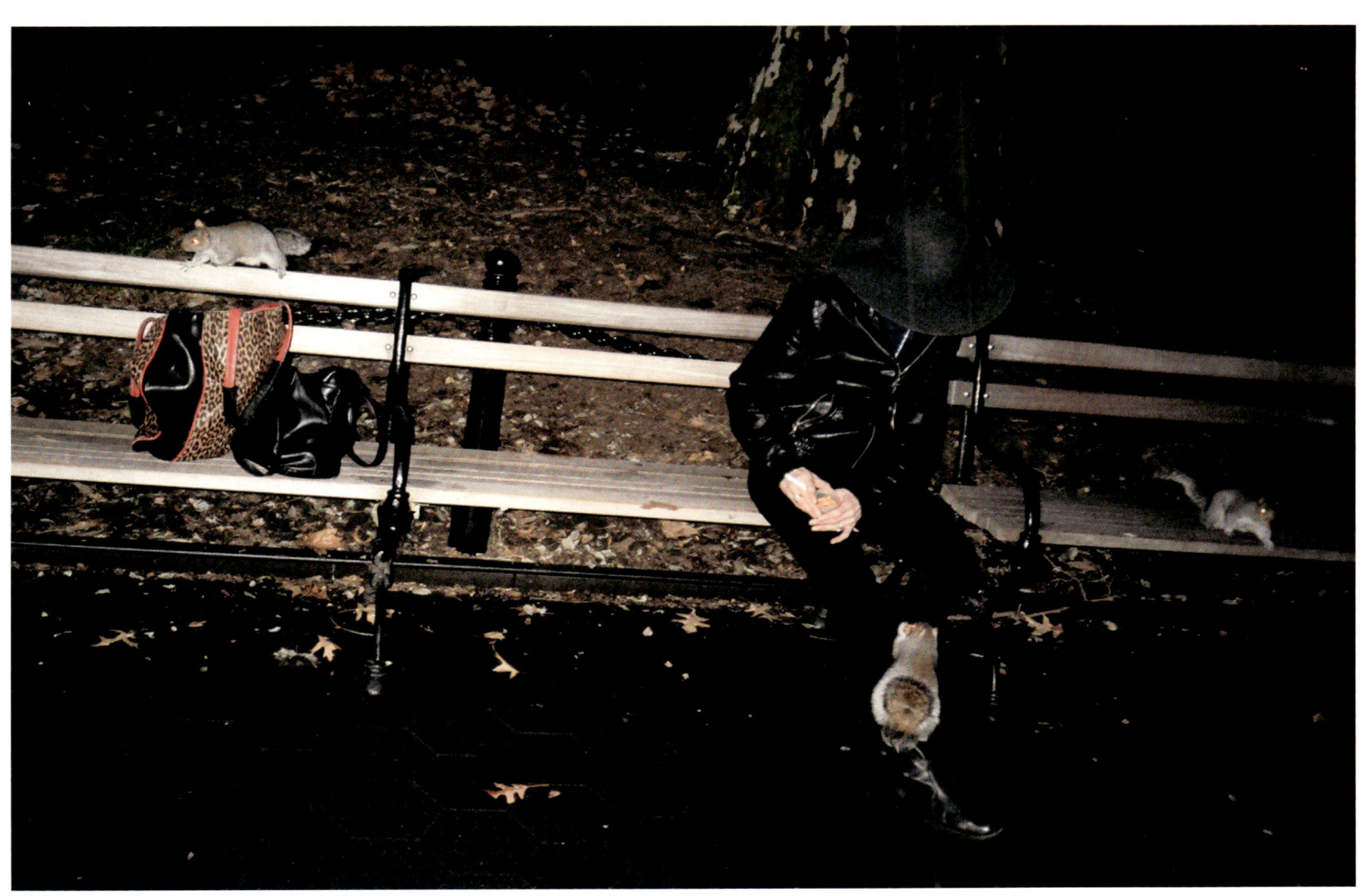

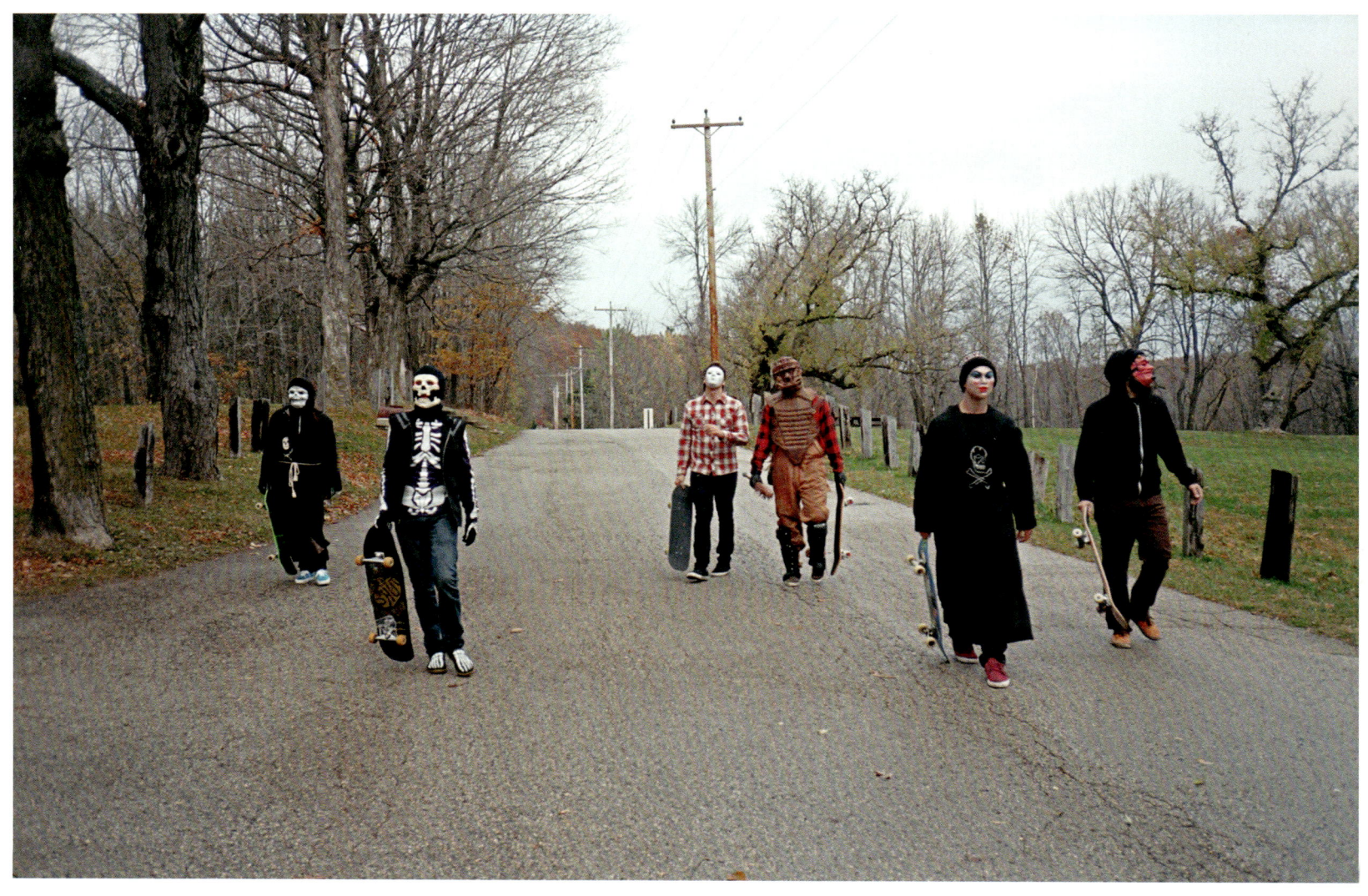

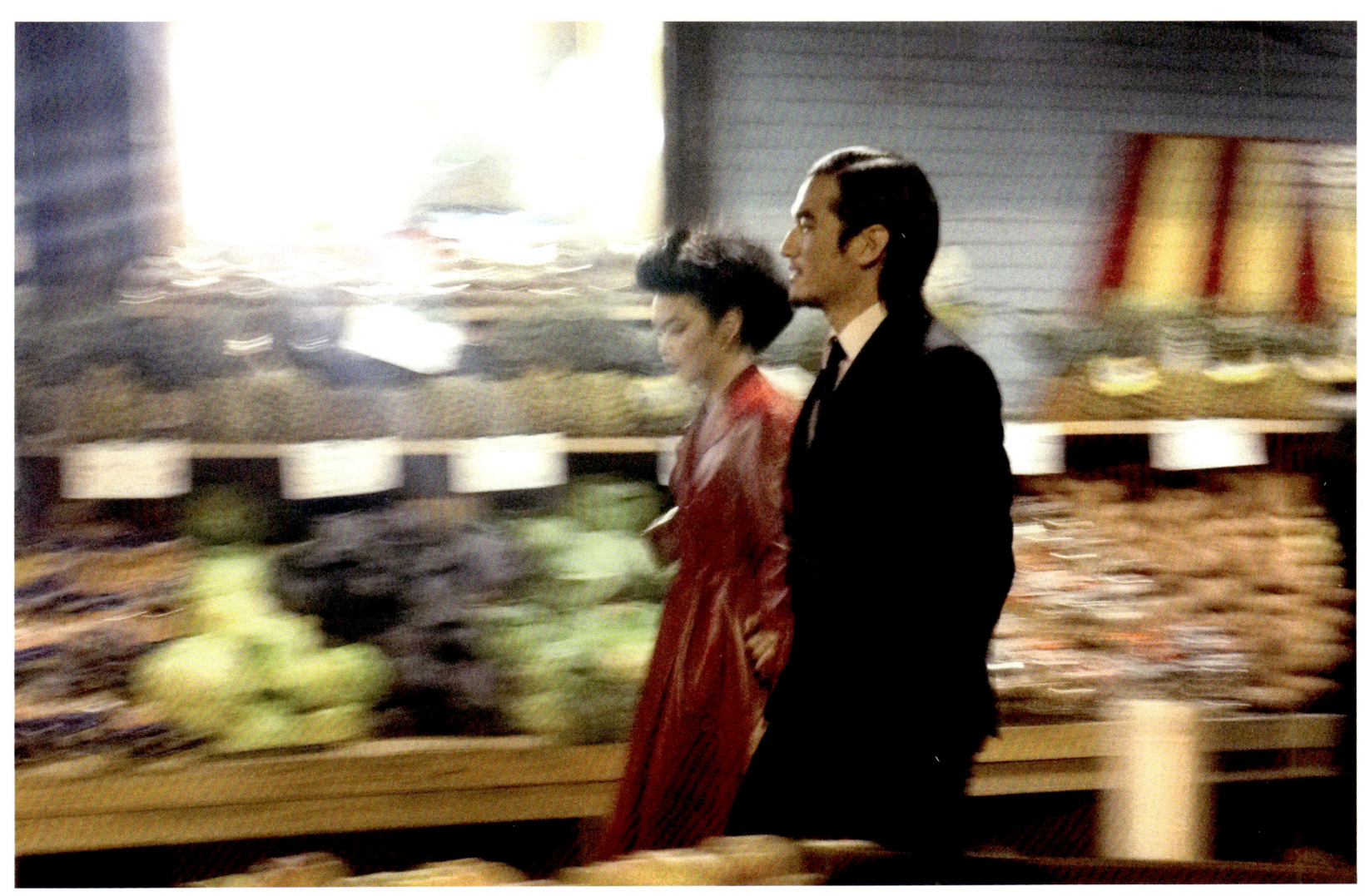

Object Lessons
Prints from *Blow-Up*,
1966

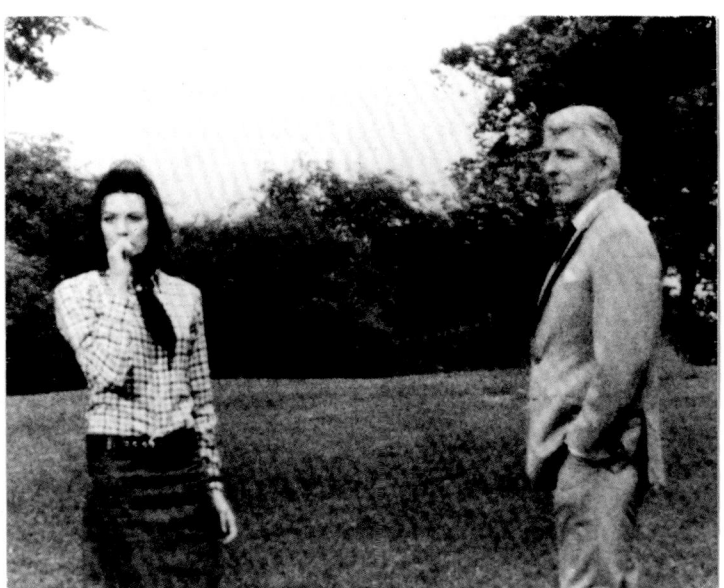 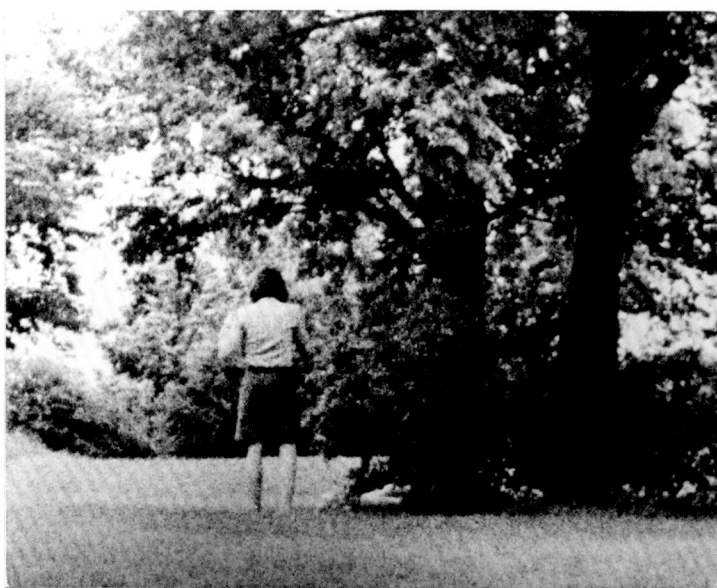

Don McCullin, photographs made for the film *Blow-Up*, 1966 Courtesy Philippe Garner

Along with *Funny Face* (Stanley Donen, 1957) and *Eyes of Laura Mars* (Irvin Kershner, 1978), Michelangelo Antonioni's *Blow-Up* (1966) is an essential fashion-photography film. Based on a Julio Cortázar short story, the film features actor David Hemmings as Thomas, a swaggering fashion photographer working in mod-era London, a character loosely modeled after several photographers including David Bailey. Thomas believes he has witnessed and photographed a murder while taking photographs of two lovers in a park. Seeking to confirm his suspicions he takes to the darkroom and enlarges his photographs but the images only become more obscured, grainy, and inconclusive. The film is a brilliant meditation on reality, perception, and the evidentiary role of photography. As Antonioni remarked, "I always mistrust everything which I see, which an image shows me, because I imagine what is beyond it. And what is beyond an image cannot be known."

The photographs in the film were made by Don McCullin, the celebrated documentary photographer known for showing the world through his searing coverage of the Vietnam War and urban poverty in England. "I was doing what the Hemmings character was supposed to be doing," McCullin has remarked. "All the blow-ups in the film were mine." However, McCullin's name does not appear in the film's credits. Around twenty of the original McCullin prints were rediscovered in 1995 at a film memorabilia auction in London, and are the only known surviving 20-by-24-inch prints used in the classic film. They bear the markings of their use as props: one can see the pinholes made when Hemmings pinned the enlargements to the walls or beams of his studio set. Two are reproduced above, and most of the set is now touring Europe in an exhibition about *Blow-Up*'s enduring influence. The film continues to be a relevant commentary on photography, and a reminder of how both the genres of fashion and documentary play with illusion and reality.
— The Editors